Toward a Critical Rhetoric on the Israel-Palestine Conflict

Abraham's Toward a Critical Rhetoric on the Israeli-Palestine Conflict *addresses traditional rhetorical artifacts (the media accounts that we have come to expect from collections like this since Said's* Covering Islam, *as well as traditional presidential public address). It also addresses less traditional rhetorical artifacts: from professional discussion lists like WPA-L, the email list for Writing Program Administrators, to the discourse around sister-city designations in Madison, Wisconsin.*

The contributions demonstrate the insights generated by rhetorical theories used to unpack texts, such as genre theory and rhetorical listening. Other essays draw on critical theorists such as Levinas and Ricoeur to inform close textual analysis about the most important ethical, political and economic conflict in the world.

—David Beard, Associate Professor of Rhetoric, Scientific and Technical Communication, University of Minnesota – Duluth

Toward a Critical Rhetoric on the Israel-Palestine Conflict

Edited by Matthew Abraham

Parlor Press
Anderson, South Carolina
www.parlorpress.com

Parlor Press LLC, Anderson, South Carolina, USA

© 2015 by Parlor Press.
All rights reserved.
Printed in the United States of America

SAN: 254-8879

Library of Congress Cataloging-in-Publication Data on File

Toward a critical rhetoric on the Israel-Palestine conflict / edited by Matthew Abraham.
   pages cm
 Includes bibliographical references and index.
   ISBN 978-1-60235-693-1 (pbk. : alk. paper) -- ISBN 978-1-60235-694-8 (hardcover : alk. paper)
 1. Arab-Israeli conflict--Public opinion. 2. Public opinion--United States. 3. Rhetoric--Political aspects--United States. 4. Intellectuals--United States--Attitudes. I. Abraham, Matthew, 1972- editor.
 DS119.7.T6717 2015
 956.9405'4--dc23
                          2015020892

Cover design by David Blakesley
Cover Image: © Diane Labombarbe. Used by permission.
Copyediting by Jared Jameson
Printed on acid-free paper.

1 2 3 4 5
First Edition

Parlor Press, LLC is an independent publisher of scholarly and trade titles in print and multimedia formats. This book is available in paper, hardcover, and digital formats from Parlor Press on the World Wide Web at http://www.parlorpress.com or through online and brick-and-mortar bookstores. For submission information or to find out about Parlor Press publications, write to Parlor Press, 3015 Brackenberry Drive, Anderson, SC 29621, or e-mail editor@parlorpress.com.

Contents

Acknowledgments *vii*

1 Editor's Introduction *3*
Matthew Abraham

2 Discourse on the Israel-Palestine Conflict: Rhetorical Memory and Uptake *7*
Anis Bawarshi

3 Reluctant Rhetoricians: Refusing to Frame the Israel-Palestine Conflict Through Jewish-Arab Antagonism *21*
Matthew Abraham

4 The Temporal Roots of Anti-Semitism and Its Impact on the Arab-Israeli Conflict *62*
Amos Kiewe

5 Deterritorialized Rhetoric; or, What Happens when We Forget We are Exiles *77*
Michael Bernard-Donals

6 Feeling the Narrative/s of the Other's Oppression: Toward a Liberatory Mutuality in the Middle East *91*
Michael Kleine

7 Dueling Visions of Israel and the World: Netanyahu and Obama at AIPAC   112
Robert Rowland

8 Traumatic Myth, the Middle Voice, and Genuine Argumentation in the Israeli-Palestinian Civil War   133
David Frank

9 Poetry and Conflict: on Civility, Citizenship and Criticism   152
Shai Ginsburg

10 The Point Is to Change It   176
James Crosswhite

11 Conclusion   187
Matthew Abraham

Contributors   193

Index   197

Acknowledgments

In addition to thanking each of the contributors, I would like to acknowledge the vital help and support of Parlor Press editor, David Blakesley, without whom this collection could not have come into print. David gave this collection a chance to see the light of day, and for that, I am most grateful.

I also must acknowledge the vital help and assistance of Chris Brown, an RCTE graduate student at the University of Arizona, who provided some vital fact-checking of the manuscript during the summer of 2014.

Finally, I wish to thank Jared Jameson, who ably copyedited the manuscript during the production phase.

Toward a Critical Rhetoric on the Israel-Palestine Conflict

1 Editor's Introduction

Matthew Abraham

In recent years, rhetoric and writing scholars have become increasingly interested in the Israel-Palestine conflict—and its attendant identity and political issues—as an object of study.[1] This interest in the ways people talk and debate about the conflict, along with all the historical and political baggage inevitably shaping such talk and debate, emerges in the context of a set of concerns about the continued cycles of conflict and violence in the Middle East. Fully believing it is imperative that the relevant issues be openly discussed and explored in the field, the contributors to this collection take it as a given that the rhetorics surrounding the Israel-Palestine conflict should become a more central part of our professional conversation—although none of us may technically consider ourselves specialists in Middle East history or politics. As specialists in persuasion, however, we do recognize that creating contexts for conversation, exchange, and debate requires continual hard work.

Laying the rhetorical ground to build affective networks conducive to deliberation about a controversial issue such as Israel-Palestine necessitates exploring how positions are drawn and maintained in the midst of discursive indeterminacy and a lack of evidence to support one's perspective. Despite such indeterminacy and a lack of evidence supporting one's expressed position, participants often engage in dogmatic position-taking. Explaining how such expressed certainty emerges and sustains itself across time is the task of rhetoric. Why should scholars, who are continually investigating the contexts within which rhetoric and the conditions of possibility for persuasion are produced, be committed to studying the rhetorical and affective contexts surrounding Middle East politics? There are a number of good reasons for this focus.

First, the intractability of the conflict has been described as being fundamentally about competing and incompatible rhetorics. The rhetoric of Zionism, with its commitment to the protection of the Jewish people in the wake of the Holocaust, clashes with the rhetoric of Palestinian nationalism, which views the Zionist presence in the Holy Land as an alien one. Of course, political Zionism's origins can be traced back to the late nineteenth century, when Theodore Herzl convened the First Zionist Congress in Basel, Switzerland, in the hopes of winning over the heart and minds of the modern European powers to create a Jewish state. The origins of Palestinian nationalism are found in the early twentieth century, as resistance grew within the Palestinian community to Zionist aspirations in Palestine. Robert Rowland and David Frank write, "Both Israelis and Palestinians have defined their identity with myth systems, which can be seen as mirror images of each other" (14). The fact that these myth systems can be seen as mirror images of each other has profound implications for rhetorical study, especially for those scholars seeking to develop deliberative models through which to reconcile political divisions between Israelis and Palestinians.

Second, as the conflict goes into its sixty-seventh year, and as the turmoil seemingly deepens in the Middle East, civic-minded rhetoricians have felt pressed to extend their professional skills to examine the dynamics of continuing cycles of violence and bloodshed for both Palestinians and Israelis. Discussion of the relevant issues surrounding the conflict is necessary within the U.S. public space. However, far too often position-taking proves a barrier to the prospect of exchanging information and perspectives. This desire to prove the Other wrong, or to be hopelessly misinformed and misguided, creates a rhetorical situation that is untenable for the production of what Krista Ratcliffe has called "rhetorical listening," which she defines as "a stance of openness that a person may choose to assume in relation to any person, text, or culture; its purpose is to cultivate conscious identifications that promote productive communication, especially but not solely cross-culturally" (25).

Third, a rhetoric of inevitability surrounds treatments of the conflict, which frames Israelis, diaspora Jews (Zionist and non-Zionist), and Palestinians as participating in a cosmic struggle, a clash of civilizations, that has no rhyme or reason. Within this rhetoric, there is an unwillingness to interrogate the grounds upon which the conflict is staged, fought, and perpetuated.

The contributors to this collection strongly believe that, while there can be no clear sense of what justice may look like in the Middle East, we are all at least committed to hearing what competing conceptions of justice might be. As a result of erroneous common places and inadequate topoi within the public sphere, a great deal of misunderstanding swirls around the conflict. These common places and missing topoi simply reaffirm a very simplistic and misleading conception of the conflict, leaving its roots unaddressed.

In a context of frequent scapegoating and the playing of the blame game, with historical forces often neglected or misunderstood, the Israel-Palestine conflict requires a fuller and more comprehensive treatment. The essays collected here attempt to do just that, to articulate a way of moving a conversation about the conflict forward, while avoiding the discursive pitfalls hampering the peace process. The contributors have thought carefully about the relevant issues dividing Israelis and Palestinians from one another, as well as about the hegemonic rhetorics surrounding the representations of this division. Whether one is discussing the conflict in an intimate setting such as a coffee shop, or in a more public space such as a political forum, the ability to recognize the historical, social, and psychological forces deforming the prospect of compassionate and empathic understanding is the first task of the concerned rhetorician.

Notes

1. For examples, see Andrea Greenbaum and Deborah Holdstein's *Judaic Perspectives in Rhetoric and Composition,* the articles in Jan Fernheimer's guest-edited special issue of *College English* (July 2010), Frank and Rowland's *Shared Land/Conflicting Identity: Trajectories of Israeli and Palestinian Symbol Use,* and my "The Rhetoric of Academic Controversy after 9/11: Edward Said in the American Imagination."

Works Cited

Abraham, Matthew. "The Rhetoric of Academic Controversy after 9/11: Edward Said in the American Imagination." *JAC* 24.3 (2004): 113-42. Print.
Fernheimer, Jan, Guest Editor. Special Topic: Composing Jewish Identities. *College English,* 72.6 (July 2010). Print.
—. "Black Jewish Identity Conflict: A Divided Universal Audience and the Impact of Dissociative Disruption," *Rhetoric Society Quarterly* 39.1 (Jan. 2009): 46–71. Print.
Greenbaum, Andre, and Deborah Holdstein. *Judaic Perspectives in Rhetoric and Composition.* Creskill, NJ: Hampton Press, 2008. Print.
Ratcliffe, Krista. *Rhetorical Listening: Identification, Gender, Whiteness.* Carbondale: Southern Illinois UP, 2006. Print.
Rowland, Robert, and David Frank. *Shared Land/Conflicting Identity: Trajectories of Israeli & Palestinian Symbol Use.* East Lansing: Michigan State UP, 2002. Print.

2 Discourse on the Israel-Palestine Conflict: Rhetorical Memory and Uptake

Anis Bawarshi

How can rhetoricians committed to a just and peaceful resolution to the Israel-Palestine conflict intervene in the entrenched set of uptakes that work to maintain the rhetorical impasse that plagues discussions of the conflict in the US, especially when the impasse has such implications for Palestinians and Israelis? For me, this question is both an academic and a personal one. As a Palestinian-Lebanese American married to a Jewish woman, with two children who are both Jewish and Palestinian, I have faced this question in my home life, as my partner and I have often struggled with, and have become increasingly better at, engaging in deliberation about this conflict. As a rhetorician, I have confronted this question repeatedly as I watch, often with a deep sense of disappointment verging on despair, as public discourse about this conflict, across various contexts and genres, often degenerates into heated accusations, personal attacks, and name-calling, even on academic listservs devoted, no less, to the teaching of academic writing and civic discourse, such as WPA-L (Writing Program Administrators' discussion list) and the Rhetoricians for Peace discussion list.[1] The striking degree to which these exchanges reflect a seemingly habitual, totalizing pattern of uptakes (whether in response to a teaching award announcement in memory of Rachel Corrie, a twenty-three-year-old student from Washington State who was killed by an Israeli bulldozer; or to Jimmy Carter's book, *Palestine: Peace Not Apartheid*; or to former DePaul University professor and political scientist Norman Finkelstein's scholarship; or to Bob Simon's January 2009 *60 Minutes* report on the West Bank occupation; or to recent reactions to Professor Steven Salaita's Twitter posts condemning Israel's airstrikes in Gaza; or numerous other examples) got me thinking about how the patterns function and how we might work to disrupt them in productive, more discerning ways—at the very least in ways that distinguish more carefully between, for instance, a racist screed by white supremacist David Duke and a critique of Israel by historian and son of Holocaust survivors, Norman Finkelstein. The stakes have never been higher. As Professor Steven Salaita's recently revoked tenured position at University of Illinois, Urbana-Champaign illustrates, the near impossibility of engaging in public debate about Israel's occupation of Palestine without incurring and having to defend oneself against charges of anti-Semitism not only threatens academic freedom but also shuts down any meaningful debate. In this chapter, I will describe some of the rhetorical patterns and normalized uptakes that have become reified around the "Israel-Palestine conflict," and then I will examine the challenges faced by those who wish to intervene in these uptakes in ways that encourage more productive inquiry and public deliberation.

In *After the Last Sky*, and speaking as a Palestinian, Edward Said writes: "There has been no misfortune worse for us than that we are ineluctably viewed as the enemies of the Jews. No moral and political fate worse, none at all, I think: no worse, there is none" (134). As I see it, this is as much a moral and political fate as it is a rhetorical fate, a rhetorical fate that has, primarily in the West and especially in the US, pitted attempts to represent Palestinian suffering and victimization against competing and more powerful representations of Jewish suffering and victimization. Within this rhetoric of incommensurability—this rhetorical dilemma of representing oneself as a victim of a victim and the competing memories and power imbalances at work there—attempts to represent or critique Israel's treatment of Palestinians are often silenced or ignored, taken up as a threat to Israel's right to exist and labeled as anti-Semitic: either because they rely on references to Jewish power or because they purportedly single out Israel for criticism. This is the rhetorical bind, entrenched and managed by a powerful set of uptakes, that Palestinians and those who speak on their behalf confront.

When Kenneth Burke helped shift the terms of how we define rhetoric from *persuasion* to *identification*, he expanded our understanding of rhetoric from a kind of discourse to a dimension of all discourse, as having to do with what David Fleming has called "the condition of our existence" (176). If rhetoric has to do with identification—with how we identify, represent, make sense of, and engage with ourselves, others, and the world—then rhetoric is bound up with memory as well, since how we identify is connected to how we remember. Evoking memory and keeping it present is therefore as much a rhetorical task as it is a cognitive task; so is denying it.

After sixty years, the twenty-seven refugee camps in Gaza and the West Bank (populated by Palestinians driven from their homes in 1948) remain permanently temporary, a liminal world: not Palestine, not Israel. According to the United Nations Relief and Works Agency figures, by 2007, nearly 950,000 of the now approximately 1.5 million people living in Gaza were refugees or their descendants (of the 3.7 million Palestinians living in the Occupied Palestinian Territories [Gaza and the West Bank], 1.5 million are refugees). The Gaza refugees, originally some 200,000, fled their homes and villages in South Palestine in 1948 to escape the approaching Israeli army, taking shelter in Gaza (then with a population of 70,000) but expecting to return to their homes. This longing to return home persists to this day and is a constant presence in Palestinian discourse.

In an essay titled "No Reconciliation Allowed," Edward Said cites Theodor Adorno, who writes: "the writer sets up house. . . . For a man who no longer has a homeland, writing becomes a place to live" (114). In the case of Palestinian refugees, who live in a world dominated to an extreme by words, stories, and memories, rhetoric indeed becomes a place to live. Several important books capture this rhetoric, including Mourid Barghouti's *I Saw Ramallah*, Amira Hass' *Drinking the Sea at Gaza: Days and Nights in a Land Under Siege*, Saree Makdisi's *Palestine Inside and Out: An Everyday Occupation*, Wendy Pearlman's *Occupied Voices: Stories of Everyday Life from the Second Intifada*, and Edward Said and Jean Mohr's *After the Last Sky*. (Not to mention the works of literature by authors such as Emile Habibi, Rashid Hussein, Fadwa Tuqan, and the great Palestinian poet, Mahmoud Darwish.) In particular, Walid Khalidi's monumental book, *All That Remains: The Palestinian Villages Occupied and Depopulated by Israel in 1948*, carefully documents the 418 Palestinian villages destroyed in the 1948 war, almost half of the Palestinian villages that existed at the time in Mandatory Palestine. While noting the depopulation and dispossession of Palestinian property in urban centers, *All That Remains* works through photographs, statistics, and narrative to retrieve the lost countryside villages from erasure. As Khalidi explains, these villages

> have remained altogether anonymous to the outside world and might as well never have existed. A dozen or so, though depopulated, were

spared or suffered only minor damage. The rest were either totally destroyed or virtually so. They have literally been wiped off the face of the earth. The sites of their destroyed homesteads and graveyards, as well as their orchards, threshing floors, wells, livestock, and grazing grounds were all parceled out among Jewish colonies. . . . The Hebrew names . . . have replaced their Arabic predecessors, sometimes faintly and mockingly echoing them. (xxxii)

In important ways, *All That Remains* is an act of rhetorical retrieval, since in most instances there is very little to no visible physical remains of the villages. Page after page includes photographs of empty fields, scattered rubble, a cactus hedge here and there, a faint row of stones marking an old boundary, scattered gravestones amid the rubble, but mostly, the photographs appear to be of stones and vegetation and nothing else. Juxtaposed alongside the photographs is text, which details as much as possible the location of the village, its original population and number of houses, and its history. In this context, the villages rhetorically become more visible.

Such preservation is also at work in everyday Palestinian narratives, which function rhetorically to keep the past alive. These narratives are poignantly chronicled in books such as Hass's *Drinking the Sea at Gaza* and Pearlman's *Occupied Voices*, where refugees "tell of their long-gone family homes in Palestine, speaking as if they had seen them only the week before" (Pearlman 3). These vivid memories permeate Palestinian refugee narratives, where children in refugee camps tell where they are from by naming their now-lost villages, and their parents and grandparents identify and form allegiances to one another in the same way. Memories of home dominate. Saber, born in Beersheba in 1943 and forced into Gaza with his family in 1948, recounts how his parents "used to talk about Beersheba all the time like a kind of paradise lost. . . . They would say that everything there was green, that there was a lot of land and fruit trees. . . . As a child, I would dream about going back to this lost paradise" (Pearlman 18–19). In her interviews with Gaza refugees, Amira Hass chronicles countless variations on this longing for an idyllic, lost Palestine: memories of corn raised so tall it came up to one's chest; fields full of bountiful olive trees, apricot trees, almond trees, and fig trees; memories of olive and eucalyptus trees that grew tall and majestic at the village entrance—"if I could take you there," one refugee tells Hass, "I could tell you who owns each plot of land" (155). As Hass explains, "In the years that I've lived in Gaza, not a day has gone by without someone mentioning his house or the number of acres that his family had or the size of his village" (160). These refugee narratives are quite beautiful and poignant, made more so by the fact that the sites of the destroyed villages are sometimes as close as fifteen miles from the refugee camps, yet accessible only in memories and narratives.[2]

In *I Saw Ramallah*, Mourid Barghouti explains that the experience of exile turns place into time: "I do not live in a place," he writes, "I live in a time" (91). Amira Hass provides an example of what Barghouti means. She recounts a conversation in which one Palestinian asks another, "Where are you from?" and each answers the other by identifying the name of his family village. Hass writes: "Both the men were born in the Gaza Strip and knew of the village only from their parents and grandparents. But in mentioning the names, the two took their place in an essential human chain that challenges history and defies the passage of time with an individual and collective inner truth that refuses to die" (161). Palestinian refugees live not only in a time but also in a rhetoric. In its persistence, this rhetoric continues to serve as a counter-argument to the myths surrounding Israel's War of Independence in 1948, which suggest that Palestinians left their homes willingly or on the advice of Arab leaders (for revisionist historical accounts of Israel's War of Independence, see the work of Israeli "New Historians" Benny Morris, Ilan Pappe, and Tom Segev) or, in then Israeli Prime Minister Golda Meir's claim in a 1969 *Sunday Times* interview, that Palestinians did not exist:

> There was no such thing as Palestinians. When was there an independent Palestinian people with a Palestinian state? It was either southern Syria before the First World War, and then it was a Palestine including Jordan. It was not as though there was a Palestinian people in Palestine considering itself as a Palestinian people and we came and threw them out and took their country away from them. They did not exist.

Meir's claim demonstrates the power of the rhetorical memories that oppose Palestinian rhetorical memories. The issue, then, is not only about competing memories or about who is more right and who is more wrong. Certainly, the impasse that plagues public discourse about Israel-Palestine in the US suffers plenty from a lack of historical and factual knowledge and from competing truth claims. More than that, the question has to do with how rhetorical memories work to shape our encounters with what we read, hear, and see and how we take these up in our responses and actions. There is a powerful affective dimension at work here that, in some cases, is manipulated by those who want to silence dialogue about Israel-Palestine in the US, but just as often works in more habitual, less conscious ways to prevent sustained engagement with the issues. It is important that we understand how these uptakes work and how we can intervene in them in respectful, productive ways.

The mainstream US public discourse surrounding the Israel-Palestine conflict and the entrenched set of uptakes that shape it is exemplified by the controversial case of John Mearsheimer and Stephen Walt's report, "The Israeli Lobby." The report was first published in article form in the *London Review of Books* in March 2006 and then posted online, in an extended format, on the Harvard Kennedy School of Government website where Walt is an endowed professor of international affairs (Mearsheimer is an endowed professor of Political Science at University of Chicago).[3] In general, the article argued that US support of Israel has been unwavering, has jeopardized US security, and has been driven by the unmatched power of the Israel "lobby," which Mearsheimer and Walt define as the "loose coalition of individuals and organizations who actively work to steer U.S. foreign policy in a pro-Israel direction" (np). Threaded through this argument is a critique of Israel's policies toward Palestinians.

Space does not permit a full contextualization, but reaction to the article was heated and ranged across contexts, genres, and perspectives, from mainstream media to op-ed pieces to letters and e-mails. Although met with some reputable support, the article was largely condemned in the US. One of the most prominent charges against Mearsheimer and Walt is that they perceive the lobby as a well-organized Jewish conspiracy. Response letters published in the *London Review of Books* noted, "Accusations of powerful Jews behind the scene are part of the most dangerous traditions of modern anti-Semitism." Likewise, the Anti-Defamation League called the article "a classical conspiratorial anti-Semitic analysis involving the canards of Jewish power and Jewish control," a charge that was echoed by Eliot Cohen (professor at Johns Hopkins School of Advanced International Studies), Harvard law professor Alan Dershowitz, Representative Eliot Engel of New York, and many others.

Dershowitz, as well, accuses Mearsheimer and Walt of recycling accusations that "would be seized upon by bigots to promote their anti-Semitic agendas" ("Letters") and compares the article to "The Protocols of the Elders of Zion," a classical anti-Semitic text which scapegoated Jews as an untrustworthy class of international conspirators plotting against the gentile nations for world domination by controlling banks and stock exchanges, etc. (the Protocols were, after the Bible, the world's most widely circulated book between 1918–1939). In a *Washington Post* editorial, Eliot Cohen summed it up: "If by anti-Semitism one means obsessive and irrationally hostile beliefs about Jews; if one accuses them of disloyalty, subversion, or treachery, of having occult powers and of participating in secret combinations that manipulate institutions and governments; if one systematically selects everything unfair, ugly, or wrong about Jews as individuals or as a group and equally systematically suppresses any exculpatory information—why yes, this paper is anti-Semitic."

Yet these accusations do not seem entirely warranted when looking at Mearsheimer and Walt's report, which explicitly states that the Israel lobby's "activities are *not* a conspiracy of the sort depicted in tracts like the 'Protocols of the Elders of Zion'" (np) and that rejects the notion that the lobby is some sort of secret cabal. The article also notes that "there is a strong moral case for supporting Israel's existence" (np). Yet to understand the reactions to the report, we need to remember, as Anne Freadman has explained, that uptakes have memories ("Uptake"). We do not simply respond to the immediate demands of a rhetorical situation, an utterance, a text, a genre. Uptakes have memories in the sense that they are learned recognitions and inclinations that, over time and through ideological reproduction, become habitual. Our uptake memory is what we bring to a rhetorical encounter, and it is what helps us select from, define, and make sense of that encounter.

In this case, we can see how Mearsheimer and Walt's report triggers uptake memory. For instance, early in the article, Mearsheimer and Walt argue that Israel does not behave like a loyal ally. They write: "Israeli officials frequently ignore U.S. requests and renege on promises (including pledges to stop building settlements. . . .). Israel has provided sensitive military technology to potential rivals like China. . . . According to the General Accounting Office, Israel also 'Conducts the most aggressive espionage operations against the U.S. of any ally.' . . . Israel is hardly the only country that spies on the U.S., but its willingness to spy on its principal patron casts further doubt on its strategic value" (np). The argument and evidence notwithstanding, this excerpt, coming early in the text, includes what Bakhtin terms "echoes and reverberations" of Jewish stereotypes—that Jews are disloyal, shifty, manipulative—that contain and trigger rhetorical memory of modern anti-Semitism.

The same thing is at work when Mearsheimer and Walt later write: "Thanks in part to the influence Jewish voters have on presidential elections, the Lobby also has significant leverage over the executive branch. Although they make up fewer than 3 percent of the population, they make large campaign donations to candidates of both parties" (np). Again, the words "influence" collocated with "Jewish" here triggers rhetorical memory that shapes how readers would encounter the text. So by the time we get to the part in the report where Mearsheimer and Walt claim that "the Lobby's perspective prevails in the mainstream media" (np), this claim can easily get taken up instead as "Jews control the media"—not because the report ever states this, but because it has previously triggered a set of uptakes that secure this response. Likewise, Mearsheimer and Walt write: "The neoconservatives had been determined to topple Saddam even before Bush became president. They caused a stir early in 1998 by publishing two open letters to Clinton, calling for Saddam's removal. The signatories, many of whom had close ties to pro-Israel groups . . . had little trouble persuading the Clinton administration to adopt the general goal of ousting Saddam. But *they* were unable to sell a war to achieve that objective. *They* were no more able to generate enthusiasm for invading Iraq in the early months of the Bush administration. *They* needed help to achieve that aim. That help arrived with 9/11" (np; emphasis added). Rhetorically, by not assigning agency in the last sentence "That help arrived with 9/11," and assigning agency in the preceding sentences "They were able," "They were no more able," "They needed help," one can imagine that the "they" can be made to rhetorically transfer to fill in the missing agent of the last sentence. Indeed, it is not difficult to imagine how some readers, after reading all the evidence of the Israel lobby's influence, would link pro-Israel groups with 9/11, in what is for some an anti-Semitic conspiracy theory, or present 9/11 as somehow a welcome event for pro-Israel groups.

Now these echoes and reverberations, appearing in a report on the role of the Israel lobby that also critiques Israel's policies toward Palestinians, inadvertently links support for Palestinian rights and self-determination with perceived anti-Semitism. In this set of uptakes, critique of Israeli policy and the Israel lobby taps into threatening stereotypes. Since Palestinian representation is linked to critiques of Israeli policy and the Israel lobby, therefore, Palestinian representation is anti-Semitic. Any salient arguments Mearsheimer and Walt make are thus lost in this rhetorical equation. And when former KKK leader David Duke writes of the Mearsheimer and Walt report, "I have read about the report and read one summary already, and I am surprised how excellent it is. . . . It is quite satisfying to see a body in the premier American University essentially come out and validate every major point I have been making since even before the war even started" (qtd in Foxman 81), this drives the threat even deeper.[4]

The uptakes I have described at work in the Mearsheimer and Walt controversy are triggered by rhetorical memories of very real, horrific, and continuing anti-Semitism. At the same time, these uptakes invariably create a rhetoric of incommensurability which too often silences attempts to represent Palestinian injustice and advocate for Palestinian rights. What makes these uptakes so powerful is that they circulate across and trump context and genre distinctions in ways that block attempts to use rhetoric to effect social change.

Within speech act theory, uptake traditionally refers to how an illocutionary act (saying, for example, "it is hot in here" with the intention of getting someone to cool the room) gets taken up as a perlocutionary effect (someone subsequently opening a window) under certain conditions. Recently, Anne Freadman has brought uptake to bear on genre theory, arguing that genres condition uptakes ("Uptake"). Genres do this by maintaining normalized, expected relationships between utterances and actions—illocutionary acts and perlocutionary effects—so that genres help us recognize and take up utterances as socially consequential actions.

According to Freadman, uptakes mediate inter-generic boundaries: for example, how a call for papers gets taken up as proposals, or, as in Freadman's more serious example, how a court sentence during a trial gets taken up as an execution. Uptake helps us understand how systematic, normalized relations between genres coordinate complex forms of social action—how and why genres get taken up in certain ways and not others and what gets done and not done as a result.

As Freadman is careful to note, uptake does not depend on causation but rather on *selection*. Uptake, she explains, "selects, defines, or represents its object. . . . Uptake is first the taking of an object; it is not the causation of a response by an intention. This is the hidden dimension of the long, ramified, intertextual memory of uptake: the object is taken from a set of possibilities" ("Uptake" 48). Our uptake memories, our learned recognitions and inclinations, are what we bring to a rhetorical/textual encounter, and they are what help us select from, define, and act within that encounter. In short, habitual uptakes guide our recognitions and responses. Knowledge of uptake, then, is knowledge of how to perform within a rhetorical situation: what to take up, how, and when, including how to execute uptakes strategically and when to resist expected uptakes.

Genres and uptakes are closely connected, and genres often help condition uptakes (indeed, through habitual uptakes, genres reliably invoke one another). What we see happening in the case of the Israel-Palestine conflict is that uptakes can likewise trump or outlast or overpower genre distinctions when they are used to select, define, or represent objects in ways that take up certain memories and block others across various contexts and genres. As Freadman notes in her discussion of uptake, this is the strategy of power.

At the same time, however, this can also be the strategy of counter-acting power, as when uptakes from one context are brought to bear on another. We see such a recontextualization of uptake memory at work in Jimmy Carter's book, *Palestine: Peace Not Apartheid*. While Carter's book is more of a personal reflection and accounting of his involvement in the region than it is a rigorously cited historical study, it gains its power by presenting two disrupting and challenging uptakes, both of which are invoked in the book's title: "Palestine" and "Apartheid." The mere mention of the name "Palestine" by a former US President constitutes a significant uptake, since it acknowledges the existence of a Palestinian homeland. Even more powerfully, Carter's use of the word "apartheid" also triggers uptake memory by transferring and applying a term for South African, legally-enforced racial segregation and using it to represent the conditions under which Palestinians are increasingly forced to live within the Occupied Territories, especially the West Bank. Indeed, the image of Israel's "Security Fence" surrounding the West Bank depicted on the book's cover, juxtaposed with the book's title, suggests fairly directly that the walled barrier (which Carter refers to as "imprisonment wall" [174] and "segregation wall" [193]) is both a symbol of apartheid and an impediment to peace.

Interestingly, the word apartheid appears minimally throughout the book: The index lists three references—by my informal count, it was four. Yet the presence of the word in the book's title permitted US mainstream public discourse about the Israel-Palestine conflict questions, comparisons, and debates about segregation and inequality that were previously less visible and generated a great deal of controversy. (It is harder to imagine, for example, that Bob Simon's January 2009 *60 Minutes* report on the West Bank occupation and his depiction of settlements and settler-only roads would have aired if not for the apartheid uptake that Carter's book permitted.)

By bringing uptake memory from one context (South African apartheid) to another (Israel-Palestine), Carter's book created the possibility for a different debate to take place. Along the way, Carter disrupts a number of other dominant uptakes. For instance, he brings the language of colonialism (to counter-balance the language of defense and security) to bear on the Israeli occupation of Palestinian territory; he challenges the perception that Yasir Arafat was responsible for the failure of the so-called peace process, having rejected Ehud Barak's "generous offer" (152); he reconfigures the narrative of historical events to highlight Israel's resistance to peace efforts (see, for example, his depiction of events that followed the Arab League resolution in 2002 [156–158]); and he allows Palestinian perspectives to emerge for a mainstream audience not used to hearing them (for example, Carter frequently uses indirect speech to report what Palestinian representatives have told him: "Abbas informed me," "he reminded me," "he responded," "He also asked"). While none of these counter-uptakes were especially revelatory or new to those who are aware of debates about the conflict, they were made especially powerful because they were performed by a former US President and addressed to a mainstream US public.

While Carter cites provocative acts by Arab militants, acknowledges corruption among Palestinian leaders, condemns terrorism as a serious threat to Israel and an obstacle to peace, and insists that "the security of Israel must be guaranteed" (207); cites his commitment to Israel's security through his negotiation of the Israeli-Egyptian peace treaty; and is careful to explain that "the driving purpose for the forced separation of the two peoples [Israelis and Palestinians] is unlike that in South Africa—not racism, but the acquisition of land" (189–190)—critics accused Carter of being one-sided, distorting facts, and contriving an accusation of ethnic cleansing against Israel in its dealing with the Palestinians. Alan Dershowitz's description of Carter in his *The Case Against Israel's Enemies: Exposing Jimmy Carter and Others Who Stand in the Way of Peace* is an example of how this uptake worked with the term "apartheid." To depict Carter as an obstacle to peace when he helped negotiate a peace deal between Israel and Egypt seemingly defies reason, yet it also reveals the power of uptake to function as a site of contestation—as both a site of instantiation and regulation of power and a site of intervention.

Dershowitz rejects the apartheid analogy as an "explosive and incorrect term" (23), arguing that it "fuels anti-Semitism in the Arab world" (47) and contributes to the irrational hatred of Israel. Instead of engaging in an argument about how the presence of settler-only roads in the West Bank, for example, serves as a kind of apartheid, Dershowitz responds instead to the uptake memory triggered by the word "apartheid." Arguing that "[r]acism is the sin qua non of apartheid" (26), Dershowitz proceeds to dispute the presence of racism in Israel: "But Israel, unlike its neighboring Arab nations, does not use religious coercion; neither is there segregation or discrimination against minorities who are not Jewish" (25). By focusing on the legal definition of apartheid and its specific systematic practice in South Africa, Dershowitz and others can then reject the analogy wholesale, claiming that the apartheid system that once existed in South Africa "does not remotely resemble Israel" (26). As noted earlier, Carter was careful to explain that "the driving purpose for the forced separation of the two peoples [Israelis and Palestinians] is unlike that in South Africa—not racism, but the acquisition of land" (189–190); likewise, to my reading anyway, it seemed fairly clear that Carter was applying the term "apartheid" only to the Occupied Palestinian Territories, not to Israel as a whole, but the uptake memory triggered by the word apartheid presents Dershowitz with an opportunity not only to reject the analogy, but also to turn it around against itself, from being a critique of Israeli occupation and segregation in the West Bank to being an existential threat to Israel. As Dershowitz argues, "To accuse Israel of apartheid is therefore to strike at the foundations of the state itself. It implies . . . that Israel is illegitimate, racist, and deserving of destruction. Just as the apartheid system in South Africa had to be dismantled entirely, the analogy posits, 'apartheid Israel' must be utterly destroyed" (23). So an analogy that Carter had purportedly used to provoke debate about the conflict, with the goal of outlining a path to peace and security, becomes taken up as a threat to Israel's existence.

Attempts to promote critical inquiry and public deliberation about the Israel-Palestine conflict in the US by and large have to contend with this rhetorical dilemma. In light of this dilemma, how can we intervene in the normalized set of uptakes we see exemplified in the Mearsheimer and Walt and the Carter controversies? How can Palestinians and those who work on their behalf speak out against human rights abuses without triggering rhetorical memories that threaten accusations of anti-Semitism and hatred of Israel? For me, the answer has to do in part with identifying and confronting the uptakes that secure and maintain habitual responses. This means we need to acknowledge when these uptakes are appropriate (as in the case of David Duke) and when they are used to silence dialogue (as in the case of Mearsheimer and Walt, Jimmy Carter, Steven Salaita, or Bob Simon's *60 Minutes* episode). But identifying uptakes is not enough. We also need to intervene in these normalized uptakes—that is, to delay, alter, or avoid triggering the habitual responses while also being accountable to truth and evidence. Part of that approach involves being careful in our rhetorical choices so as to avoid loaded, memory triggering words, but part of it is also about imagining alternative uptakes as well as allowing genre and context distinctions to *matter*—to help us distinguish between uptakes in more nuanced, genre- and context-specific ways so as to allow for a greater selection of responses (something art and humor, for example, afford).[5] There are not easy solutions, but these are some of the challenges I think we have to confront if we as rhetoricians wish to intervene in dominant uptakes in order to promote civic discourse about the Israel-Palestine as well as other conflicts.

NOTES

1. In May 2006, a colleague and I posted an announcement on the WPA-L for the Fourth Annual Rachel Corrie Award for Courage in the Teaching of Writing, sponsored by the Progressive Special Interest Groups and Caucuses Coalition that meets at the Conference on College Composition and Communication. The award was created to honor the memory of Rachel Corrie, a twenty-three-year-old student from Washington State who was killed by an Israeli bulldozer in Rafah, Gaza Strip in 2003 while she was blocking the demolition of a Palestinian home as part of the International Solidarity Movement. The award announcement was followed by five days of heated exchanges, personal attacks, facts and counter-facts, and accusations of anti-Semitism. Similar exchanges and accusations have taken place on the Rhetoricians for Peace discussion list about the Rachel Corrie award as well about debates over boycott and divestment campaigns against Israel.

2. For other accounts, see Ra'anan Alexandrowicz's *The Inner Tour*, a powerful documentary of a group of Palestinian refugees on a bus tour of Israel, and Sandy Tolan's *The Lemon Tree*, which recounts a young Palestinian man's encounter and subsequent friendship with an Israeli woman after he returns to visit his lost family home she and her family now inhabit. See also Joe Sacco's graphic novel, *Palestine*, as well as Saree Makdisi's recent book, *Palestine Inside and Out: An Everyday Occupation*.

3. Since the publication of the report in 2006, Mearsheimer and Walt have published a book length version of their research titled *The Israel Lobby and U.S. Foreign Policy* (Farrar, Straus and Giroux, 2008).

4. Mearsheimer and Walt have rejected the praise from David Duke, writing in response: "We have no control over who likes or dislikes our article, but we regret that Duke used it to promote his racist agenda, which we utterly reject" ("Letters").

5. For example, Joe Sacco's graphic novel series *Palestine*, the recent award-winning film *Waltz with Bashir*, the Israeli television series *Arab Labor*, and the song "Look into My Eyes" by the Danish-based hip-hop band *Outlandish* all explore the Israel-Palestine conflict in ways that are as critical as Mearsheimer and Walt's and Carter's, but in examining the uptakes in response to these productions, the artistic expression seems to produce more nuanced, alternative uptakes, which suggests that art and humor have the potential to delay and defamiliarize uptakes in productive ways.

Works Cited

Barghouti, Mourid. *I Saw Ramallah*. New York: Anchor Books, 2000. Print.

Burke, Kenneth. *A Rhetoric of Motives*. Berkeley: U of California P, 1950. Print.

Carter, Jimmy. *Palestine: Peace Not Apartheid*. New York: Simon and Schuster, 2006. Print.

Cohen, Eliot. "Yes, It's Anti-Semitic." *The Washington Post* (5 April 2006). Web. 7 June 2010.

Dershowitz, Alan. *The Case Against Israel's Enemies: Exposing Jimmy Carter and Others Who Stand in the Way of Peace*. New Jersey: Wiley and Sons, 2008. Print.

—. "Letters." *London Review of Books* 28.8 (20 April 2006): 3–12. Web. 7 June 2010.

Fleming, David. "Rhetoric as a Course of Study." *College English* 61.2 (1998): 169-91. Print.

Folman, Ari, and David Polonsky. *Waltz with Bashir: A Lebanon War Story*. New York: Metropolitan Books, 2009. Print.

Foxman, Abraham H. *The Deadliest Lies: The Israel Lobby and the Myth of Jewish Control*. New York: Palgrave, 2007. Print.

Freadman, Anne. "Anyone for Tennis?" *Genre and the New Rhetoric*. Ed. Aviva Freedman and Peter Medway. Bristol: Taylor and Francis, 1994. 43–66. Print.

—. "Uptake." *The Rhetoric and Ideology of Genre: Strategies for Stability and Change*. Ed. Richard Coe, Lorelei Lingard, and Tatiana Teslenko. Cresskill, NJ: Hampton Press, 2002. Print.

Hass, Amira. *Drinking the Sea at Gaza: Days and Nights in a Land Under Siege*. New York: Henry Holt, 1996. Print.

Khalidi, Walid. *All that Remains: The Palestinian Villages Occupied and Depopulated by Israel in 1948*. Institute for Palestine Studies, 1992. Print.

Makdisi, Saree. *Palestine Inside and Out: An Everyday Occupation*. New York: W.W. Norton, 2008. Print.

Mearsheimer, John, and Stephen Walt. "The Israel Lobby." *London Review of Books* 28.6 (23 March 2006): 3–12. Web. 7 June 2010.

—. "Letters." *London Review of Books* 28.9 (11 May 2006). Web. 7 June 2010.

Meir, Golda. "Interview." *The Sunday Times*. 15 June, 1969. Web

Pearlman, Wendy. *Occupied Voices: Stories of Everyday Life from the Second Intifada*. New York: Thunder's Mouth Press/Nation Books, 2003. Print.

Sacco, Joe. *Palestine*. Seattle: Fantagraphics Books, 2006. Print.

Said, Edward W. *After the Last Sky: Palestinian Lives*. New York: Pantheon Books, 1986. Print.

—. "No Reconciliation Allowed." *Letters of Transit: Reflections on Exile, Identity, Language, and Loss*. Ed. André Aciman. New York: The New Press, 1999. 91–114. Print.

3 Reluctant Rhetoricians: Refusing to Frame the Israel-Palestine Conflict Through Jewish-Arab Antagonism

Matthew Abraham

> *A harsh reality needs harsh words to describe it, live, and survive it. Laundered words allow us to perceive soiled realities as clean. We did not invent this method, but we improved it, as if we learned nothing from the evil ones who laundered words before us.*
>
> —Avraham Burg, *The Holocaust Is Over We Must Rise From Its Ashes*

In 2014, Steven Salaita, who had been offered a tenured position in the University of Illinois's American Indian Studies Program, found himself in the fight of his life. Salita was effectively fired when his position was rescinded by Chancellor Phyllis Wise on August 1, within weeks of Salaita assuming his appointment. UIUC's administration responded to key donors who were disturbed by the tone and content of Salaita's supposedly "anti-Israel" comments on Twitter about Israel's destruction of Gaza. Salaita continues his campaign for due process and reinstatement.

Salaita's firing created a national backlash against UIUC, as scholars considered the implications of the case for academic freedom, free speech, and contractual rights. To date, the University of Illinois's administration has characterized Salaita's twitter remarks as uncivil; disrespectful of opposing points of view; and a possible obstacle to the recruitment of students, faculty, and staff. Many of Salaita's tweets were misrepresented in the media to portray him as a racist and anti-Semite, including this one: "Zionists: transforming anti-Semitism from something horrible into something honorable since 1948." As Phyan Nugen demonstrates in his two-part essay, "Reading Salaita in Illinois—By Way of Cary Nelson," Salaita's tweets were cherry-picked and taken out of context to portray Salaita as a racist.

Several key organizations, including the American Association of University Professors, The Center for Constitutional Rights, and the Modern Language Association have denounced UIUC's actions in this case. Unfortunately, no official organization associated with the field of Rhetoric and Composition chose to endorse a public statement in support of Salaita. Litigation is now pending in the case. The controversy demonstrates how the charge of anti-Semitism takes on a promiscuous aspect, as Israel's most ardent defenders seek to remove the prospect of serious debate about the Israel-Palestine conflict by denouncing Israel's critics as racists and anti-Semites, and in turn, confusing the relevant issues.

As this essay seeks to explore, the conflation of criticisms of Israeli militarism with anti-Semitism constitutes a distinct rhetorical strategy geared to ensuring that Israel's ethnonational project will be identified with Judaism, despite many Jews' rejection of Zionism as being inconsistent with the tenets of Judaism. I attempt to work through the rhetorical production of such conflations, focusing on how and why they take place.

Reflecting on the Impasse

In assessing the many different efforts I have undertaken over the years to raise awareness about the hidden assumptions shaping the US citizen's understanding of the Israel-Palestine conflict, I have been continually struck by how little headway has been made in our field to address the argumentative dynamics informing how people talk about and debate competing claims informing the conflict.[1] These argumentative dynamics are clearly driven by the demands and claims of history, cultural and religious identifications, the affective attachments accompanying competing positions, and the embodied states of the participants. While it is impossible for these participants to divorce themselves from their embodiments and affective attachments, it is possible for participants to develop a more nuanced understanding of why they react to certain knowledge claims about the Israel-Palestine conflict in the ways that they do, seeking to contextualize these reactions in relation to the present historical moment instead of through the reverberations of the past that so often distort perceptions. As Lynn Worsham notes in her "Going Postal: Pedagogic Violence and the Schooling of Emotion," "Without a fundamental revision in our conception of subjectivity and of our affective relationship to the world, the radical potential of recent pedagogy to reconstitute our emotional lives may be re-contained, in spite of its best intentions and the euphoria of its claims, as a strategy of condescension" (240). Worsham invites us to consider how our subjectivity and affective relationships are constructed and maintained over time, cautioning that—without a fundamental revision to our conceptions of both—the prospects of radical pedagogy will be channeled into strategies of condescension. For the purposes of this article, I think it is important to keep Worsham's cautionary note in mind as it reminds us how easily claims to liberation and transgression within current pedagogies can slide into simply telling others what to think or believe, or how to act, if they are to be considered ethical subjects. This tendency to insist that one is being ethical, while others are unethical or completely blind to the demands within an ethical system, is particularly pronounced in discussions about the Israel-Palestine conflict.

Burkean and postmodern conceptions of identification teach us that just as we inhabit history as situated subjects, history (with all its hauntings) inhabits us. To speak of an "I" is to simultaneously also to speak of a "We." If, as Diana Fuss reminds us, identification is the name of the psychical mechanism through which one achieves self-recognition by detouring through the Other, position-taking cannot be simply viewed as an individual "act," but emerges in negotiating the border between the inside and the outside, the border between the self and one's environment (49). To identify where one stands is to simultaneously also identify where one stands in relation to a community of other voices, a community characterized by identification and division. As Burke teaches us, "put identification and division ambiguously together, so that you cannot know for certain just where one ends and the other begins, and you have the characteristic invitation to rhetoric" (25). How we answer this "characteristic invitation" determines the conditions of possibility for achieving community.

As committed public intellectuals, rhetoricians have a great deal to contribute in elucidating how history, conscious and unconscious identifications, affective attachments, and "embodiment" shape one's understanding of—and the ability to make claims about—the Israel-Palestine conflict; including identifying how history and language, all too frequently, serve or obscure a particular politics. However, these uses (and possible abuses) of history and language to advance a particular viewpoint are not always in our conscious control, as I will try to elaborate. Indeed, history often "returns" to us like a boomerang with sometimes unexpected and startling effects.[2] By virtue of its returning to us in a different form, and within a potentially deformed context, this history necessarily becomes ripe for misrecognition and possibly illegitimate activation and deployment as part of (and within) a hegemonic politics.

Perhaps the reason so little substantive discussion about the Israel-Palestine conflict takes place in our field is because participants within these debates rarely seem to have an interest in exchanging information; instead, interlocutors seem intent upon silencing or damaging the Other.[3] While this might seem like a provocative and far too sweeping claim about scholarship and debate within our field, I have witnessed how gingerly journal and press editors approach the topic of Israel-Palestine when it comes to determining whether a manuscript will see its way into print, suggesting that certain sensitivities around the conflict should not be explored for fear of offending the readership. These journal and press editors seem to prefer hewing to a very protective discourse around the Israel-Palestine conflict than to deal with some relatively straightforward dimensions of it that support the Palestinian narrative about the oppressive effects of Israeli colonization and militarism on the indigenous inhabitants. Among these relatively straightforward dimensions of the conflict are the international consensus on the Question of Palestine and the relevant international law, including UN 242, which requires Israel to withdraw to its pre-June-1967 borders and immediately evacuate the settlements in the West Bank.

Even establishment politicians such as Barack Obama and Jimmy Carter have insisted that Israel must comply with this aspect of international law if the Israel-Palestine conflict is to be resolved.[4] In this context, the ridiculous charges of anti-Semitism and bigotry that have been leveled against Carter and the silly attempts to portray Obama as harboring anti-Israel sentiments create an interesting discursive predicament. Concerns about the rise of the so-called New Anti-Semitism has also imposed an unhealthy and stifling form of political correctness on the field that has resulted in the censorship of hard-hitting scholarly criticisms of Israel's occupation and its effects on the Middle East peace process. To work past this predicament, we must reframe our identifications with respect to Israeli and Palestinian nationalism if rhetoricians are to find a way out of the discursive impasse that currently hampers discussion about the historical and diplomatic record.

When debates a nomination for a teaching award emerge out of the discourse of anti-Semitism, as they did in the listserv exchange I will describe below, with participants angrily withdrawing because the Other is either hopelessly racist or uninformed, it is a small wonder that serious discussion about the historical and diplomatic record around the Israel-Palestine never takes place. Debate, or an exchange of views, seems not to be the point. Instead, the rhetorical situation enables participants to unleash aggression and to employ a particular affective stance against those with whom they disagree. The position one may have held at the beginning of the debate is simply reaffirmed. I would like to examine some ways out of this troubling discursive impasse, exploring why the Israel-Palestine conflict is particularly susceptible to this sort of dynamic. Let me begin by examining the debate that touched upon our professional community.

Disavowals

In a 2004 *JAC* article entitled "The Rhetoric of Academic Controversy: Edward Said in the American Imagination," I examined how the life and legacy of Edward Said tend to become objects of transference within debates about Middle East politics. I would like to extend the analysis I developed in that article to assess how the memory of the late Rachel Corrie, for whom the Rachel Corrie Courage in the Teaching of Writing Award is named, took on a similar transferential role when a call for nominations for the award was posted to the Writing Program Administrators list in May 2006.

How could the circumstances surrounding the death of an American college student in Gaza become the object of intense discussion on a list-serv for writing program administrators? How could the politics surrounding the Israel-Palestine conflict and the Middle East, as the controversy over this college student's act of seeming martyrdom, come to ever so briefly grip the attention of our field? What seemed like a relatively straightforward decision to post a call for nominations for the Rachel Corrie Courage in the Teaching of Writing to the Writing Program Administrators list in May of 2006 quite unexpectedly led to an interrogation of the values informing our professional organization and its supposed politics. What narrative, if any, was the umbrella organization for writing instruction, College Composition and Communication, forwarding about Rachel Corrie's death and Middle East politics, some asked, by allowing the Progressive Special Interest Caucuses and Coalitions (PSCC) to promote the Rachel Corrie Courage in the Teaching of Writing Award—an award seeking to recognize courage and risk-taking in the academy—and to present the award at the national conference (the CCCCs)? According to the award organizers, the Rachel Corrie Courage in the Teaching of Writing Award seeks to honor "a teacher in the CCCC who has taken professional risks in order to promote social justice through the teaching of writing" (Abraham, "Nomination Call"). In response, one list-serv member pointed out that the call for nominations was filled with "very disturbing loaded language," noting that the award was a polarizing and offensive way to pursue peace and justice: "I'm uncomfortable with an announcement that asserts its interest in peace while also subtly (or perhaps not so subtly) repeating some of the anti-Israel rhetoric that has become so common among us liberals lately" (Writing Program Administrators Archive). Another member stated that he felt the award to be problematic because it takes the tragedy that befell Rachel Corrie and raises it above "the thousands of other tragedies that have been going on in that region for decades." This person asked, "Where is the award for the busload of Israeli school children which was stopped so that children could be shot, execution style, at close range, for example?" This award, then, in this person's estimation, is a not-so-subtle way of expressing solidarity with the Palestinian people—and as a consequence—demonizing Israel.

According to other critics of the award, to make a value judgment about Corrie's actions—that they were in fact courageous—and to accept a specific reading of these actions as consistent with anti-colonial and liberationist struggle improperly politicized an organization committed to writing and rhetorical studies. To endorse a tendentious reading of Corrie's actions, according to some, was to uncritically accept a pro-Palestinian politics, essentially confirming that Corrie had been deliberately killed by the Israeli Defense Forces in March of 2003, when she was supposedly defending a Palestinian home in Rafah, Gaza against demolition. Could Rachel Corrie necessarily be framed as a victim, some asked, implying that she may have been responsible for own death. One participant, who was hesitant to get involved in the discussion because he was still a graduate student, felt obligated to point out that there is a tendency to align Jews, who ask legitimate questions about how Rachel Corrie died, with the repressive policies of the Israeli government. As this person noted, when Jews question whether Rachel Corrie was actually murdered, they are inevitably assumed to be automatic supporters of Israel and its policies, which is precisely the type of anti-Semitism that is at the heart of Zionism—an anti-Semitism that must be vigilantly guarded against. In other words, Zionist ideology has enabled a logic that identifies Judaism with Israel and Zionism; this is the oldest form of anti-Semitism going back to biblical times because it identifies Jews with a nation and a national ideology, positioning Jews to be spoken for by leaders serving national ambitions. According to this logic, of which the participant mentioned above seemed to be unaware, to even question the appropriateness of the Rachel Corrie Courage in the Teaching of Writing Award enables anti-Semitic accusations of siding with murder and Israel's occupation. As this participant wrote, " . . . a person who raises concerns about the naming of the award suddenly finds him or herself directly, or by implication, identified with murder, violence and injustice." Furthermore, this interlocutor suggests that when Jewish supporters of Israel raise legitimate questions about the appropriateness of the Rachel Corrie Courage in the Teaching of Writing Award, as well as the circumstances surrounding Corrie's death, they often become stand-ins for the Israeli government. That Jews become stand-ins for the Israeli government is perhaps more an operationalization of Zionist ideology, and not necessarily a manifestation of the anti-Semitism frequently attributed to critics of Israel.

Another discussion participant brought up the example of Alyssa Flatow, a young Jewish student who went to study in Israel in 1995 and was killed by a suicide bomber. According to him, "The courage of her convictions led her to study in Israel, despite the risk of suicide attack, and she died in the pursuit of learning." He expressed the opinion that the Corrie award represents "a skillful rhetorical move designed to draw attention to a particular perspective on the Israel-Palestine conflict." He then encouraged list participants to think about how we would go about talking about an award meant to honor Alyssa Flatow. Would this award be any more or less appropriate than the Rachel Corrie award? To ask this question, according to this participant, would lead "into a battle over the relative values of injustices, the moral status of different peoples, the tortured history of the region—and suddenly we are taking sides on the Israel/Palestinian conflict—a conversation I don't think is appropriate for the list." Despite the calls for list-serv propriety, the debate continued, with several participants insisting that the conversation about the Rachel Corrie Courage in the Teaching of Writing Award was appropriate for the WPA list precisely because it involved questions about the CCC's values and its advocacy of social justice for disadvantaged populations.

Furthermore, disagreement revolved around the clear incommensurability between the courage Corrie displayed—in supposedly facing down an Israeli Defense Forces Bulldozer—and the risks adjuncts and the untenured take in confronting the political economy of the academy, as they cope with the unstable labor conditions that make their employment situation tenuous at best. In the context of this labor uncertainty, the untenured do in fact demonstrate courage when they challenge the labor conditions within their universities by asking administrators hard questions about the institution. In addition, for these untenured faculty to pursue controversial lines of inquiry within their scholarship and teaching could also possibly jeopardize their ability to later obtain a contract renewal or a tenure-track position. Labor uncertainty often produces conformity within institutional and cultural domains, whereby pleasing authority figures ensures one's economic survival. While there is a clear lack of parity between Rachel Corrie losing her life by standing in front of an Israeli Defense Forces bulldozer—as an act of resistance against Israeli colonization and in solidarity with Palestinian dispossession—and the brave adjunct who places her employment prospects in jeopardy by questioning her Dean or department chair about the casualization of labor within her college and department, both actions seek to disrupt the status quo.

As the award creator noted, the Rachel Corrie Courage in the Teaching of Writing Award is designed to recognize work that often goes unrecognized, work that advances social justice, grassroots, and maverick opinions that are threatening to stalwarts in the CCCCs. The award positions the CCCCs leadership as the status quo (seemingly with respect to Middle East politics and academic institutional politics), and unresponsive to the demands of colonized populations, placing the CCCC's leadership on the defensive and representing it as quiescent, disengaged, and uninterested in political struggle that might lead the organization to clash with political forces bigger than itself. As the nomination announcement makes clear, the award seeks to recognize an untenured scholar who "has taken professional risks in order to promote social justice through the teaching of writing." Furthermore, the nomination announcement advances the following claim: "It is well known that the politics of hiring, tenure, and promotion often motivate graduate students and junior faculty to write, teach, and serve in 'safe' subject and project areas; many are encouraged by mentors to shy away from genuinely 'controversial' or 'risky' subjects until they are tenured."

While many may disagree with this characterization of the CCCC's leadership and the politics of the profession, it is clear that the Rachel Corrie Courage in the Teaching of Writing Award challenges academics to think about and through their location within the US academy and this location's relationship to other parts and populations of the world. The purpose of the award, then, is to " . . . encourage writing teachers early in their careers to take on research, pedagogy, and service projects that promote commitment to peace, justice, and human dignity—even when hazarding the ire of deans, chairs, editors, and hiring and review committees." While I do not think that deans, chairs, editors, and hiring and review committees are necessarily opposed to research; pedagogy; and service projects that promote commitments to peace, justice, and human dignity, they might be reluctant to endorse work that is perceived as engaging in advocacy for a despised population such as the Palestinians living under Israeli occupation.[5] If a young American citizen dies in the course of defending such a population, it only stands to reason that there might be attempts to smear this citizen's motives and actions.

Attempts to undercut the memory of Rachel Corrie take the form of questions about the circumstances around Corrie's death, as well as questions about those seeking to memorialize Corrie as a martyr who died at the hands of the Israeli government: Did the driver of the IDF bulldozer deliberately run over Rachel Corrie? Was the IDF bulldozer driver being unjustly blamed for causing Corrie's death in what was in fact an accident? Did the driver actually see Rachel Corrie in her orange vest, standing on top of a pile of dirt with the bulldozer in front of the soon-to-be demolished home? Had anti-Semites and anti-Israel activists in their zeal to condemn Israel seized upon Rachel Corrie's death, memorializing her to unfairly highlight and condemn the Israeli occupation? If one were to suggest that the circumstances around Corrie's death—and her parents' efforts to involve the US and Israeli governments in an investigation of those circumstances—had been underreported or purposely embargoed in the US, would one then be engaging in the classic anti-Semitic canard that "Jews control the media"? These were just a few of the questions encircling this debate one May morning in 2006 on the Writing Program Administrators list-serv.[6]

As a white, privileged American woman, and a member of the International Solidarity Movement who was allegedly murdered by the Israeli Defense Forces (IDF), Corrie served as a tragic reminder of how US support for (and defense of) Israel's occupation seemingly knows no bounds, even when an American citizen is killed under troubling circumstances. According to the nomination announcement, "Rachel was attempting to block an Israeli military bulldozer from demolishing the house of a pharmacist and his family when the driver of the bulldozer ran over her, then backed up and ran over her again." Furthermore, "Wearing a bright orange jacket and using a bullhorn, Rachel was, by all eyewitness accounts and in horrifying photographs published on the Internet, exceptionally visible." For many participants on the WPA list, both of these claims were far from factual. For some, claims that were being reported as factual by the award creators were tendentious and partisan, deliberately slanted against the Israeli government. Perhaps equally controversial was the claim within the nomination announcement that Corrie's "parents, some members of Congress, and grassroots organizations including several Jewish peace groups have called for an independent U.S. investigation into her death. Such an investigation has yet to happen, and the U.S. media virtually buried the story—though it was featured prominently in the U.K. and in many other countries." As I explain below, the lack of US media coverage about the circumstances around Corrie's death became a focal point of controversy among participants on the WPA list, with some insisting that to merely suggest that there was a dearth of coverage about Corrie's death is to traffic in the anti-Semitic canard that "Jews control the media."

While Corrie's actions have been praised by certain members of the progressive community, others have described here as a naïve idealistic young woman who took her ideals too far, someone who had been duped by "left-wing propaganda" on the conflict. For many participants, what justice looks like in the Middle East is far from clear; therefore, the Rachel Corrie award is inappropriate because it presents the Palestinians as the only group with a legitimate grievance in a war-torn region, portraying a complex situation in a simplistic binary of right and wrong. As one participant complained, the award supporters "treat extremely complex situations in [a] simplistic manner and the price for doing so is continued conflict and lack of resolution." This same participant insisted that I had opened the way for expressions of racism against Jews because of my attempts to bring discussions of the Israel-Palestine conflict into the field, suggesting that criticism of Israel—or critical discussion about the conflict—is tantamount to anti-Semitism. This person insisted that the Rachel Corrie Courage in the Teaching of Writing Award, based on the same martyrdom that was behind Palestinian extremism, represented a denial of one group's nationalism (Jewish nationalism, apparently), and sought to portray what justice might look like in the Middle East without taking into account the various complexities of the situation. According to this person, the award creators sought to carry on as "almighty" by portraying a clear "right" and "wrong" in the Middle East.

Some critics of the award questioned whether Corrie's motives as an activist for peace were as pure as her supporters believed, stating that they had read news accounts that described Corrie as protecting terrorist tunnels in Gaza, and as a member of the ISM (International Solidarity Movement), harboring and providing comfort to known terrorist organizations.[7] What some viewed as an altruistic act of sacrifice, Corrie's decision to stand in front of an Israeli Defense Force's bulldozer to protect a Palestinian pharmacist's home, others viewed as anti-Israel activism, which had been capitalized upon by the award creators to promote a political agenda. While there can be little dispute that the politically charged circumstances surrounding Rachel Corrie's death make it difficult to separate Corrie's sentiments toward Israel and the United States from those of the award creators and winners, it is important to remember that the purpose of the Rachel Corrie Courage in the Teaching of Writing Award is to recognize pedagogical courage and risk-taking. Such courage and risk-taking may very well have nothing to do with the Middle East. Indeed, most of the winners of the award have not focused on the Middle East in either their teaching or scholarship.

One critic of the award stated, "Imagine putting this award down on your c.v.," suggesting that no reasonable person would consider doing so. This participant implied that applying for and winning the award were demonstrations in themselves of one's bias and bigotry, apparently against Israel, and that no one in their right mind would list the award as a legitimate professional accomplishment—apparently the award is something to be hidden rather than advertised. Furthermore, according to this person, the creators of the award designed it to "push buttons politically (propaganda), not pedagogically." These are somewhat curious claims that were generated when the award announcement was sent out through the WPA list. One might be left to wonder, "Who is afraid of Rachel Corrie?" Clearly, the memorialization of Corrie's actions in Gaza touches upon some sensitive issues, issues that are disturbing to some members of our professional community. The attempts that were made to frame the award as "inappropriate," "unprofessional," and "as propaganda" sought to blame Rachel Corrie for her death, to deprive the moral, legal, and historical basis for the justice of the Palestinian national movement, and to smear those associated with advancing criticisms of Israel. Instead of recognizing these dimensions of the debate, it was far easier to frame the disagreement about the award as a matter of professional decorum and propriety.[8]

In his "Dignity and Solidarity," a speech delivered on June 15, 2003 before the American-Arab Anti-Discrimination League, Edward Said described Rachel Corrie's actions as "heroic and dignified at the same time," a recognition of Corrie's sacrifice for something larger than herself. Said discussed the circumstances around the US government's decision not to investigate Corrie's death: "An American citizen willfully murdered by the soldiers of a client state of the US without so much as an official peep or even the *de rigeur* investigation that had been promised her family." According to Said, Corrie had traveled to Gaza "to stand with suffering human beings with whom she had never had any contact before." Finally, Said noted the significance of Corrie's actions:

> What Rachel Corrie's work in Gaza recognized, however, was precisely the gravity and the density of the living history of the Palestinian people as a national community, and not merely as a collection of deprived refugees. That is what she was in solidarity with. And we need to remember that that kind of solidarity is no longer confined to a small number of intrepid souls here and there, but is recognized the world over ("Dignity and Solidarity").

Despite Said's solemn remembrance, other accounts of Corrie's death (and its significance) have been less than respectful. According to Joshua Hammer,

> If Corrie thought that a white, American, female college student putting her life on the line could somehow change hearts and minds,

she would, in death, be little more than a news blip, convincing people of nothing more than what they already believed. What remained unclear were the precise circumstances of her death—and why a 23-year-old woman from Olympia, Washington, would have placed her body in front of Israeli military bulldozers in the first place.

Given these disparate accounts of how Rachel Corrie died and what she represented, it is perhaps unsurprising that heated discussion ensued when a call for nominations for an award created in her memory came across a major list-serv. The dynamics of this discussion in our field, among our colleagues, did surprise me, however. As Barbara Herrnstein Smith reminds us, "The dynamics of intellectual controversy often mirror, shadow, and predict quite closely the dynamics of larger human conflict."[9] Smith's statement certainly seems to ring true as I turn to an examination of some of the specific exchanges between participants on the WPA list about the Rachel Corrie Courage in the Teaching of Writing Award.

The Memory of Rachel Corrie in the Present

Consider the following response to me from an interlocutor on the WPA list in May of 2006:[10] "Abraham, you know damn well that what Luisa said had heavy racist overtones in it: JEWS CONTROL THE MEDIA. If you don't admit that, you are lying or believe it." In this context, the person identified as "Luisa" had alleged that "we are all under the influence of a group that can readily draw sympathies from the horrible crimes against them during WWII." As one might expect, several list-serv participants found this assertion, or at least the assertion they believed Luisa had made, offensive and beyond the pale. One person noted that

> [t]o assign Jews some kind of mystical influence over the thoughts of Americans, that's beyond the pale. And to treat Jewish memory of the Shoah and the loss of a third of the Jewish population of the world, along with entire cultures of Jews—Yiddish speaking Jews of Eastern Europe, the Jews of Salonika—as merely an industry run by a highly influential cabal of Jews who want to play on the sympathies of the world, well, it's a willful caricature of Jewish history and community and shows a lack of familiarity with the role of history and memory in Judaism.

As I quickly pointed out, one must draw the crucial distinction between "Jews" and "Zionists" before alleging that someone has engaged in anti-

Semitic rhetoric. To criticize Zionism, which is an ideology derived from European romantic nationalism, is not to criticize Judaism, Jews, Holocaust survivors, or the use of the Holocaust. As Marc Ellis insists through the title of his recent book (*Israel≠Judaism*), Judaism and Israel are not equivalent; although, Zionism as a nationalist ideology seeks to promote Israeli actions as Jewish actions. Furthermore, might one also insist that to take issue with the Rachel Corrie Courage in the Teaching of Writing Award is to be blind to the history of Palestinian suffering?

I defended Luisa, insisting that she was referencing "Zionists," not Jews, suggesting that Zionism itself has historically engaged in anti-Semitic caricatures in its attempts to position Israel as the Jewish state, even though many Jews refuse to allow Israel to speak for them. My interlocutor, however, insisted that I was either being willfully ignorant in asserting that Luisa meant Zionists, not Jews, or that I really did believe that "Jews control the media." In other words, if I did not agree with my interlocutor I was either turning a blind eye to racism or lying. To some, Luisa appeared to suggest that Jewish "influence" has successfully manipulated the Holocaust for political purposes in the context of diminishing Israel's culpability in its treatment of the Palestinians. Any suggestion that the Holocaust has somehow been misused by Israel's defenders to justify Israel's occupation of the Palestinians immediately creates controversy, including the allegations that one is suggesting "Jews control the media." As the award creator noted, the fact that "Jewish media control" even came up in a debate about whether or not this award is appropriate "utterly trivializes the reality of anti-Semitism by claiming that just about anything under the sun that strikes the imagination of a speaker rightfully fits that category."

That Corrie's actions were of historical significance, providing an exemplar through which to recognize a courageous teacher advancing vital issues through teaching and scholarship, was too much for some list-serv participants who believed that Corrie's death had been misused within the professional organization of the Conference of College Composition and Communication to advance a distinctly pro-Palestinian politics. As another participant noted, "Being a Palestinian sympathizer hardly aligns a person with violence and injustice. To say that there is no clear side of justice in the Middle East is to ignore a lot of history and to succumb to the propaganda campaign that has allowed so much unnecessary death to continue." Assigning blame and responsibility to parties in the Middle East conflict, particularly in the context of Israel-Palestine, creates immediate controversy, allowing for the invocation of the "cosmic struggle" argument, i.e., no side can be blamed for what is happening because the conflict has been going on since time immemorial for reasons that are beyond human comprehension.

Instead of assigning blame, the most common retort is that the conflict is too complex for comprehension, or that so much propaganda swirls around the conflict due to excessive partisanship that it is impossible to know the truth about where justice resides. In response to the participant who claimed that to assert that there is no clear justice in the Middle East is to succumb to the propaganda campaign that is responsible for so much bloodshed, another participant stated, "One can easily go after the rhetorical stance taken up by this award and show how it IGNORES history and how this award is a very specific case of PROPAGANDA" (emphasis in original). As to who was being propagandized by whom was not at all clear, as those supporting the award accused the award's critics of having succumbed to propaganda and vice versa. As one critic insisted, "I don't believe I ignore history or have succumbed to a propaganda campaign by feeling that there are legitimate competing interests at play in the Middle East, even for the very liberal, sensible, non-religious-fanatics among us."

The circumstances around Corrie's death came to represent a more general debate about the politics informing the Israel-Palestine conflict. In other words, Corrie became an object of transference in this controversy, representing a conduit through which the controversy could develop and play out.[11] Participants seemingly either strongly identified with Corrie and her actions or completely disavowed that she could possibly stand for what the award named after her claimed she did. Corrie's actions in Gaza and their significance were also taken up in discussants' affective transmissions, with each message to the list seemingly escalating the political and professional stakes of the exchange. Furthermore, participants who agreed with one another solidified their identifications by situating themselves as reasonable and compassionate, while seemingly characterizing those who supported or criticized the award as somehow biased or uninformed. In this debate, Corrie was either a victim of IDF aggression or a terrorist (Hamas, Hezbollah, etc.) sympathizer. In other words, she was either defending an innocent Palestinian's home or protecting a terrorist's stash. Establishing whether Corrie was to be remembered as the victim of a tragedy, and by inference a victim of Israel's colonization project, or as a naïve college student who had been manipulated by the International Solidarity Movement to stand in front of an IDF bulldozer as part of a publicity stunt gone terribly wrong, became the very object of debate.

When a contested figure such as Corrie becomes an object of transference, through which participants debating her legacy have a tendency to repeat the very problems they are supposedly subjecting to critique and analysis (the use and seeming repetition of violent metaphors to examine violence or the recycling of anti-Semitic tropes in a discussion about the Holocaust and Israel, for example), the debate itself becomes susceptible to resuscitating echoes (or *uptakes*) of the past. These uptakes tend to seize upon a particularly affective-laden event or meaningful signifier from the past, re-deploying it in the present for the purpose of maintaining a unified meaning and coherence. When one speaks of Jewish History, the Jewish People, or Jewish suffering, there is a tendency to lump a good bit of history together, say, from 70 A.D. (the destruction of the Second Temple) to 1948 (the founding of the state of Israel), for example. While this strategy contributes to the circulation of a lachrymose narrative about Jewish suffering, it simultaneously enables a conflation of memory, whereby supposed threats to Jewish memory in the present seemingly enable one to reach for events from the past, as part of an effort to suture together—what is in fact—a rather fragmented history.[12] That the controversy about the Rachel Corrie Courage in the Teaching of Writing Award became an occassion to express concerns about anti-semitism, while also affirming a lachyrmose narrative about historical Jewish suffering, should hardly be surprising. Add to this the communal response that was seemingly demanded in the wake of the "We are all under the control of a group" comment, one is left to wonder if we are fully aware of the forces shaping our perceptions of conflict in the Middle East.

According to some WPA list-serv participants, since the evidence was far from clear as to how Corrie was killed, or in what capacity Corrie was acting when she was killed, the CCCCs should stay far away from endorsing Rachel Corrie's memory or the award meant to recognize an untenured faculty member taking risks in teaching and scholarship to advance peace and social justice. The PSCC (Progressive Special Interest Caucuses and Coalitions), not the CCCCs, sponsored the award. According to some, embracing Corrie as the epitome of courage was neither professionally responsible nor neutral; to embrace Corrie's memory as a victim of Israeli violence was to be partisan, unprofessional, and un-objective. This is an interesting discursive move: suggesting that those who were convinced that Corrie had, in fact, been deliberately killed by the IDF—instead of simply being the victim of an accident—were simple-minded, seeing clear justice in the Middle East conflict while also promulgating propaganda as part of that vision. It is not that those making this accusation had done the research to conclusively determine that Corrie was the victim of an accident, but that Corrie's death had not been reported as a deliberate killing in the US mainstream media.[13] In brief, according to many, Corrie had been taken up as part of a propaganda campaign to defame and delegitimize Israel, at a time of supposed increasing anti-Semitism through the world. To name an award seeking to recognize courageous teaching and scholarship after Corrie was a controversial idea because some did not think that Corrie's actions were in themselves courageous, particularly if her memorialization was being employed to criticize Israel. As one astute observer insisted, political choices are made all the time in the course of memorialization, such as when a museum, airport, or in this case, an award is named after a person—controversial or not. How many objected to the naming of Reagan National Airport in Washington D.C. out of principled objections to the Reagan administration's involvement in the mining of the Nicaraguan harbors throughout the 1980s, which was condemned as international terrorism? According to this person, objecting to the Rachel Corrie Award, without objecting to the naming of Reagan National Airport, was hypocritical. Perhaps some found Corrie's actions, or at least the way in which they have been memorialized, potentially anti-Semitic because they frame Israel—as the Jewish state—in a bad light. In brief, the debate seemed to revolve around several questions.

First, what were the exact circumstances around Rachel Corrie's death in Gaza? Could these circumstances be objectively verified to satisfy all interested parties? For example, could Corrie's death have been the result of negligence or even a willful disregard for her life by the IDF? Furthermore, what was Corrie doing when she died? Yes, she was seeking to block an IDF bulldozer as it attempted to demolish a Palestinian pharmacist's home, but she must have realized such an action was pointless. Perhaps she was trying to reach the bulldozer driver on some human level, appealing to him to stop acting as an extension of Israel's state policy. Furthermore, we might ask what Corrie believed herself to be doing when she stood in front of the six-ton D9 Caterpillar bulldozer, specially built to demolish homes. Was she doing more than reminding the bulldozer driver of the illegality of his actions according to international law? Those who were standing with Corrie watched as she was run over.[14] Do they share any culpability in Corrie's death? They claimed to have tried to warn the bulldozer driver that Corrie had fallen down and was struggling to climb up the mound of earth that was accumulating in front of her.[15] The driver maintained that he could not see Corrie. However, as one participant pointed out, " . . . the pictures that the International Solidarity Movement presented in an effort to prove that he [the bulldozer driver] could not have missed seeing her were later revealed to have been presented out of sequence." Furthermore, "While they seem to suggest that Corrie was easily visible and that the driver would have had to go out of his way to hit her, the photos were not taken in quick succession but several hours apart." As another participant aptly put it, "Readers [of the call for nominations] are urged to view the pictures of her [Corrie], as if this absolved the situation of its complexity."

If, as some critics of the award alleged, Corrie was anti-Israel and anti-American because she was critical of Israeli and US policies in the Middle

East, does this present a problem for the CCCCs if the PSCC sponsors an award named after her? What does it mean to be anti-Israel or anti-American after all? Answers to these questions are complex, particularly as these questions are debated in a discursive space where criticisms of Israel appear strange and are easily classified as anti-Semitic. There are some theoretical concepts that can help us move beyond this discursive impasse, **radically reconfiguring our understanding of how to discuss the Israel-Palestine conflict within the profession and beyond: affect, belatedness, and transference.**

Figure 1. Rachel Corrie. Reproduced with the permission of the Rachel Corrie Foundation.

These three concepts are applicable to understanding the hidden energies and psychological forces at work in our argumentative dynamics about the

Israel-Palestine conflict. These psychological forces are so powerful because of the history of anti-Semitism, the discursive dimensions of the Holocaust, and what Michael Rothberg calls "multidirectional memory," the ways in which a particular memory can flow in different directions based upon one's experience, history, and positionality.[16] Multidirectional memory is particularly relevant in the context of examining what happens when the discourses around the Holocaust clash with discourses around anti-colonial struggle, including the Palestinian struggle for national liberation.

The Affective Component

In describing the affective dimension of the conflict, I am drawing upon the work of Teresa Brennan, who in her *The Transmission of Affect* defines affect as "the physiological shifts that accompany a judgment" and "the energy transfer or exchange between aggressor and passive recipient" (49). Far too often, interlocutors debating the Israel-Palestine conflict become enmeshed within affective environments, within which it becomes extremely difficult to separate position-taking from assignments of moral culpability. As one WPA participant astutely pointed out in the discussion of the Rachel Corrie Courage in the Teaching of Writing Award:

> Not much interest in *inter*locution going down here among us-rhetoricians. . . . but lots of interest in ranting in the name of justice against the other on the list who is classically and hopelessly stupid or biased or prejudice or uninformed or insert-your-slam-here. In fact, it seems that the other is so morally or intellectually out of it that engaging with him or her in honest-to-the-gods deliberation would be like shooting fish in a barrel. This thread—on a Writing Program Administrators list, no less—seems to operate as a microcosm of the broader realm of "civic discourse," which makes sense but which also sure does deflate any self-important claims rhetoricians make about the need for the sorry-ass political body to study rhetoric. And it reminds me of why I have no faith in "argumentation" or the "civic" model of operative rhetoric.

The affective dimensions around this conflict, which include libidinal energies and investments, cannot be accounted for by the "'civic' model of operational rhetoric."[17] The reason for this is quite simple: the energy exchanges suffusing any affective environment are not even recognized, much less accounted for, in this model because bodies are treated in isolation instead of in context and in concert. In other words, the notion that my affective energy in the heat of debate would interact with and change someone else's physiological responses is not something traditional theories of argumentation consider. In other words, the debate ensures its own polarization because of the over-determined affective environments within which it occurs. Each point meets a counterpoint, leading to a sure escalation of heated rhetoric and an increased affective energy pitched at higher and higher intensities.

How does one achieve the necessary intellectual and affective distance from the complex issues surrounding the Israel-Palestine conflict before entering into an informed and good-faith discussion about them? Appropriate "distance" in this instance refers to the achievement of a certain ability to recognize and avoid the polarizing influences and affective transmissions that often infuse analyses of issues such as nationalism, occupation, ethnic exclusion, and the historical grievances accompanying dispossession. These influences and transmissions, which often infuse defenses of nationalistic commitments, are often intense and irrational, verging on a type of fundamentalism. Indeed, these transmissions have a contagious quality to them, ensuring controversy once they are unleashed.

In her *Toward a Civil Discourse*, Sharon Crowley describes how fundamentalist ideologies develop, noting how "densely articulated belief systems" that preclude the kind of inventiveness that makes for flexible and contingent thinking take root. Fundamentalism interferes with one's capacity to process new information and to notice evidence that does not confirm one's strongly held perspective. A fundamentalist ideology literally gives one tunnel vision with respect to how one views the world and processes events within it. Drawing on Clore and Gasper, Crowley argues that "densely articulated ideologies construct bad affective grammarians who pay intense notice to objects and events that can be threaded into the intricate tapestries of their belief system(s)." As Crowley notes, "They notice because almost everything that is made legible by their belief system(s) is weighty with affect for them" (85).

When someone interprets an event through an interpretative framework weighty with affect, one can only view that event as either contributing to or undermining one's worldview because of how the structure of feeling informing the event shapes one's very understanding of—and relationship to—it. In other words, as the fundamentalist subject encounters an event within the social field, she processes this event as consistent with what she already believes, even if the event itself has no relation to the belief in question. In this sense, the fundamentalist maintains her tunnel vision. If she were to lose it, she would lose her very identity. Finally, Crowley draws this conclusion: "If this account is correct, extremists have difficulty taking notice of events or objects that neither support nor attack their beliefs. That is to say, whatever is new and neutral in relation to their system of beliefs is unlikely to pass unremarked" (85). Crowley works, then, to build a rhetoric of fundamentalism by noting just how resilient and impervious to change some belief systems can become. We see such impervious belief systems at work within debates about the Israel-Palestine conflict.

Belatedness

It is a commonplace of psychoanalysis that the past frequently intrudes upon the present, often in unexpected and novel ways.[18] A bad romantic relationship, for example, can return and influence all future relationships, persistently exercising control over us and shaping how we view others, while all the while not announcing itself in any definable or visible way. Similarly, a bad educational experience in high school or early in college can reappear in terms of a confidence problem in graduate school or in a first job. The reason such experiences exercise such a hold on our attention, seemingly reappearing in other contexts, is because they have played a formative role in shaping our identities, establishing an important place in the solidification of our self-esteem and our ability to understand our positionality in the world. Jean Laplanche reminds us, "It takes two traumas to make a trauma," by which he means that the first trauma instills in us the fear that that we will re-experience the absence and loss of the original traumatic event.[19] When the second trauma overtakes us, it has so much resonance because we experience and feel the second trauma through the framework created by the first.[20]

When certain traumatic experiences are reawakened in us because of a particularly painful memory, we tend to react quite defensively, insisting upon removing the conditions that have led us to revisit the past, or more precisely, that has led the past to revisit us. Certain triggers can quickly and quite unexpectedly bring the past "back" into the present, surprising even the most astute and critical observer of a particular social scene. That there is a degree of uncontrollability to these intrusions is consistent with the notion that the unconscious exercises its influence upon the conscious mind in slightly detectable ways, from a slip of the tongue to a particularly realistic dream that corresponds to—or embellishes—upon the events of the previous day or a particularly memorable moment. How the past will "return" to us is enigmatic, defying any easy explanation.

The past continually seeks to catch up with and exercise its hold on the present, erupting into the contemporary scene, even as we work diligently to keep this past at bay. As the past makes its way into the present, either through unconscious language choices or conscious manipulation of certain tropes, we are often surprised at how quickly the past can literally dictate the unfolding of the present. This phenomenon, which Freud labeled "belatedness," or deferred action, (*nachträglichkeit*) reminds us that past events take on more and more significance and often become more and more meaningful (affect-laden) in our conscious minds because it takes time for the memory—particularly a memory about a traumatic event—to develop or catch up with the present.[21] These belated memories seem to have a boomerang effect upon the psyche of the subject, "returning" the full force of the prior event with particular energy. When these forces are unleashed, there is a tendency for subjects to seek narrative dominance.

Belatedness is certainly operative with respect to contemporary discussions of the Israel-Palestine conflict, as day-to-day events in the Middle East seem to inevitably become refracted through the prism of Jewish suffering leading up to and during the Holocaust. Perhaps it is only to be expected that this history of Jewish suffering should be invoked to contextualize and explain the violence and religious hatred that drives the "clash of civilizations" mentality of the disputants and partisans in the conflict. Israel, as a Jewish state, is often described as being under siege and in a battle for its very survival against the various Islamic organizations who seek to advance the nationalist aspirations of the Palestinian people.[22] These organizations are described as anti-Semitic because they seek the physical destruction of Israel, in its form as a state dedicated to the preservation of a Jewish majority, and the return of the Palestinian refugees who lost their homes to invading Zionist forces in 1947 prior to Israel's creation. Writing in his *My People* in 1968, the renowned Israeli statesman Abba Eban claimed, "There is not a single image, phrase, or adjective in the Nazi vocabulary which Arab propaganda, directed from Cairo, has not adopted and diffused in the political warfare against Israel . . . The murder of six million Jews by Nazis was alternately denied and applauded . . . Israel's very existence was portrayed in Arab writings and politics as a crime for which the only expiation lay in Israel's disappearance" (quoted in Isacoff 52). This transposition of Nazi rhetoric into the Arab's struggle with Israel after 1967, particularly with respect to the demands of dispossessed Palestinian refugees, only contributes to the conflations of historical moments identified above.

Since the claims these Palestinian refugees make upon Israel involve providing redress for dispossession and ultimately a return to Israel, which would disturb Israel's demography as a Jewish state, these claims are often characterized as threatening Israel's existence. In other words, any political action or statement that makes a gesture toward disturbing Israel's Jewish character seems to become configured—by definition—as anti-Semitic. These actions and statements create an affective energy, drawing participants into an endless labyrinth of accusations and counter-accusations about ideological purity, victimization, and the authority of cited sources.

This configuration becomes operable because Zionism posits that criticisms of Israel, as a Jewish state, are anti-Semitic because Israel is the state of all Jewish people, both prior to Israel's creation and into perpetuity, and because the history of anti-Semitism is understood to have reached its zenith in the Holocaust, a culmination of centuries of gentile hatred against Jews. This positioning of Israel within Zionist ideology as a Jewish homeland, even before Israel officially existed as a nation, allows for an easy transposition of historical events, enabling the anti-Semitism of one age to become identified with the words and actions directed against Israel in the context of the contemporary crisis in the Middle East. Often, these transpositions are inappropriate and lead to incorrect conclusions about people's motives as they participate in furthering discussion and understanding about the Israel-Palestine conflict.[23]

As rhetoricians, we should be concerned by this possible misuse of history in these debates; indeed, the charge of anti-Semitism, if it is to be taken seriously, must be leveled with precision and not as a scatter-shot propaganda device for scoring cheap political points.[24] In this discursive environment, every statement introduced into the debate contains a hidden motive, or at least a hidden rhetorical or historical resonance whereby nothing can be interpreted as being offered in good faith: "You claim that the Rachel Corrie Courage in the Teaching of Writing Award is about X (rewarding courage, risk-taking, innovation, etc.) but it is really about Y (anti-Israelism, pro-Palestinian politics, and anti-Semitism)." It is this displacement of a particular conception of anti-Semitism, a conception that had a particular meaning and resonance at a particular point in history, which tends to confuse participants in contemporary debates about the Middle East. As rhetoricians, we should be much more vigilant about the prospects of importing this flawed conception of anti-Semitism into the field of rhetorical studies, particularly when doing so has the potential to harm prospects for dialogue and understanding.

Perhaps no caricature of Jews provokes as strong and quick a response as the suggestion that American Jews exercise undue "influence" over the media, particularly in the context of discussing media coverage of the Israel-Palestine conflict, or US Middle East policy. Of course, many Jews do not agree with Israel's policies and refuse to believe that Israel is *the* Jewish state since its actions do not speak for them. If a Jew condemns Israel, given this ideological economy, does she then renounce her Judaism? Or has Zionism, through Israel, illegitimately usurped Judaism for its purposes, engaging in anti-Semitic caricatures ("All Jews think alike" or "All Jews are capable of having Israel represent them") to silence dissent against its policies? This is the most prevalent form of anti-Semitism animating our contemporary historical moment, as Zionism and Israel seek to speak for Jews throughout the world.

The presentation of Israel as a Western rampart in the Middle East, an offshoot of Europe posed as a defender of Western values, holding nothing in common with its Arab neighbors, provides a comforting narrative to those seeking to use Huntington's "clash of civilizations" model to provide tacit endorsement to Israel's increased militarization within the Middle East and colonization of Palestine. In this context, resisting Israel's colonization project either through physical actions or in written and spoken words is configured as anti-Semitism, the same anti-Semitism that created the environment within which the Holocaust was conducted. Surely, every critic of Israel is not being critical of what Israel (as the Jewish state) does because she is anti-Semitic.[25] The usual refrain to this observation is that mere criticism of Israel is not anti-Semitic, but when criticism becomes intemperate and is continually generated without proper context and proportion—singling out Israeli actions without comparing them to the actions of other countries facing similar threats—then such criticism crosses into anti-Semitism.[26]

Transference

Related to the phenomenon of *nachträglichkeit* (belatedness) and affect is the psychoanalytical concept of transference, which as I mentioned earlier, is the tendency to repeat the very problems one sets out to study and identify, e.g. using anti-Semitic tropes in the course of studying anti-Semitism or employing sexually violent rhetoric in the course of discussing sexual violence. Or, more directly related to the concerns of this article: the tendency to repeat the use of war-like metaphors in discussing various positions within the Israel-Palestine conflict. There indeed seems to be a tendency for interlocutors to adopt the same rhetorical stances as the actual disputants in the conflict, unwittingly repeating the very same problems they set out to discuss and solve. According to Dominick LaCapra, one can cope with the problem of transference either by engaging in greater empathic identification or by working through the very tendency one seeks to analyze and study.[27]

The potential for transference exists in the relationships professors develop with their graduate students and in the relationships psychoanalysts develop with their patients; these are situations within which a sufficient power differential exists, leading to the introduction of inappropriate feelings from the past into the present. In other words, we tend to repeatedly seek out the same kinds of relational dynamics in our personal and professional lives without realizing we are inappropriately transporting the feelings and desires from another time and place into the present. So, we may transfer a libidinal investment or aggressive drive in a relationship from the past into the present, recognizing something in the formation of an opposing point of view that reminds us of that past relationship. So, a bad relationship with my father may emerge later in my life if I recognize a behavior of my father in someone else. This tendency to repeat my feelings of anger or resentment existing in the relationship with my father in a completely different context is a function of my not recognizing the source of my psychological pain.

The return of the past through the mention of a name or an event and the different memories that are evoked in the process of remembering those names and events represents a complex process of reconciling personal histories with events in the world. In other words, our libidinal investments (the ways our narcissistic identifications and attachments become mobilized) manifest themselves in the social field when we remember a controversial event or an individual associated with a controversial event. An analysis of libidinal attachments, then, requires us to suspend conceptions of justice and "right and wrong" and to concentrate on how individuals approach social antagonisms in the ways they do, noting how they create identifications with respect to social conflicts based on race, gender, ethnicity, religion, and class.

For example, I must continually interrogate why I find the Palestinian claims to justice in the conflict so compelling. Is it because I am, as an Indian-American man, a postcolonial subject? By this logic, I am committed to Palestinian liberation because of the history of European colonialism, which directly touched my ancestral heritage, although I am unaware that my commitment springs from this aspect of my identity. Naturally, there are limitations to this sort of identity-based psychoanalysis. Perhaps the sources I find compelling are written by people with my politics and are written within an intertextual chain that I understand. In other words, I agree with the conclusions of Israel's New Historians because they write about the conflict in ways that I have come to understand based on my anti-colonial perspective and politics. So, if the scholarship of Illan Pappe, Neve Gordon, Tom Segev, Avi Shlaim, and others is attractive to me, it is because these scholars' once-considered radical opinions, which have rendered a more accurate accounting of the historical events surrounding Israel's creation than previous historians, conform to international law and the international consensus for a just resolution of the Question of Palestine. This body of scholarship largely refutes the long-held belief that Israel fought a war for independence in 1948, prior to it being granted statehood by the UN, and that it is a weak, beleaguered nation fighting for its survival.

A Wider View

One of the reasons the WPA discussion about the Rachel Corrie Courage in the Teaching of Writing Award went so awry is because many participants seemed to have a fundamental misunderstanding of the balance of forces within the conflict. In addition to positioning Corrie as a martyr who had been seized upon by those seeking to score cheap political points against Israel, some participants seemed to genuinely believe that Israel is the weaker party in its struggle with the Palestinians, seemingly vulnerable because it is surrounded by Arab countries supposedly eager to see its destruction. If to memorialize Rachel Corrie as an example of the kind of courage worthy of emulation within the profession is to advance an anti-Israel politics, then Corrie is standing in as a sort of metonymic replacement for something called "anti-Israel activism," which is really tantamount to advancing Palestinian human rights. When Palestinians living under Israeli occupation exert agency, in framing and advancing their rights as part of an anti-colonial struggle under international law, Holocaust discourses often construct them as seeking to contest Israel's "right to exist," an abbreviated reference to Israel's "right" to exist as a state dedicated to preserving a Jewish majority; with the "as a state dedicated to preserving a Jewish majority" portion of this discursive construction almost always absent in the context of popular representations of the conflict.[28] However, for many, the preservation of a Jewish majority in Israel is particularly important in the wake of the Holocaust, even as Israel refuses to truly become a part of the Middle East, acting instead as an offshoot of Europe, "the portion of the rampart of Europe against, an outpost of civilization as opposed to barbarism."[29]

Israel, as the Jewish state, is a modern nation with one of the best militaries in the world, reserving the right to use its nuclear arsenal if threatened. Israel's determination to rid Iran of its nuclear arsenal, for example, is often framed by media pundits as a struggle to defend civilization against the maniacal aspirations of Mahmoud Ahmadinejad, who supposedly seeks to wipe Israel off the map of time. In fact, Israel has long feared Iran as a competitor because of its pretensions toward modernization and because of the challenge it might pose to Israeli regional hegemony. If one suggests that Israel has engaged in immoral or illegal conduct in its dealings with the Palestinians, due this affective dimension whereby to criticize Israel is to somehow criticize the Jewish people, one is likely to be constructed as issuing an indictment of Jews, even if one goes to great lengths to insist that this is not what one is doing.

Inevitably, interlocutors seem to draw comparisons between Jewish and Palestinian suffering, without realizing that these comparisons are not only inappropriate, but quite unnecessary. Herein resides the dilemma: the Israel-Palestine conflict brings together two distinct histories of oppression and suffering that are simply incompatible and incomparable, leading to easy conflations of memory—where both Hamas and Israeli settlers in the West Bank can be compared to either Nazis or freedom fighters, depending upon the point to be made. Hamas can be compared to the Nazis because as an organization it is dedicated to the destruction of Israel as a Jewish state; however, one cannot simply state that Hamas is driven to destroy Israel because of anti-Semitism. Instead, one must recognize that Hamas seeks Israel's destruction because Israel is viewed as occupying and colonizing Palestinian land. The reason Palestinian resistance against Israeli occupation is often configured as anti-Semitic is because the occupiers of Palestinian land are Jewish. Just as American Indian resistance against European settlers in the New World could not be credibly framed as arising from "anti-Europeanism" or "anti-Whiteism," we should be equally skeptical of framing Palestinian resistance to Israeli domination as arising from anti-Semitism.[30] What allows for these easy conflations and transpositions?

A theme that consistently animates discussions of the Israel-Palestine conflict is that Israel is fighting a war for its very survival and that its fight against various Islamic enemies is simply a continuation of the Jewish fight against the Nazis, which if lost, will result in another holocaust against the Jewish people. Leaders as diverse as Yasser Arafat, Saddam Hussein, and Mahmoud Amadinejad have been compared to Hitler because of the supposed threat they posed to Israel's existence.[31]

Israeli exceptionalism enables an abuse of history and historical memory and a general confusion about what constitutes a legitimate threat to Israel's existence.[32] What allows for this transfer between historical moments? Is it simply a matter of politics whereby Israel's defenders are trying to win a propaganda war, or is it a conflation of memory where the modern-day "war on terrorism" is a continuation of the war for Jewish survival that was part of the Holocaust, the creation of Israel, etc.? With such an expansive sense of history and Jewish memory, which allows for the threat against Jewish survival to take the same general motivation in different forms across history, it only stands to reason that what will trigger a conflation of memory may be something as innocuous as raising the issue of Palestinian victimage, or preserving the memory of a young college student who was attempting to defend a Palestinian home against demolition by an IDF bulldozer.[33] The faces of these victims are threats to the historical narrative about Jewish suffering, as they refute conceptions of Jewish victimization, while simultaneously suggesting that Jews can also be victimizers.

If to embrace Rachel Corrie as a heroine is to embrace a Palestinian politics, what does that politics look like exactly? Is it pro-terrorism and anti-Israel? The Exodus narrative about the creation of a Jewish state in the midst of a hostile Middle East has created an affective environment within which it is difficult to be critical of Israeli military actions because of the victim status Jews have been assigned historically. Although this victim status disappeared long ago, it still plays a powerful affective role in shaping contemporary discussions about conflict in the Middle East. In insisting that that the victim status of Jews disappeared long ago, I am referencing the fact that Jewish prosperity and success in the Western world since World War II have been unmatched by any other ethno-religious group.[34]

As Marc Ellis explains in his *Judaism ≠ Israel*, "When Jews see themselves as cosmic actors on a universal stage, those who critique aspects of Jewish power find themselves in the Jewish existential drama" (19). Edward Said notes in his *After the Last Sky*, "There has been no misfortune worse for us than that we are ineluctably viewed as the enemies of the Jews. No moral and political fate worse, none at all, I think: no worse, there is none" (134). That the Palestinians have been necessarily positioned as somehow metaphysically opposed to Jews because of the Israel-Palestine conflict, instead of being viewed as engaging in a resistance struggle within a particular historical context, does serious damage to any deep understanding of the roots of the conflict. As scholars committed to understanding the specific circumstances informing rhetorical situations, we must be diligent in understanding how the easy conflation and transposition of the highly charged language from events in the past with/into the present can greatly hamper efforts to create the conditions of possibility for reconciliation and dialogue. Many constituencies are finding alternative ways to express their dissatisfaction with the dominant configurations governing understandings of the Israel-Palestine conflict.

In his *Out of the Ashes*, Ellis notes that a civil war has developed in the Jewish community between Jews of conscience—who refuse to forget how Israel's politics of occupation produces Palestinian suffering—and Jews who continue to turn a blind eye to what years of Israeli conquest have wrought upon the Palestinian community. Similarly, Avraham Burg in his *The Holocaust is Over, We Must Rise from its Ashes* states that "We, the Jewish Israelis, are the core of the world's Jewish superpower, and must act toward our enemies as a moral superpower: forcefully, uncompromisingly, and fearlessly" (158). In his *The Myths of Liberal Zionism*, Yitzhak Loar argues that Israel's use of Jewish suffering in the Holocaust to justify its territorial expansion and colonization of Palestinian land is reaching a crisis point, with many Jews walking away from what they see as the abuse of the past for political ends.

Many younger, progressive, American Jews, for example, are refusing the facile formulation that Israel's ongoing dispossession of the Palestinian population is about defense or securing the Jewish community against anti-Semitism. This abuse of memory and history has produced a level of cynicism within the Jewish diasporic community, as many younger Jews are refusing to become wholesale defenders of Israel's actions in the West Bank and its increased militarization.[35] This abuse of memory and history has produced a level of uncertainty within the diaspora, as many younger American Jews are resisting to reflexively defend Israel whenever its actions are publically criticized. For these reasons, organizations such as *J Street* are emerging as a political alternative to the American-Israel Public Affairs Committee (AIPAC), otherwise known as one of the major arms of the "Israel Lobby." *J Street* and other progressive organizations have realized that the perversion of the past in the service of a distinct politics—purposefully geared to conflate issues within the Israel-Palestine conflict such as anti-Semitism and Palestinian resistance—prevents meaningful dialogue. These progressive organizations understand that the Holocaust has been effectively employed as a weapon to advance a politics that relies upon a particular activation of the past to serve a distinct politics in the present, as my final example will demonstrate.

The Holocaust and the Israel-Palestine Conflict

In January 1998, Yasser Arafat visited the United States as part of a US negotiated peace effort between Israel and the PLO at Camp David. Arafat expressed interest in visiting the Holocaust Museum in Washington D.C. as part of this visit. A great deal of controversy ensued as plans for the proposed visit went forward. Wilhelm Reich, director of the Museum, refused to extend Arafat the standard courtesies given to other world leaders and VIPs, arguing that Arafat's presence at the hallowed sight would be an affront to the memory of the dead. When the Clinton White House learned of Reich's resistance to Arafat's visit, it expressed its displeasure.

The Museum's Board of Directors became involved with deliberations over the visit, reversing Reich's initial decision, insisting that Arafat be allowed to view the Museum and afforded the same privileges during his visit as other world leaders. From the Board of Director's perspective, Arafat's visit could be used for public-relations purposes: Arafat, as a Palestinian leader, through his very presence at the Museum would represent an open acknowledgment of Jewish suffering in the Holocaust, and by extension, an acknowledgment of the legitimacy of Israel's right to exist as a Jewish state.

The controversy around Arafat's visit was not simply a matter of logistics, it was a battle over political signification, as various factions debated what it would mean for the PLO leader to visit one of the most significant sites devoted to documenting Jewish suffering. The Board of Directors decided that having Arafat visit the Museum would signal to the world that Arafat acknowledged the Holocaust as a legitimate event and expressed an interest in learning something about it. What would it mean for a Palestinian leader, in the context of Israeli-Palestinian peace talks, to visit the Holocaust Museum? It was undoubtedly an opportunity ripe for political manipulation as Zionist organization sought to characterize the visit as a Palestinian capitulation to Jewish history, but in actuality it was a capitulation to Zionist history. Through his visit to the Holocaust Museum, Arafat would be acknowledging the centrality of the Holocaust for Jews, those Jews living in Israel as well as those in the diaspora. This acknowledgment would help to solidify Zionism's claim that the Holocaust is the event through which Israel gains its legitimacy as a protectorate against any threat to the existence of the Jewish people.[36]

In arguing to Lerher that Arafat should have been allowed to visit the museum, Hyman Bookbinder claimed that "Whatever arguments can be made about not opening wide the welcome gates to an Arafat, they are overwhelmed by the central argument that the [M]useum exists because of its potential—demonstrated over and over again—to move even the most skeptical" (Dorf and Kurtman). As Joseph Massad states in his *The Persistence of the Palestinian Question*, "The fact that neither Arafat nor the PLO had ever denied the Jewish holocaust and had always expressed solidarity with its victims was immaterial to such propaganda" (138). By visiting the museum, Arafat would seemingly be giving tacit endorsement to Zionism's wedding of Jewish and Zionist history and the manipulation of Jewish history to serve Israeli political aims. Once again, the past returned like a boomerang to influence the present, encircling the participants in an emotional drama involving events that have been molded for a specific emotional effect, subjecting all those who enter the scene to be sorted as either "good" or "evil." Given the tendency to sort interlocutors within such discursive environments in this way, as a result of the affect-laden pull that is often at work, it is relatively easy to understand why Rachel Corrie's memory—like Arafat's presence at the Holocaust Museum represented an anomaly to some constituencies—symbolized such a monumental threat to some list-serv participants. Instead of substantively engaging the significance of Corrie's actions, it was easier to scapegoat and diminish Corrie and what she supposedly represented, e.g. anti-Semitism, anti-Israel activism, anti-Americanism, etc.

Similarly, John Mearsheimer and Stephen Walt faced abuse and vilification for exploring the power of the Israel Lobby in shaping discussion and perceptions about the Middle East in the United States. Mearsheimer and

Walt's book *The Israel Lobby* goes to great lengths to make clear that the Israel Lobby does not involve a conspiracy and is not a shadow organization controlled by a Jewish cabal. Indeed, Mearsheimer and Walt insist that the Israel Lobby represents a loosely organized grassroots organization that engages in old fashioned politics, demonstrating that the most active elements of the Israel Lobby involve Christian Zionists and not only, or just, Jews.[37] Despite Walt and Mearsheimer's insistence that the Israel Lobby is anything but a conspiracy, Abe Foxman in his *The Most Dangerous Lies* and Alan Dershowitz, in his *The Case Against Israel's Enemies* invoke the anti-Semitic forgery, *The Protocols of the Elders of Zion*, suggesting that Walt and Mearsheimer traffic in anti-Semitic stereotypes in their descriptions of the Lobby's power.[38] Similar tendencies were seemingly at work in the language choices of some WPA list-serv participants, especially among those who insisted that the Corrie award was inherently anti-Semitic and anti-Israel.

In retrospect, what was so fascinating about the WPA discussion was the participants' complete avoidance of international law and the international consensus on a just resolution of the Question of Palestine. Only two participants briefly mentioned UN 242, UN 194, the Fourth Geneva Convention, etc. According to international law, Israel's occupation, by which I mean settlement expansion beyond the established 1967 Green Line, constitutes the major obstacle to a comprehensive peace agreement in the Middle East. President Jimmy Carter asserted as much in his book *Palestine: Peace Not Apartheid*, when he wrote that the major stumbling block to achieving peace in the Israel-Palestine conflict is Israel's unwillingness to comply with international law. It is almost as if the majority of the WPA participants were not aware of the international consensus or the relevant international law, indicating that "what justice would look like in the Middle East" is actually pretty straightforward from the standpoint of the international community, United Nations resolutions, and thousands of pages of human rights reports. Invocations of the region's "tortured history," "complex politics," and "terribly fraught and nuanced situations" are studious ways of avoiding how Israel's militarism and territorial expansionism play a key role in creating the conditions of possibility for "cycles of violence," resistance, and repression. Assertions that the Rachel Corrie Courage in the Teaching of Writing Award represents "a denial of nationalism," "an instance of ignoring history," "a specific case of propaganda," and an instance of "the rhetoric of martyrdom" are clearly diversionary techniques employed to prevent a substantive discussion of the historical and diplomatic record enveloping the conflict. Those participants to the WPA discussion who responded to the call for nominations for the Rachel Corrie award in May 2006 with, "I'm uncomfortable with the anti-Israel rhetoric that seems to be beneath it," were seeking to protect their own knowledge claims about the conflict: I am uncomfortable; therefore, what is making me uncomfortable must be inappropriate. If to state that "Israel is in violation of international law" is beyond the pale, reflecting that one harbors anti-Semites animus, then it is completely understandable why public figures such as Jimmy Carter and Desmond Tutu are so often accused of engaging in anti-Israel rhetoric. This tendency to condemn criticism and critics of Israeli policy as anti-Semites enforces a type of political correctness at the cost of refusing to promote greater understanding about the conditions producing conflict in the Israel-Palestine conflict.

As rhetoricians, we must make public interventions into debates about the Israel-Palestine conflict. Events such as the ones I have described in this article are relatively representative of the kinds of opportunities that are available to those seeking to identify and clarify the psychological forces and energies infusing the rhetorical situations surrounding these debates. The abuse of history and historical memory in the service of a politics does not enable productive dialogue, but instead creates affective environments that disable the potential for experimentation, risk-taking, and exchange. In such an environment, participants are particularly susceptible to the kinds of inappropriate transfers of the past into the present that I have examined. If we refuse to engage the relevant issues with respect to the Israel-Palestine conflict, particularly when these issues are directly part of our professional conversation (as the discussion of the Rachel Corrie Courage in the Teaching of Writing Award clearly was), then we cede the discursive field to the past, without considering the demands for political and rhetorical action in the present. Indeed, as one participant aptly noted toward the end of the controversy, in an attempt to explain the surprising level of passion and vitriol that had been expressed in a seeming moment of communal division,

> We're revealed as less unified than we might imagine and that we would find comfortable. It's the revelation that what seems "obvious" to us isn't so to others—most significantly, those others we imagined to be so like us. It may be the kind of shock (even betrayal) that I felt when students were no longer like me, that what I thought we shared had sobering limits. I knew I'd have to work harder, but I think I got smarter then, too.

Dealing with such divisions in our communities, when we are hit with the realization that we are not as unified as we previously believed ourselves to be, forces a reevaluation of our most sacred and entrenched belief systems. Such moments should be viewed as opportunities for persuasion, rhetorical action, and material interventions.

Postscript

In a report dated March 24, 2008, a Task Force headed by Paul Puccio, and charged by then CCC's chair Cheryl Glenn, offered guidelines to distance the CCCCs from the SIGs (special interest groups). According to the report, "CCCC respects the right of self-organizing groups to act as their members deem appropriate, as long as those actions are clearly represented as the group's and not, for example, as an aspect of CCCC." Furthermore, the Task Force offered the following policy recommendations:

- *Any award conferred by a SIG or Caucus must include the following disclaimer: "This Award is not sanctioned by CCCC. It represents the sole judgment of the independent group conferring it and does not reflect the opinions or honors of CCCC." SIGs and Caucuses should communicate to award recipients that they must represent the award in any document or venue as SIG/Caucus-based and not as a "CCCC Award." This should be seen by SIGs and Caucuses as an opportunity for proudly claiming their own field of inquiry and practice—as well as authoring their own endorsements and appreciation for accomplishments in those fields.*
- *Should such an award be so mis-represented as a "CCCC Award," we propose that the SIG, Caucus, or award recipient responsible for the misrepresentation be approached by the Executive Committee in a collegial manner and asked to amend the misinformation to the best of his or her ability. We discussed at some length the thorny issue of consequences for a SIG, Caucus, or individual that does not comply with this policy. Some members of our group favor particular sanctions to be levied against such groups or individuals, while others believe that enforcing this policy would be logistically difficult for the officers or members of the Executive Committee in any case. It was proposed that perhaps CCCC assign a compliance officer to be responsible for the enforcement of this policy; Ira Shor volunteered to serve in that capacity, should the organization pursue this option. Everyone on the Task Force agreed that it is important for the organization to communicate these policies to all SIG/Caucus representatives annually.*

Perhaps the Task Force's most arduous discussion revolved around the issue of announcements, calls, and notices regarding SIG- and Caucus-Awards in CCC. The Task Force could not arrive at a consensus. Some members strongly affirm that SIGs and Caucuses in good standing have a right to access in CCC. Others do not believe that a journal editor should be mandated regarding announcements—especially when announcements, more generally, are at the discretion of the editor because of space constraints. It was also observed that an announcement in CCC can be (mis)read as an indication that an Award is sanctioned by the organization when, in fact, it is a SIG- or Caucus-Award. All of these recommendations and issues require further deliberation. Several members of the task force wished for a clearer statement of context for the charge of the task force; they strongly felt that the exigency for this charge was not explicit enough. Most particularly, they resist opening the door to punitive policy changes in the absence of particular exigencies.

It is difficult not to view the controversy around the Rachel Corrie Courage in the Teaching of Writing on the WPA list in May 2006 as having provided the exigence for the creation of this Task Force and the resulting recommendations. However, no one on the Task Force—in an official capacity—would acknowledge such an exigence.

Notes

This essay originally appeared in the *Journal of Advanced Composition,* Vol. 33, Issues 1&2 (2013). Thanks to the editor for granting permission to reproduce that essay in this volume.

1. See: http://condor.depaul.edu/~mabraha5/pretext1.pdf; http://condor.depaul.edu/~mabraha5/pretext2.pdf; http://condor.depaul.edu/~mabraha5/pretext3.pdf; http://condor.depaul.edu/~mabraha5/pretext4.pdf; http://condor.depaul.edu/~mabraha5/pretext5.pdf; http://condor.depaul.edu/~mabraha5/pretext6.pdf (accessed on September 1, 2010).

2. In his *Multidirectional Memory: Remembering the Holocaust in the Age of Decolonization,* Michael Rothberg, drawing upon Hannah Arendt's *Origins of Totalitarianism* and Aime Cesaire's *Discourse of Colonialism,* develops the notion of *choc en retour,* literally "boomerang effect," "backlash," or "reverse shock" (23).3. See Cheryl Glenn's *Unspoken: The Rhetoric of Silence.* Glenn writes, "Silence exists in overlapping states: environmental, locational, communal, personal. It can be self-or other-initiated, self-or other-derived. Silence can be something one does, something that is done to someone, or something one experiences" (9). Last year, a former editor of *College Composition and Communication* in an afterword questioned whether an edited collection devoted to the examination of a "critical rhetoric on the Israel-Palestine Conflict" should be "burned," arguing that the collection was being published under false pretenses with a major commercial publisher in Rhetoric and Composition. This former *CCC*'s editor claimed that she had been led to believe that the collection would explore positions on the conflict through rhetorical analysis, instead the essays she was handed supposedly engaged in "entrenched position-taking." Within the Afterword, this former *CCC*'s editor characterized Norman G. Finkelstein, the son of Holocaust survivors, as "a denier of historical fact," suggesting that Finkelstein "denies" the Holocaust. Actually, Finkelstein has argued that the Holocaust is often used as an ideological weapon to silence critics of Israel's human rights record and its continual violation of international law. It's ironic that this former *CCC*'s editor called for full scholarly accountability, when she herself did not meet the minimum benchmark for accountability.

4. See Jimmy Carter's *Palestine: Peace Not Apartheid* and Barack Obama's May 19, 2011 State Department Speech. Carter notes, "The bottom line is this: Peace will come to Israel and the Middle East when the Israel government is willing to comply with international law, with the Roadmap for Peace, with official American policy, with the wishes of a majority of its own citizens—and honor its own previous commitments—by accepting its legal borders. All Arab neighbors must pledge to honor Israel's right to exist in peace *under these conditions*. The United States is squandering international prestige and good will and intensifying global anti-American terrorism by unofficially condoning or abetting the Israeli confiscation and colonization of Palestinian territory" (216, emphasis added). As Obama noted in this speech, "The borders of Israel and Palestine should be based on the 1967 lines with mutually agreed swaps, so that secure and recognized borders are established for both states. The Palestinian people must have the right to govern themselves, and reach their potential, in a sovereign and contiguous state." Also, see Zalman Amit and Daphna Levit's *Israeli Rejectionism: A Hidden Agenda in the Middle East Peace Process*.

5. See http://u.arizona.edu/~mabraham1/chart.pdf (accessed on 22 March 2015) for an example of how university administrators may not always support scholarship promoting peace, human dignity, and justice.

6. For a list of all the emails posted on the topic of the Rachel Corrie Courage in the Teaching of Writing Award, see: http://u.arizona.edu/~mabraham1/chart.pdf (accessed on 22 March 2015).

7. See Bruce Ticker's "The Case Against Rachel Corrie" and Joshua Hammer's "The Death of Rachel Corrie. For a critique of Hammer's article, see Pham Nguyen's "Mother Jones Smears Rachel Corrie Specious Journalism in Defense of Killers."

8. See Hussein.

9. See Barbara Herrnstein-Smith's *Belief and Resistance: The Dynamics of Intellectual Controversy*. Cambridge: Harvard UP, 1999, p. vii.

10. The call for nominations read as follows:

> Fourth Annual Rachel Corrie Award for Courage in the Teaching of Writing 2007
>
> RACHEL CORRIE
>
> Rachel Corrie was a 23-year-old peace activist and senior at Evergreen State College in Olympia, Washington. She was killed on March 16, 2003 in Rafah in the Gaza Strip. She was on leave from school to work in Palestine with the International Solidarity Movement, a group using and promoting "nonviolent, direct-action methods of resistance to confront and challenge illegal Israeli occupation forces and policies." Rachel was attempting to block an Israeli military bulldozer from demolishing the house of a pharmacist and his family when the driver of the bulldozer ran over her, then backed up and ran over her again. Wearing a bright orange jacket and using a bullhorn, Rachel was, by all eyewitness accounts and in horrifying

photographs published on the Internet, exceptionally visible. Her parents, some members of Congress, and grassroots organizations including several Jewish peace groups have called for an independent U.S. investigation into her death. Such an investigation has yet to happen, and the U.S. media virtually buried the story—though it was featured prominently in the U.K. and in many other countries.

Corrie took courses like "Labor and the Environment" and "Public Art and the Middle East Conflict"; she also wrote detailed emails from Palestine. The late Edward Said, who met with her parents in May, 2003, wrote, "Her letters back to her family are truly remarkable documents of her ordinary humanity that made for very difficult and moving reading. . . ."

THE AWARD

The Progressive SIGs and Caucuses Coalition (PSCC) of the CCCC wishes to honor the memory of this extremely courageous student by recognizing a teacher in the CCCC who has taken professional risks in order to promote social justice through the teaching of writing. It is well known that the politics of hiring, tenure, and promotion often motivate graduate students and junior faculty to write, teach, and serve in "safe" subject and project areas; many are encouraged by mentors to shy away from genuinely "controversial" or "risky" subjects until they are tenured. In making this award, the PSCC hopes, conversely, to encourage writing teachers early in their careers to take on research, pedagogy, and service projects that promote commitment to peace, justice, and human dignity—even when hazarding the ire of deans, chairs, editors, and hiring and review committees.

Also, see: http://www.discoverthenetworks.org/groupProfile.asp?grpId=7046.
    11. See my "The Rhetoric of Academic Controversy after 9/11: Edward Said in the American Imagination," for a discussion about how transference can develop around an individual or school of thought.
    12. See Shlomo Sand's *The Invention of the Jewish People.*
    13. See Rory McCarthy's "British activist saw Rachel Corrie die under bulldozer, court hears."
    14. For eyewitness accounts of Corrie's death, see Dale et al.'s "Four Eyewitnesses Describe the Murder of Rachel Corrie."
    15. See Sandersock's *Peace Under Fire: Israel/Palestine and the International Solidarity Movement* for the eyewitness testimony of those who were near Rachel Corrie when she was attempting to block the bulldozer's path.
    16. See *Multidirectional Memory: Remembering the Holocaust in the Age of Decolonization.*

17. See Patricia Roberts-Miller's *Deliberate Conflict: Argument, Political Theory, and Composition Classes*.

18. See Dominick LaCapra's *History in Transit* and *History and Memory after the Holocaust*.

19. Thomas Rickert makes this observation, through LaPlanche, in his *Acts of Enjoyment: Rhetoric, Žižek, and the Return of the Subject*.

20. According to Thomas Rickert in his *Acts of Enjoyment: Rhetoric, Žižek, and the Return of the Subject*, "Žižek understands trauma to be our response to an impossible limit or radical antagonism; it is an experience of constitutive anxiety or unease at the terrifying prospect of the impossibility of achieving harmonious resolutions to personal and social relations. Furthermore, trauma is more intensified by the fact that is also 'resists' symbolization, totalization, symbolic integration (*Sublime* 6)" (219).

21. See Freud's "From the History of an Infantile Neurosis."

22. See Ian Lustick's "Abandoning the Iron Wall: Israel and the Middle Eastern Muck," "To Build and to Be Built By: Israel and the Hidden Logic of the Iron Wall," and "Negotiating Truth: The Holocaust, Lehavdil, and Al-Nakba"

23. See the Introduction to *Judaic Perspectives in Rhetoric and Composition*, p. 3. Greenbaum and Holdstein allege that anti-Semitism has crept into composition studies, citing comments made during the WPA list-serv debate about the Rachel Corrie Courage in the Teaching of Writing Award.

24. See Norman Finkelstein's *Beyond Chutzpah: The Misuse of Anti-Semitism and the Abuse of History*. For additional perspectives on the "New Anti-Semitism"and Alexander Cockburn and Jeffrey St. Clair's *The Politics of Anti-Semitism*. For a contrasting view, see Bernard Harrison's *The Resurgence of Anti-Semitism: Jews, Israel, and Liberal Opinion*.

25. See Judith Butler's "It's Not Anti-Semitic" and Sara Roy's "Short Cuts."

26. See p. 210–211 of Dershowit'z *The Case for Israel* for a list of features constituting the New Anti-Semitism.

27. See LaCapra's *Writing History, Writing Trauma*.

28. In speaking to the disconnect between popular and scholarly knowledge on the Israel-Palestine conflict and the attacks that have been enabled against serious scholarship on the conflict, Joseph Massad notes, "What makes these anti-scholarship attacks possible and popular is the existence of a major discrepancy, even a radical disconnect, between popular knowledge and media coverage about the Palestine/Israel conundrum and established scholarly knowledge about the topic. It is this disconnect that the witch hunters mobilise against scholarship as proof that it is not media and popular knowledge, which defends Israeli policy and Zionism's axioms, that is ideological, but rather academic scholarship which has largely uncovered unsavory facts about both." See Massad's "Targeting the University: Witch hunt at Columbia."

29. This phrase appears in Theodore Herzl's *The Jewish State*. According to Joseph Massad,

Herzl affirms that it is not a question of taking Jews away from "civilized regions into the desert," but rather the transformation "will be carried out in the midst of civilization. We shall not revert to a lower stage we shall rise to a higher one" (119)

30. See Norman Finkelstein's *Image and Reality in the Israel-Palestine Conflict.*

31. See Jonathan Cooke's *Israel and the Clash of Civilizations: Iran, Iraq, and the Plan to Remake the Middle East.*

32. In his *Writing the Arab-Israeli Conflict: Pragmatism and Historical Inquiry*, Jonathan Isacoff uses the phrase "teleological exceptionalism" to describe how "some of Israel's most cosmopolitan elites, such as [Abba] Eban," described the unique circumstances surrounding Israel's birth in terms that did not conform to traditional liberation movements, emphasizing the reuniting of the Jewish people with the land after a nineteen-hundred-year separation (55).

33. For very thoughtful discussions of "conflation of memory," see Michael Bernard-Donals "Conflations of Memory; or, What They Saw at the Holocaust Museum after 9/11" in *Forgetful Memory: Representation and Remembrance in the Wake of the Holocaust.* Albany: SUNY P, 2009, pp. 125–143.

34. See Yuri Slezkine's *The Jewish Century* and Karen Brodkin's *How Jews Became White Folks and What That Says About Race in America.*

35. See Norman G. Finkelstein's September 16, 2009 interview with Amy Goodman on *Democracy Now* about the Goldstone report at http://www.norman-finkelstein.com/democracy-now-analysis-of-goldstone-report/ (accessed on August 31, 2010).

36. Ultimately, Arafat chose not to visit the Museum at all, bringing the controversy to a premature end. For news coverage of the controversy, see Baer's "Holocaust Museum Reverses Self, Offers VIP Tour to Arafat"; Kurtzman's "Controversy Bedevils U.S. Holocaust Museum Again"; *Washington Post*, "U.S. Holocaust Museum Scuttles Visit by Arafat"; and Miller's "Arafat at Holocaust Museum? Issue Stirs Emotions in Israel."

37. According to Walt and Mearsheimer,We use 'Israel Lobby' as a convenient shorthand term for the loose coalition of individuals and single, unified movement with a central leadership, however, and the individuals and groups that make up this broad coalition sometimes disagree on specific policy issues. Nor is it some sort of cabal or conspiracy. On the contrary, the organizations and individuals who make up the lobby operate out in the open and in the same way that other interest groups do" (112).

38. Dershowitz writes, in his *The Case Against Israel's Enemies: Exposing Jimmy Carter and Others Who Stand in the Way of Peace*,To summarize: Mearsheimer and Walt accuse American Jews of creating a mechanism of social and political control in order to further their loyalty to Israel—which, Mearsheimer and Walt imply, trumped American Jews' loyalty to the United States—by steering U.S. foreign policy in directions that suited Israel's and not America's interests. American Jews and their friends are not only disloyal, Mearsheimer and Walt suggest, but dangerous to the United States" (52).

Furthermore, as Dershowitz claims, "The accusations leveled by Mearsheimer and Walt share the same themes as the notorious *Protocols of the Elders of Zion*, the czarist forgery whose motifs became a staple of anti-Semitic propaganda" (52).

In his *The Deadlies Lies: The Israel Lobby and the Myth of Jewish Control*, Foxman contends,

> Naturally, scholars like Mearsheimer and Walt don't directly tap into this vein of fantasy ("the whole bizarre rigmarole of paranoid fantasies that finds its classic expression in the notorious czarist forgery *The Protocols of the Elders of Zion*"). In fact, they explicitly disavow it. But the tenor of their argument, intentionally or not, activates that fantasy and draws upon the emotions it evokes (109).

WORKS CITED

Abraham, Matthew. Nomination Call. WPA-L (Discussion List). 6 May 2006. Web. 6 January 2013.

—. "The Rhetoric of Academic Controversy after 9/11: Edward Said in the American Imagination," *JAC* 24.3 (2004): 113-42. Print.

Amit, Zalman and Daphna Levit. *Israeli Rejectionism: A Hidden Agenda in the Middle East Peace Process*. London and New York: Pluto Press, 2011. Print.

Arendt, Hannah. *Origins of Totalitarianism*. New York: Houghton Mifflin Harcourt, 1973. Print.

Baer, Susan. "Holocaust Museum Reverses Self, Offers VIP Tour to Arafat," *Baltimore Sun*. 21 January 1998. Web. 1 September 2010.

Berg, Avraham. *The Holocaust is Over: We Must Rise From Its Ashes*. New York: Palgrave, 2008. Print.

Bernard-Donals. *Forgetful Memory*. Albany: SUNY P, 2009. Print.

Brennan, Theresa. *The Transmission of Affect*. Ithaca and London: Cornell UP, 2004. Print.

Brodkin, Karen. *How Jews Became White Folks and What That Says About Race in America*. New Brunswick: Rutgers UP, 1998. Print.

Burke, Kenneth. *A Rhetoric of Motives*. 1950. Berkeley: U of California P, 1969. Print.

Butler, Judith. "No, It's Not Anti-Semitic." *London Review of Books* 26.16 (August 21, 2003): 1921. Print.

Carter, Jimmy. *Palestine: Peace Not Apartheid*. New York: Simon and Schuster, 2006. Print.

Cesaire, Amie. *Discourse of Colonialism*. New York: Monthly Review Press, 2001. Print.

Cockburn, Alexander and Jeffrey St. Clair. *The Politics of Anti-Semitism*. London: AK Press, 2003. Print.

Cooke, Jonathan. *Israel and the Clash of Civilizations: Iran, Iraq, and the Plan to Remake the Middle East*. London: Pluto Books, 2008. Print.

Crowley, Sharon. *Toward a Civil Discourse: Rhetoric and Fundamentalism*. Pittsburgh: U of Pittsburgh P, 2006. Print.

Dale, Tom, et. al. "Four Eyewitness Describe the Murder of Rachel Corrie." *Electronic Intifada*. 19 March 2003. Web. 6 January 2012
Dershowitz, Alan. *The Case Against Israel's Enemies*. New York: Wiley & Sons, 2008. Print.
Discover the Network. "Rachel Corrie Award." 18 August 2010. Web. 27 April 2015.
Dorf, Matthew and Daniel Kurtman. "Arafat's Invitation to Holocaust Museum Arouses Ire, *Jewish Telegraphic Agency* 23 January 1998. Web. 26 May 2010.
Ellis, Marc. *Judaism ≠ Israel*. New York and London: New Press, 2009. Print.
—. *Out of the Ashes: The Search for Jewish Identity in the Twenty-First Century*. London: Pluto Press, 2002. Print.
Finkelstein, Norman. *Beyond Chutzpah: The Misuse of Anti-Semitism and the Abuse of History*. Berkeley: U of California P, 2005. Print.
—. *Image and Reality in the Israel-Palestine Conflict*. London and New York: Verso, 2004. Print.
Foxman, Abraham. *The Most Dangerous Lies: The Israel Lobby and the Myth of Jewish Control*. New York: Palgrave Macmillan, 2007. Print.
Freud, Sigmund. "From the History of an Infantile Neurosis." *The Standard Edition of the Complete Psychological Works of Sigmund Freud*. Trans. James Strachey. London: Hogarth, 1964. 17.7–122. Print.
Fuss, Diana. *Identification Papers*. New York: Routledge, 1995. Print.
Glenn, Cheryl. *Unspoken: A Rhetoric of Silence*. Carbondale: Southern Illinois UP, 2004. Print.
Hammer, Joshua. "The Death of Rachel Corrie." *Mother Jones*. September/October 2003. Web. 31 August 2010
Harrison, Bernard. *The Resurgence of Anti-Semitism: Jews, Israel, and Liberal Opinion*. Lanham: Rowman and Littlefield, 2006. Print.
Herzl, Theodore. *The Jewish State*. . New York: Dover Publications, 1988. Print.
—. *Old-New Land*. Trans. Lotta Levensohn. New York: Block Publishing Company and Herzl Press, 1960. Print.
Andrea Greenbaum and Deborah Holdstein. *Judaic Perspectives in Rhetoric and Composition*. Creskill: Hampton Press, 2008. Print.
Hussein, Abu Hussein. "Rachel Corrie: Blaming the Victim." *Common Dreams*. 2 September 2012. Web. 6 January 2013.
Isacoff, Jonathan B. *Writing the Arab-Israeli Conflict: Pragmatism and Historical Inquiry*. Lanham: Rowman and Littlefield, 2006. Print.
Kurtzman, Daniel. "Controversy Bedevils U.S. Holocaust Museum Again," *J-Weekly.com*. 26 June 1998. Web. 1 September 2010.
LaCapra, Dominick. *History in Transit*. Ithaca: Cornell UP, 2004. Print.
—. *History and Memory after Auschwitz*. Ithaca: Cornell UP, 1998. Print.
—. *Writing History, Writing Trauma*. Baltimore: Johns Hopkins UP, 2001. Print.
Laor, Yitzhak. *The Myths of Liberal Zionism*. London and New York: Verso, 2009. Print.
Lustick, Ian. "Abandoning the Iron Wall: Israel and the Middle Eastern Muck." *Middle East Policy*. 15:3 (Fall 2008): 30–56. Print.

—. "To Build and to Be Built By: Israel and the Hidden Logic of the Iron Wall," *Israeli Studies*. 1:1 (Spring 1996): 196–223. Print.

—. "Negotiating Truth: The Holocaust, Lehavdil, and Al-Nakba." *Journal of International Affairs*. 60:1 (Fall/Winter 2006): 51–77. Print.

Massad, Joseph. *The Persistence of the Palestinian Question: Essays on Zionism and the Palestinians*. London and New York: Routledge, 2006. Print.

—. "Targeting the University." Counterpunch. 3 June 2005. Web. 29 May 2012.

Mearsheimer, John and Stephen Walt. *The Israel Lobby and U.S. Middle East Policy*. London: Giroux & Strauss, 2007. Print.

McCarthy, Rory. "British activist saw Rachel Corrie die under bulldozer, court hears." *Guardian*. 10 March 2010. Web. 25 August 2010

Miller, Marjorie. "Arafat at Holocaust Museum? Issue Stirs Emotions in Israel." *Sun-Sentinel.com*. 25 January 1998. Web. 1 September 2010.

Nguyen, Phen. "Mother Jones Smears Rachel Corrie Specious Journalism in Defense of Killers." *Counterpunch*. 19–21 September 2003. Web. 31 August 2010.

Obama, Barack. State Department Speech. 19 May 2011. *YouTube*. Web. 29 May 2012.

Puccio, Paul. *Report of the Task Force on CCCC Awards and Guidelines*.24 May 2008. Print.

Rickert, Thomas. *Acts of Enjoyment: Rhetoric, Žižek, and the Return of the Subject*. Pittsburgh: U of Pittsburgh P, 2007. Print.

Roberts-Miller, Patricia. *Deliberate Conflict: Argument, Political Theory, and Composition Classes*. Carbondale: Southern Illinois UP, 2007. Print.

Rothberg, Michael. *Multidirectional Memory: Remembering the Holocaust in the Age of Decolonization*. Stanford: Stanford UP, 2009. Print.

Roy, Sara. "Short Cuts," *London Review of Books*26.7 (April 1, 2004): 24. Print.

Said, Edward. *After the Last Sky: Palestinian Lives*. New York: Columbia UP, 1998. Print.

—. "Dignity and Solidarity."*Counterpunch*. 25 September 2003. Web. 30 August 2010.

Sand, Shlomo. *The Invention of the Jewish People*. London and New York: Verso, 2010. Print.

Sandersock, Joyce, et al. *Peace Under Fire: Israel/Palestine and the International Solidarity Movement*. London and New York: Verso, 2004. Print.

Slezkine, Yuri. *The Jewish Century*. Princeton: Princeton UP, 2004.

Ticker, Bruce. "The Case Against Rachel Corrie." *Israel National News*. 30 May 2004. Web. August 2010.

Washington Post. "U.S. Holocaust Museum Scuttles Visit by Arafat." LATimes.com. 17 January 1998. Web. 1 September 2010.

Worsham, Lynn. "Going Postal: Pedagogic Violence and the Schooling of Emotion." *JAC* 18:2 (1998): 213–45. Print.

Writing Program Administration (WPA) Archive. WPACouncil.org. *1419 May 2006. Web. 6 January 2013.*

Žižek, Slavoj. *Sublime Object of Ideology*. London and New York: Verso, 1989. Print.

4 The Temporal Roots of Anti-Semitism and Its Impact on the Arab-Israeli Conflict

Amos Kiewe

Introduction

I begin my exploration into the temporal roots of anti-Semitism with a working premise that politics, flexibly and generally considered, is but a discursive process that encompasses a collection of arguments that seek to persuade others of specific positions as justification for action. Under the umbrella usage of the word "arguments," I put concepts such as ideologies, beliefs, opinions, attitudes, values, and convictions, each with the objective of arguing a specific point that can secure adherence by others. Such a variety of arguments can take both positive and negative directions, as "necessary" to justify a course of action. Here, the list could expand to include support, reinforcement, and conformity, but also prejudices, stereotypes, and biases. Anti-Semitism is a prejudice, often resorting to vile stereotypes that border on hate speech. It is also as a metaphor to the extent that anti-Semitism is a rhetorical construct or a cover for base hatred. As I wrote elsewhere, anti-Semitism "is a rhetorical construct prompted by theological precepts in order to create mass persuasion. Anti-Semitism is a means whose ultimate end is often obscured but its victims are always the Jews" (2).

Anti-Semitism, then, clearly falls under the large heading of political discourse or political communication. More specifically, it is a prejudice that has been used throughout history to justify political, religious and social actions of one sort or another, all based on a fundamental hatred of Jews. The topic of anti-Semitism has been investigated at length, especially following World War II and the Holocaust, seeking an explanation for the worst act of anti-Semitism—the Holocaust and its planned objective of decimating European Jewry. Though the topic of anti-Semitism is complex and its motivations and practices have evolved over two millennia, the root cause has by and large remained constant. The transformation of religious hatred into racial, ethnic, and national animosity has remained for centuries rooted in Christianity's primary act—the events surrounding Jesus' crucifixion and the charge that Jews are forever guilty of this act. In Islam, anti-Semitism, a recent development closely associated with the State of Israel, has sought to ground this relatively new hatred in events surrounding Muhammad's struggle to establish a new religion and the charge that Jews rejected the Prophet's plan to establish Islam. Out of these root causes, hatred of Jews developed to include a host of related and unrelated manifestations, piling charges including being cosmopolitan, usurer, capitalist, socialist, communist, arrogant, coward, and parasite.

Most crucial is the fact that anti-Semitism has been practiced with great zeal for some two thousand years, in the case of Christianity, and to a lesser extent for some fourteen hundred years in Islam. Charging Jews with eternal guilt of crimes against the founders of Christianity and Islam and their hatred thereof is the focus of this chapter, specifically, pointing to the temporal variable that has allowed such hatred to be sustained eternally and the impact of the hatred of Jews on the Arab- and Palestinian-Israeli conflict. Anti-Semitism, or the more accurate phrasing, the hatred of Jews, began in antiquity and has continued into contemporary times with no signs of weakening or abating relative to other examples of group hatred that have long disappeared.

The longevity of anti-Semitism as a specific form of hatred and its theological projection into the future, in my view, stands at the heart of the Arab-Israeli conflict and only its eradication can open the path to a more peaceful relationship between Muslims and Jews. Indeed, when contemplating anti-Semitism, the longevity and eternity of this hatred must be raised as a surprising feature. Put in a question form, why has the hatred of Jews lasted so long and with no signs of ending this century-old prejudice? The longevity of this hatred, or what I refer to here as the temporal roots of anti-Semitism, must have a life and reasoning of its own. But what has allowed this longevity in the first place and what variables made anti-Semitism survive despite the many historical, political, geographical and social changes? I begin my exploration by discussing the notion of temporality in rhetoric. I then turn to identifying the temporal causes of anti-Semitism in Christianity essential to understanding anti-Semitism in Islam and how central it is to comprehending the Arab-Israeli conflict.

Temporality in Argumentative reasoning

The longevity of Christian and Islamic anti-Semitism, despite the ebbs and flows, is rooted in the identification of "original causes" that both faiths selected to consider, perhaps strategically so, as continuous and timeless. Time froze for centuries once an inherent cause has identified Jews as guilty of a major religious offence against the founders of Christianity and Islam. In Christianity the offense is that of deicide—the killing of Jesus as God, and in Islam the charge of rejecting Muhammad's teaching and quarreling with him. The theology of these charges as timeless was made possible by the temporality that allowed time to be extended to eternity. This very formula is a unique and powerful argumentative and rhetorical stance since any logical assessment of the inherent argument therein would lead one to quickly dismiss the extension of guilt from one person to another, not to speak of from one generation to another and from one century to another. Yet, put in a theological context and argued as divinely inspired, the charge of eternal guilt gained ultimate power and authority precisely because in theology, claims are ultimate and infallible. Anti-Semitism's very presence over centuries proves that such an argumentative stance has been possible, functional, and with dire consequences.

I rely on the work of Paul Ricoeur whose conceptualization of time and temporality has guided my work on the charge of eternal guilt and the longevity of anti-Semitism.[1] As I have explored elsewhere Ricoeur distinguishes chronological time from rhetorical time or narrated time, arguing that temporality is rather elastic and open to manipulation.[2] My contention, in view of Ricoeur, is that rhetorical time allows for the stretching of time, condensing it, rupturing it as well as punctuating it. Humans can designate an arbitrary starting point, investing it with much symbolism, and calling it sacred time or condensing what chronologically is a long spread of time such that "yesterday" was actually a decade earlier. Time, then, can be manipulated and molded such that it serves as grounding for specific claims. A starting point or the moment of initiation can also imply rupture with that which preceded it, allowing the erasure of an "undesired" past.

Religions, in particular, are prone to temporal manipulation as their foundations require an agreed-upon starting point heavy on symbolism befitting divine intervention. In religious narratives, time can stretch, sometimes to eternity; condense or rupture relative to the theology at hand. The metaphor in particular allows humans to connect different temporal points. Thus for example, time lost or time regained is possible only via the metaphor (Ricoeur 151). No wonder, then, that Time takes on religious metaphors and functions interpretively as in a theological construct whereby "God is more than just the source of a 'physical' time: God is the *agency* of time" (Stevenson 149–150). Brockmeier conjures up time "as an organizing principle of human life, an instrument by means of which we structure our activities and, on the basis of these, order our thoughts about the world and about ourselves" (243). Theology is prone to the usage of a starting point that is invested with sacredness, a condensing of metaphors that allows, for example, the "father/mother" and "child" relationship between the deity and followers and, hence, a familial, immediate, and temporal relationship that chronological temporality could not allow. The imperatives of theology are often timeless as the primary vehicle for continuation including projection into the life after.

Time, then, is a rhetorical construct, a metaphor punctuated and molded to fit a coherent, argumentative narrative, be it by stretching time, condensing, rupturing or expanding it to eternity. Time expanded, ruptured, continued or constricted can warrant the foundation of appealing mythic narratives. Such mythic narratives are also the root causes of anti-Semitism, constructed for public consumption without it being charged as illogical, unethical, or immoral. This charge of the eternal guilt of the Jew was taken as "necessary" given the unique evolution of Christianity from Judaism and the need to separate the two such that Judaism would forever be the scorned religion.

The Temporal Roots of Anti-Semitism in Christianity

Anti-Semitism is entrenched and enduring, and its practices ranging from antiquity to the present must yield a profound surprise at the longevity of such hatred.[3] While anti-Semitism may appear in different forms, and at different times to include religious hatred, social antagonism, economic blame, psychological scapegoating, intellectual elitism, and others, events of two thousand years ago are still the primary reason for such persistent hatred.

Religious temporality that grounds the eternal guilt of the Jew for crucifying Jesus on the cross stands at the foundation of Christian anti-Semitism. The Church Fathers who sought to extend Jewish guilt centuries after the charge of deicide was first leveled, succeeded in doing so by developing simple but appealing mythic narratives that identified a culprit who would carry the guilt temporally to eternity. This very temporality explains much in defining Christ's death on the cross as a timeless act and so is the hatred of Jews as "deserving" of the crime of deicide. Recent development in Islam has employed this very concept and for the very purpose of turning anti-Semitism perpetual and timeless.

The Council of Nicaea in 325 CE had Roman Emperor Constantine declare that in killing Christ, the Jews committed a horrendous act and that they should suffer for it, and that subsequently, "let us have nothing in common with their odious people" (Caroll 55). The sin of crucifying Christ has mandated a separation between the two religions, but as St. Augustine suggested, "[t]he continued preservation of the Jews will be a proof to believing Christians of the subjugation marked by those who, in the pride of their kingdom, put the Lord to death" (Julius et al 5). The charge of Jews as carrying the guilt of Christ's crucifixion to eternity also carried with it their subjugation to eternity as a memory sign of their punishment.

The restrictions on Jews put by Emperor Constantine's policy that intensified Christian hatred toward Jews were formalized in 438 AD, in the *Code of Theodosius II* which thereafter charged Jews as a collective and accused them of deicide, responsible for killing Jesus.[4] From here onward, "the blood of Jesus falls not only on the Jews of that time, but on all generations of Jews up to the end of the world" (Julius et al 5). The eternal charge of deicide, once turned into liturgy, insured its adherence as well as its repetition from one generation to another.

Hence, performances such as the annual "passion play" which repeated (in some place they still do) the narrative of Christ's birth and death on the cross function to reinforce the deeds of the Jew, often resulting in attacks on Jews throughout the Middle Ages, their segregations in ghettos, restrictions put on many occupations, and overall denigration and humiliation reaching a dramatic climax with the Holocaust. That the charge of eternal guilt of deicide was accepted though lacking good reasoning only proves how powerful religious edicts could be, and how temporality can sustain them by stretching time to its endless possibility and thus grounding this theology.

The proof that the temporal variable is inherent to Christian anti-Semitism has been furnished by no other than the Catholic Church itself. In the 1965 Synod, known as Vatican II, the Church has focused precisely on the temporal issue, claiming belatedly that though "[t]rue, the Jewish authorities and those who followed their lead pressed for the death of Christ; still, what happened in His passion cannot be charged against all the Jews, without distinction, then alive, nor against the Jews of today." The statement went as far as to ask that "the Jews should not be presented as rejected or accursed by God, as if this followed from the Holy Scriptures. . . . Furthermore, in her rejection of every persecution against any man, the Church, mindful of the patrimony she shares with the Jews and moved not by political reasons but the Gospel's spiritual love, decries hatred, persecutions, displays of anti-Semitism, directed against Jews at any time and by anyone."[5] The statement by Vatican II known as *Nostra Aetate* (in our time), identified the primary cause of Christian anti-Semitism to lie in the charge of the eternal guilt of the Jew, seeking now to correct this early theology by correctly zeroing in on the temporality inherent to anti-Semitism and questioning the eternity claim.

Cardinal Bea who drafted *Nostra Aetate*, wrote that the Church now questioned that very claim stating that "[T]he Jews of our time can hardly be accused of the crimes committed against Christ, so far removed are they from those deeds. Actually, even in the time of Christ, the majority of the Chosen People did not cooperate with the leaders of the people in condemning Christ . . . If therefore not even all the Jews in Palestine or in Jerusalem could be accused, how much less the Jews dispersed throughout the Roman Empire? And how much less again those who today, after nineteen centuries, live scattered in the whole world?" ("Catholic Attitude Toward Jews"). Not all supported this foundational change then or even now, voices in the Church have argued against dropping the charge of eternal guilt of the Jews thus exposing the centrality of temporality—eternal guilt—as foundational to anti-Semitism (Lewis 162).

THE TEMPORAL ROOST OF ANTI-SEMITISM IN ISLAM

By comparison with Christianity, virulent Islamic anti-Semitism is a relatively new development, and its practices were influenced much later by imported Christian anti-Semitism of the nineteenth century but much expanded in the second half of the twentieth century.[6] It is truly unfortunate that just as the Catholic Church in 1965 had come around, after some two millennia of anti-Semitism, to repudiate its own responsibility for anti-Semitism, the very same anti-Semitic slogans of medieval Europe have found attractive adherents in the Islamic world. Islamic anti-Semitism has adopted long-standing European anti-Semitism, including tracts and slogans that have long been considered passé. Such attitudes were interjected into verses from the Quran and other religious tracts to prove a much greater animosity than warranted between the Prophet Muhammad and the Jewish inhabitants of the Arab peninsula during the early Seventh Century CE than initially formulated. This hindsight interpretation and theology thereof was constructed specifically to suit the Arab-Israeli conflict.

Until the twentieth century, anti-Semitism was an unknown concept in the Islamic world. Some anti-Jewish sentiments accompany the rise of Islam from inception and the Quran carries several invectives against the Jews, but Jews are also respected as the "People of the Book (The Bible)." By and large, Islam has had for many centuries a fairly consistent view of Jews and other non-Muslims as *Dhimmi*—a protected minority. As a matter of fact, Jews were not singled out among other minorities as deserving special hostile treatment. There are simply no parallels between European and Islamic anti-Semitism until the twentieth century.

Muslims' relationship with Jews is based on two different contexts: The first and short phase center on Mecca when Muhammad's struggle with various pagan tribes was supported by Jews. Muhammad learned much from his Jewish neighbors and the Islamic reference to the Jews as the "People of the Book [the Bible]" is attributed to this peaceful period. The second phase is related to emigration to Medina when Muhammad and his followers began to spread Islam and the Jews of the Arab Peninsula resisted these efforts. The antagonism toward Jews sprung from the Jewish resistance to accepting Muhammad's religion. From this period come few negative verses in the Quran, verses that nonetheless, have not been operationalized until the rise of Islamic anti-Semitism in the nineteenth and twentieth centuries. Such negative verses describe Jews as "afflicted with humiliation and poverty, and [that] they felt the wrath of God. This was because they used to disbelieve the signs of God and kill his messengers unjustly."[7] Jews are also described as monkeys and apes, despised, rejected and the "enemies of the believers."[8] Jews were now described as "base, contemptible, scorns all moral values, gnaws on live flesh and sucks blood for a pittance . . . let us cast side this distinction [between Jews and Israelis] and talk about the Jews" (Yadlin 318). The focus centered not on Jews as Israelis but on Jews as Jews.

For centuries, Islam's attitude toward Judaism was of measured relationship and devoid of anti-Semitism (Lewis 118). Early hints of a change in attitude toward Jews in Judaism began in the nineteenth century and were primarily due to the influence of European anti-Semitism in the form of Greek and Catholic clergy spreading anti-Semitic tracts (Lewis 132). The infamous *Damascus Affair* in 1840 (a blood libel reminiscent of numerous Middle-Age accusations that Jews need to drink the blood of a Christian child, hence, the kill), prompted by the French Council in Damascus, was a sign of things to come (Lewis 132). In 1869, the first anti-Semitic publication is translated from French into Arabic. The *Dreyfuss Affair* in the late nineteenth century and the forged document known as *The Protocols of the Elders of Zion* that first appeared in 1895 and later in wider distribution since 1921, further intensified Islam's hostile view of Judaism. The most devastating development in introducing a new phase of the Muslim-Jewish relationship into the Middle East was in the form of Nazi anti-Semitism that spread quite effectively by the Nazi propaganda machine in the 1930s.

Initially, the imported European anti-Semitism was not shared by all Muslims and facts on the ground prove how fast the cordial relationship between Muslims and Jews underwent a major change. Though Jews always resided in the Holy Land and the larger Middle East, initial immigration of European Jews into Palestine did not begin until 1888 was not resisted but was welcomed by local governments and people. Ziwar Pasha, later the Prime Minister of Egypt, took part in the celebrating of the *Balfour Declaration* of 1916. Jewish leaders met with Arab representatives and found support in the Zionist project. When the Hebrew University was opened, the Egyptian Minister of Interior traveled to Jerusalem to participate in the opening ceremony. Sports competition in the 1920s included Jewish and Arab delegations (Lewis 137, 194). These are but few of numerous instances of Arab-Jewish collaboration and an overall positive relationship and support of Jewish immigration viewed as contributing to the development of the Near East.

Arab hostility toward Jews would intensify tenfold during the 1920s following growing waves of Jewish immigration. It would significantly intensify with the introduction of Nazi anti-Semitism in the Middle East in the 1930s, as it quickly fused with Islamism in Palestine and Egypt, producing intense anti-Semitism that was never part of the Islamic world. Jews were now described as the enemy of Islam and with it the opposition to Jewish immigration into Palestine became a focused campaign. Yet, even as late in 1936, for example, the rector of Egypt's premier university, Al-Azhar, "forbade his Palestinian students from indulging in any anti-Jewish propaganda" (Kuntzell 22). The forces of moderation, however, could not stop the Muslim Brotherhood in Egypt and the Husseini tribe in Palestine from their anti-Semitism despite strong resistance by other Arabs in Palestine. As world affairs quickly took over local tensions, the Jewish-Arab relationship would be absorbed by the larger world-wide conflict.

Islamist anti-Semitism would further intensify after the war of 1948 with the establishment of the State of Israel, a hostility that was now grounded in theological claims. Looking back at the early days of Islam, Sayyib Qutb's founding essay "Our Struggle with the Jews," published in 1950, argued that Jews were hostile to the Prophet Muhammad, that they conspired against him and that the Jews fought the Prophet. This struggle, argued Qutb, was not over and it continued because Jews would not be satisfied until Islam is destroyed (Netter 98–105). Accordingly, the war with the Jews is an eternal one and theological. The temporality of eternity was inserted to define the hostility as never-ending and thus insoluble. A new and virulent chapter in the relationship between Jews and Muslims was underwritten and its effects are clearly visible today. In the words of Matthias Kuntzell, in today's Islam "not only is everything Jewish evil, but everything evil is Jewish" (Kuntzell 84).

Clearly, the establishment of Israel in 1948, the defeat of Arab armies and the Nakba (catastrophe) it brought on Palestinians is the context for this religious view. After the war of 1967 and the further defeat of Arab armies brought even more intense anti-Semitism. Now, Islam charged that "Jews had strayed from the Law of Moses, killed Jesus, and were cursed by God through the Prophets *forever*" (Fackenheim 33). The religious cause has framed the Arab-Israeli conflict absorbing the Palestinian struggle as a unifying feature and as providing the theological cover that is most authoritative in Islam and thus can easily yield followers. As historian Bernard Lewis opines, modern Islam has taken minor references to Jews in the Quran and made the focus on Jews an obsession and the cause of all misfortunes that befell the Islamic world (Lewis 193). This obsession and the specific accusations of Jews as hostile enemies of the Prophet and the argument that the conflict continues, I argue, is akin to the temporality in Christianity's charge of deicide and with it the cause of the eternal fight with Judaism. In Shia Islam, the eternal temporality is even more profound. Here, Muslims await the Imam-Mehdi and upon his arrival a great war and upheaval would bring a Shi'ite rule in the world and a messianic era.[7] The end of days or the messianic era would be possible only with the killing of Jews. The Shi'ite messianic idea is rather similar to the end of the days prophecy in Christianity and with both, the Jew is the agency on whose literal body, the messianic days are prophesied (Kiewe 129). Both visions are essentially narratives of temporality—the end of days, but with dire consequences for Jews.

Though Nazi Germany was defeated some seventy years ago, the Nazi swastika continues to be used as the ultimate image of anti-Semitism and is often physically attached to images of Jews. Throughout the world, the swastika is often used when seeking to oppose Israel for one reason or another. This experience is especially acute in the Islamic world where cartoons in particular are replete with the Nazi symbol. For a region that often denies the Holocaust, the use of the swastika image is intriguing. Several examples illustrate this point. In one cartoon, Israel's Prime Minister Benyamin Netanyahu is looking in the mirror, but instead of seeing himself he is seeing the image of Hitler (*Al-Kahlij*, United Arab Emirates, July 20, 2014). Another cartoon depicts an Israeli soldier with a Star of David affixed to the front of his Nazi helmet (*Fars*, Iran, July 21, 2014). A variation on this cartoon has an Israeli soldier with a Star of David on one arm and the swastika on the other while the arm is stretched in a Nazi salute (*Al Bayan*, United Arab

Emirates, July 15, 2014). And yet, another cartoon takes a stereotypical view of the Jew, with a hooked nose complaining of his injured finger while a pile of bodies next to him are identified as Gaza (*Al-Madina,* July 11, 2014). One cartoon depicts a religious Jew telling an Israeli soldier pointing at an Arab nailed to the cross "this way Israel will become a Jewish state." Above the cross, the caption reads, "1948 Arabs." (*Al Raya*, Qatar, March 11, 2013). A final example has Secretary John Kerry depicted twice; once hugging Abbas of the Palestinian Authority and handing him a balloon, and one hugging a generic Jew identified with a hat and a Star of David on it and handing him a bag of money (*Al Jazeera*, July 30, 2013).[10] In these examples, the Jew-Nazi takes center stage as well as the portrayal of the ugly Jews as money hungry, perpetuating old stereotypes that are European in origin. These cartoons, and many like them, seek to associate the Jew with the Nazi, killing, and crucifying (a clear reference to the charge of deicide), and subsequently blurring the distinction such that the true nature of the Nazi such as he is no longer recognized, at the least in the Islamic world, and with it the Nazi and the Jew have become one and the same. Ultimately, the Jews as the victims of the Nazi regime are now the victimizers and their victimage is thus erased.

The Durban Conference in South Africa in 2001 can be considered an exemplar and a turning point in virulent Islamist anti-Semitism of recent years. The conference devoted to eradicating racism and discrimination across the world turned into a festival of hate against Israel and was replete with anti-Semitism, the likes of which, the world had not seen since Nazi Germany in the 1930s (Kiewe 109–134). Pamphlets and cartoons depicting Jews with hooked noses and Nazi emblems attached to Israelis with blood on their hands were displayed at demonstrations outside the conference while inside delegates debated the replacement of the capital "H" in Holocaust with a lower-case "h" as a clear attempts to downplay the Jewish Holocaust if not to erase it altogether and thus allowing the charge that Israel has committed the same (Kiewe 110). The term anti-Semitism was "struck from the conference's official register of bigotries because it is not a contemporary form of racism" (Kiewe 110). One flyer distributed at the conference suggested that if Hitler won in World War II, there would not be a State of Israel, implying that there would have been no Jews left to build it (Kiewe 110).

One might ask why use the Nazi swastika that proves the Holocaust did exist while at the same time denying the Holocaust ever happened. Here, anti-Semitism's rhetorical grounding is front and center; seeking to deprive Israel of the Holocaust often understood in the Islamic world as justification for its creation but also, and relatedly, seeking to take away the Holocaust cover under which the Arab world sees Israel fighting its wars of defense and survival. Hence, the constant attempts to attach the Nazi symbol to Israel is an argumentative stance that claims that Israel's actions are identical to those of Nazi Germany, while at the same time also seeking to downplay the Holocaust by usurping its impact. The objective of associating Israel with Nazism is also motivated by the historical development that early Muslim supporters of Nazi Germany in the Middle East did not anticipate when they were first attracted to Nazi ideology in the 1930s. That things did not develop as planned, and that Nazi Germany became synonymous with evil has not helped the Islamic world and thus what better way to distance oneself from an evil than to attach it to one's enemy, especially when evidence exists that Haj Amin Al-Husseini, the Grand Mufti of Jerusalem, not only supported Hitler's "final solution" but also organized Muslim SS troops in Bosnia-Herzegovina (Kuntzell 36–45).

And though in Islam there is no room for any other religion in the territories it controls, namely, the entire Middle East, the presence of a Jewish State in its midst is simply unacceptable to Muslims. The toleration of non-Muslims is managed only within a specific set of limitations put in place by local communities. Yet, none of this explains the anti-Semitism of the modern Islam. The explanation for intense anti-Semitism in Islam, as I argue here, is possible only if one considers Christian anti-Semitism as foundational to Islamic anti-Semitism. The rhetorical process of establishing a successful campaign of anti-Semitism in the Islamic world is quite similar to the process undertaken by the Church for some two thousand years earlier, whereby a religious quarrel becomes foundational to the origin of the faith. Just as killing Christ allowed for the eternal guilt of all Jews, Muslims have re-discovered Quranic verses to "prove" an eternal and religiously sanctioned hatred. With such verses lashing against the Jews, uttered by Muhammad himself, all contemporaries have the right to repeat them and to follow their sentiments. Thus, a foundational story functions as a legitimate cause for hatred, absolving Muslims from contemplating a more realistic assessment of the contemporary Arab-Israeli conflict. Clearly, it is easier to fall back on foundational archetypes of hatred than to deal with the more complex realities of the contemporary Middle East, especially the Palestinian-Israeli conflict.

The foundational story of Muhammad and his struggle with Jews as the perspective from which the Arab-Israeli conflict is now assessed leaves no room for a much needed compromise or accommodation between the warring parties. Yet, this foundational narrative works only if time is frozen, whereby events in the early seventh century CE are used as a justification for contemporary and eternal attitudes and actions toward Jews and Israel, now and forever. Considering Jews hostile to the founder of Islam is akin to the Christian's timeless accusation of Jews as Christ killers. The eternal charge that Jews conspired to hurt the Prophet Muhammad is the equivalent charge of killing Christ, whereby Jews are evil for their designs on the founders of other religions, both of which sprung from Judaism. The reverse charge, that Christianity and Islam are forever indebted to Judaism, to one degree or another, for its monotheistic theology, for its being the mother religion, and for its establishment of the land of antiquity as Holy, is downplayed if not resisted altogether precisely because any recognition of Judaism would negate hatred and require accommodation with Jews and Israel.

Despite the clear distinction between the accusation of killing the founder of Christianity and the charge of the Jews' struggle with the founder of Islam, contemporary Islamic anti-Semitism is so vicious, so crude, and so outmoded, that the only explanation for its intensity must be put in the context of anti-Zionist hatred. Temporality in the case of anti-Semitism has had a devastating impact on the Jewish people as it sustained the hatred beyond all logical extensions. Generation after generation, were made to suffer anew an act committed centuries and millennia earlier. But temporality by itself does not explain anti-Semitism beyond its eternal perpetuation. Temporality implies something else that is simple yet sinister—that people inherit guilt. This is precisely how anti-Semitism has remained eternal and rationalized as such. The ability to accuse Jews as accursed and guilty of crimes committed against the founders of Christianity and Islam is possible only if one accepts the premise of transference of guilt from one generation to another, even those not born yet.

The corrective is possible given the profound change the Catholic Church undertook in 1965 by repudiating anti-Semitism and its eternal foundation. Though the Church understood how foundational the Jews' rejection of Christ and the separation of Christianity from Judaism was necessary for the new religion to set foot during earlier centuries, it now rejected anti-Semitism and embraced Judaism and "the patrimony she [the Church] shares with the Jews." Islam can do the same and with a much easier process and convoluted theology since its foundation has much less to do with the Jew. The corrective is also possible if all trappings of anti-Semitism are to be avoided in the context of the Arab-Israeli conflict. Criticism of Israel devoid of anti-Semitic references in speech or cartoon may allow a better focus on the issues of contention and will likely narrow the gap between the two sides as they seek to find a peaceful solution to the long and intractable conflict.

SUMMARY

My overriding conceptualization is that Anti-Semitism has been sustained by the narrative of temporality that has allowed its extension, longevity and future continuation in two separate religious contexts. Yet, the temporal causes of anti-Semitism in both Christianity and Islam are but convenient narratives that mask the more serious and genuine root causes. Both religions sprung from Judaism, borrowed heavily from its biblical narratives, relied heavily on its primary symbols and the land of antiquity, and claimed to be a perfected form of the Judaism With such proximity to Judaism, it is no wonder that hatred of Jews soon developed. After all, how can one borrow heavily from another and claim to be original? It is this very proximity that stands at the root of anti-Semitism and the cause for its longevity. Judaism's presence is a constant reminder that Christianity and Islam would not have come to life without Judaism as their religious predecessor and that Judaism's prior existence does justify claims to the originality of theology and geography. Only the elimination of Judaism can allow Christianity and Islam to claim theology and geography with no recrimination. As long as Judaism stands, a constant doubt creeps into the other two religions, casting suspicion about various theological claims.

In the words of the rhetorical scholar, Kenneth Burke, I contend that an inherent guilt pervades Christianity and Islam and it is this rhetorical variable that stands at the root of continuous anti-Semitism. Put differently, as long as Jews are present, Christian and Islamic anti-Semitism could exit as well, at least until a more accommodating theology is advanced. Yet, it still begs the question why resort to anti-Semitism in the context of the Arab-Israeli conflict? Because it may be easier to resort to the trope of the tried-and-true anti-Semitism than dealing with the complexity of the Arab-Israeli conflict, or put differently, "it may be easier to attack Israel by focusing on its Jewish identity than dealing with specific Israeli infractions" policies and claims (Kiewe 111). The religious argument inherent in anti-Semitism is more universal, in longer use and thus more amenable to quick persuasion and reception. Relatedly, the focus on the Holocaust, denying it but in the same breadth wishing Hitler succeeded in killing all Jews, allows the critic a window into Islam's view of the Holocaust as the sine-qua-non reason for the establishment of the State of Israel, Hence, the attempts to usurp the Holocaust, diminish its importance, or deny it altogether, are rhetorical approaches that work to negate the cause of Israel's existence. Yet, what this premise misses is that all institutions of a future state were in existence and evolving since the British Mandate began in 1920, and a state would have been established even without the Holocaust, though the Holocaust and the devastation it incurred likely hastened the establishment of Israel. Equally important is the fact that anti-Semitism in Islam, imported from Europe in the mid-nineteenth century, preceded the first wave of Jewish immigration into Palestine by several decades and appears some one hundred years before the establishment of the State of Israel. Likewise, the intensification of anti-

Semitism in the 1930s was possible because it began to set foot much earlier. Put differently, linking anti-Semitism to the establishment of the State of Israel is a convenient argument but a false one.

The implications of Vatican II and the repudiation of anti-Semitism and the charge of eternal guilt is thus a most significant development in the history of anti-Semitism, as it showed that theological precepts can be altered and dramatically so. It is not beyond reason that Islam can resort to the same process, returning to earlier history when the Prophet's relationship with the Jewish tribes of the Arab Peninsula were rather friendly and respectful. A more accommodating argument and practice whereby Islam acknowledges its Judaic roots, just as the Catholic Church did in Vatican II, would allow not only for a more comfortable shared usage of the holy sites, but also better respect between the three religions and, in my opinion, a prerequisite for solving the Arab-Israeli conflict. The Arab-Israeli and Palestinian-Israeli conflicts cannot be solved with intense anti-Semitic attitudes hovering above the political.

NOTES

1. Paul Ricoeur, *Time and Narrative*. Volume I (Chicago: University of Chicago Press, 1983); *Time and Narrative*. Volume II (Chicago: University of Chicago Press, 1985).

2. Kiewe, *Confronting Anti-Semitism*, 155–158.

3. The European Monitoring Centre of Racism and Xenophobia (EUMC) defined anti-Semitism in 2005 the following way: "Anti-Semitism is a certain perception of Jews, which may be expressed as hatred toward Jews. Rhetorical and physical manifestations of anti-Semitism are directed toward Jewish or non-Jewish individuals and/or their property, toward Jewish community institutions and religious facilities. In addition, such manifestations could also target the state of Israel, conceived as a Jewish collectivity. Anti-Semitism frequently charges Jews with conspiring to harm humanity, and it is often used to blame Jews for 'why things go wrong. It is expressed is speech, writing, visual forms and action, and employs sinister stereotypes and negative character traits." (http://www.marilynstowe.co.uk/2011/06/03/the-experts-is-the-ucu-antisemitic/ accessed, Dec. 8, 2014).

4. Cited in James Carroll, *Constantine's Sword: The Church and the Jews* (Boston: A Mariner Book, 2001), 55.

5. Anthony Julius, Robert S. Rifkind, Jeffrey Weill and Felice D. Gaer, *Antiemitism: An Assault on Human Rights* (New York: The Jacob Blaustein Institute, The American Jewish Committee, 2001). This document was submitted to The United Nations World Conference Against Racism, racial Discrimination, Xenophobia and Related Intolerance, Durban, South Africa, August-September 2001), 5.

6. Qtd. in, Kiewe, *Confronting Anti-Semitism*, 149.

7. Qtd. in, Kiewe, *Confronting Anti-Semitism*, 151.

8. http://vaticaniiat50.wordpress.com/2013/11/19/text-of-cardinal-bea-on-draft-of-catholic-attitude-toward-jews/ accessed, Dec. 7, 2014.

9. Strong opposition to Vatican II's repudiation of anti-Semitism came from Near East bishops. See Bernard Lewis, *Semites and Anti-Semites: An Inquiry into Conflict and Prejudice* (New York: W. W. Norton & Co., 1999), 100; Kiewe, *Confronting Anti-Semitism*, 162.

Works Cited

Carroll, James. *Constantine's Sword: The Church and the Jews*. Boston: Mariner Books, 2001. Print.

Julius, Anthony, Robert S. Rifkind, Jeffrey Weill and Felice D. Gaer. *Antiemitism: An Assault on Human Rights*. New York: The Jacob Blaustein Institute, The American Jewish Committee, 2001. Print.

Kiewe, Amos. *Confronting Anti-Semitism: Seeking An End to Hateful Rhetoric*. Leicester: Troubadour Publishing, 2011. Print.

Kuntzel, Matthias. *Jihad and Jew-hatred: Islamism, Nazism and the Roots of 9/11*. Trans. Colin Meade. New York: Telos Press Publishing, 2007. Print.

Lewis, Bernard. *Semites and Anti-Semites: An Inquiry into Conflict and Prejudice*. New York: W. W. Norton & Co., 1999. Print.

Wistrich, Robert S. *A Lethal Obsession: Anti-Semitism from Antiquity to the Global Jihad*. New York: Random House, 2010. Print.

5 Deterritorialized Rhetoric; or, What Happens when We Forget We are Exiles[1]

Michael Bernard-Donals

> By the Rivers of Babylon,
> there we sat,
> sat and wept
> as we thought of Zion.
> . . .
> How can we sing a song to the Lord
> on alien soil?
> If I forget you, Jerusalem,
> let my right hand wither
> let my tongue stick to my palate . . . (Psalm 137)

The last ten years have seen a reinvigoration of the discussions surrounding questions of rhetoric's public dimension. Much of this work takes as its point of departure the classical Greco-Roman tradition of rhetoric, beginning with Plato's Socrates and running through Aristotle and the civic rhetoric of republican Rome, in which rhetoric's deliberative dimension was seen not just as an instrument for conceiving national policy and debating matters of community and the state, but was integral to the construction of a civic self. This civic subject participates *with others* in building and maintaining a common space—a polis—and in so doing constantly renegotiates the boundaries of "the good" along with the boundaries of the self and the space in which she resides. Contemporary models of deliberation—that share a notion of the common good, a civic space, and the primacy of reason and good sense—tend to founder when confronted by interlocutors who do not share our sense of the good, a common vocabulary, or even what we think of as reasonability. In such cases, deliberation deteriorates into the taking of positions, the dissolution of the public sphere into enclaves, and pitched battles. Much of the problem involves our understanding of, and our models for, the public sphere, and of deliberation within those models (much of the foregoing is clearly laid out in Roberts-Miller's *Deliberate Conflict*).

These problems are, at least in part, due to the fact that even the most inclusive deliberative models for argument do not go far enough to examine the position of the radically "exogamous" individual, the subject that, for whatever reason, is excluded from the social or civic space and hence the argument, and who in fact is not seen as *present* at all. What do we make of the altogether other, the one who resides "on alien soil," and who for that reason is outside the parameters of the nation or polis, the one to which all other interlocutors' backs are turned? The position of the excluded other, it seems to me, is the position that has characterized Jews since antiquity: exiled from the nation and dispersed to other nations, Jewish participation in civic life has been defined, even in modernity, by its marginalization and precariousness. The Jew, in other words, provides a salient example of the position of the exile whose participation in the discursive life of the political or community body is sorely vexed.

In this essay I want to propose what could be called an exilic rhetorical position, one founded on the understanding that one is never quite at home in one's place of residence, that one's position when one speaks is always fraught and never secure (that one is always, to some measure, by the rivers of Babylon). To foreground the problem of exile and the marginal, voiceless other, and how an exilic rhetorical stance might better account for the stranger, I want to examine an instance of deliberative rhetoric whose very subject was the nature of civic space. That case—a proposal that came before the Madison, Wisconsin, common council to enter into a sister-city relationship with Rafah, in Palestine—brings into stark relief the question of exile and participation, inclusion and banishment, that underwrites any discussion of argument and deliberation, particularly since 1948, and particularly when the subject is Israel/Palestine.

Publicity and the Other

As I've argued elsewhere,[2] there are two principal emphases in work that attempts to recuperate a strong notion of publicity, and to study how individuals use discourse to situate themselves into social orders, negotiate their identities within them, and in so doing work together to forge, to the extent possible, a common good. One turns to the classical tradition, citing the inherent connection between rhetoric and democracy from Aristotle through the Roman republic for our current predicament, while noting that while we live in a decidedly post-rational age, the point of deliberation isn't necessarily—or only—rational consensus but *action*. The other weds the classical tradition, often as it winds itself through Habermas's ideal speech situation in the public sphere, with more contemporary theoretical notions of human agency, countering Habermas's privileging of rationality and the face-to-face negotiation involved in argument with an acknowledgement of error, the extra-rational, and the always-present Other in the discursive situation. Often enough in this public sphere, we come into contact with strangers with whom we share nothing else except that we are thrown together in a common space and so are forced to come to a communicative "being-together" without consensus or even necessarily a common vocabulary.

Alain Badiou, in the first two chapters of his book *Ethics*, identifies the principal difficulties inherent in these rhetorical stances (though Badiou does not use that term). First, an ethics based on the "recognition of the other" or "the ethics of differences" or "multiculturalism" has little force because it's founded on *mimesis*. The other is other only to the extent that we can identify features of an interlocutor—our co-inhabitants in the public sphere—that can be distinguished from those we hold in common. Difference is never altogether different.[3] Alternatively, if the other is found to be so unlike us as to be unable to find a language or feature they hold in common with us, the argument stops dead in its tracks or breaks down into something entirely other than discourse (and more often than not this "something" is violent). Badiou's second difficulty, a corollary to the first, is that if discourse insists upon our respect for difference in our interactions with others, there ought to be some *principle* of difference to which instances of difference refer, something beyond our direct experience to which instances of difference point. If differences are to be perceived as such—if difference is not just some anomalous case to be dismissed or to be interpreted in the language of sameness (as in "she *seems* different, but really she is very much like me in the following ways")—one would have to refer those differences to something beyond what we know and yet, because of the first difficulty noted above, mimesis *depends upon* figure, the establishing of relations between and among known quantities.

So for Badiou—and I agree with him—other-oriented notions of argument and publicity simply cannot account for the interlocutor who is altogether unrelated to us—even as an other—because under such notions there is no idea or utterance or individual whose difference from our own idea or utterance or self is not ultimately subsumed by contiguity or similarity, and thereby brought into relation, finally, with some idea or utterance or sense of self that originates with us. There is always some prior or originary idea or entity—call it God or "the good" or civic organization—in relation to which all parties to an argument, and all ideas advanced in the argument, must be placed. Even the most preposterous or offensive proposal may finally be brought into relation to a more reasonable one because it bears a relation, after all, to a position or proposal I myself might make, and even the most preposterous or offensive proposal or utterance bears a relation to a reality to which both propositions ultimately correspond.

Israel, Palestine, and Community

But often enough this is not what really happens. When presented with a proposition—or an interlocutor—that is altogether other, maybe even horrifyingly so, to one's understanding, that other often enough seems to defy reasonableness and, in the person of the interlocutor, presents a threat to one's identity and even the ground on which one stands to argue. In such a case, identity and the location of utterance themselves are called into question. What I want to do here is describe such a case in order to suggest just how rapidly the civic body can become shattered, particularly when questions of belonging, participation, and exogamy—the attempt to integrate the altogether other—are in play. After presenting this case, I'll lay out why what might be called an exilic rhetorical stance—one that takes exile, deterritorialization, and otherness as central to that stance—may well be preferable when confronted with a discursive situation marked by the calling into question of principles of common space, mutual respect, and the potential for inclusion. It is such a rhetoric that allows us to meet the problem of exile and the alien head on.

On March 24, 2004, a group called the Madison-Rafah Sister City Project submitted to the Madison, Wisconsin Common Council (the city's legislative body) a proposal to enter into a formal relationship with the city of Rafah in the occupied Palestinian territory of Gaza, a relationship meant to foster mutual understanding between the two communities. Members of the Sister City Project's Advisory Committee included a number of prominent community members, one of the city's rabbis, as well as nationally prominent individuals like Noam Chomsky and the parents of Rachel Corrie.[4] They spent the better part of 2003 making the proposal, forging connections with individuals in Rafah, including its mayor, and with members of the Palestinian community in the United States and abroad, some of whom provided letters of support for the proposal. The proposal was presented at a meeting of the Common Council on March 30, 2004, which, along with its committees, functions as a representative democratic deliberative body, in which its members represent aldermanic districts in the city whose residents vote every four years for their alder. By design (and in accordance with the city's and the State of Wisconsin's open meetings law), members of the community attend to speak in favor of or against a pending proposal or piece of legislation, and a few individuals—mostly sponsors of the resolution—did just that in March.

Between March 30 and May 18, the Common Council's Organizational Committee (the body's executive committee) took up the proposal, and the discussions in the Committee became widely known and very much a part of the discussion particularly in the city's Jewish, activist, and civic communities. Among the most vocal opponents of the proposal was the director of the city's Jewish Community Council, who wrote in a letter, urging the Mayor to reject the proposal, that it was "nothing more than a thinly veiled mechanism to bash the State of Israel. That it is also about anti-Semitism only makes it more offensive" ("Letter"). At the Organizational Committee meeting, over fifty citizens had signed up to either support or object to the proposal, and of that number, ten spoke in support and three spoke in opposition to it. For those who spoke against the proposal at the May meeting, its "anti-Israel" and "anti-semitic" nature were particularly problematic. Several speakers cited the alleged ties between Al Mezan, an NGO that promotes human rights in Gaza and one of the proponents of the relationship with Madison, and statements Al Mezan made about the Holocaust at the Durban Conference Against Racism in 2001, and others cited the accusation that the mayor of Rafah was a member of Hamas. For members of the Organizational Committee, on the other hand, the main question was whether the debate being held at its meeting—and a proposal to hold community forums as well as talks between the Common Council, the Jewish Community Council, and the Sister City Project—would help create a consensus on the proposal (see "Minutes 5/18/2004"). It became clear, even at this early stage of the discussion, that its reasonableness was being put into question by issues having to do with identity and membership in a community of one sort (the civic forum of Madison, Wisconsin) or another (one's filiation with Judaism, Zionism, or Palestinian sovereignty).

The discussions at that May meeting, along with two subsequent meetings of the Organizational Council in June and July and a Common Council Meeting in late July at which the proposal fell two votes short of approval, were anything but deliberative. Instead, those present spoke mostly past one another. While some involved in the debate, including members of the Common Council and those in support of the resolution, painted the discussion as civil and productive, far more saw the discussion as divisive or, worse, as offensive (see Davidoff). Complicating matters was an email sent by one of the members of the Sister Cities Project to the *NGO Monitor*, an organization whose self-stated aim is to ensure "neutrality" among non-governmental organizations; the email took issue with the *NGO Monitor*'s reports on the Madison Sister City proposal. That email—which was posted on the *NGO Monitor*'s website on July 5, 2004—accused the local Jewish Community Council's Executive Committee of being "deeply racist." Rather than discuss whether a sister city relationship between Rafah and Madison would be productive for either city's citizens, those involved in the subsequent Organizational Committee meeting described instead the Israeli policy of violence against Palestine, Hamas-sponsored terrorism in Palestine and Israel, Jewish self-hatred, Islamo-fascism, and the Israeli army's incursion into Gaza in early 2004. The sister city proposal was deferred twice, meetings were loud and boisterous, and the proposal was ultimately defeated in late July by a narrow margin.

What happened in Madison in the summer of 2004 was an extreme but otherwise typical case of the dissolution of the public sphere over questions of identity, difference, and membership in a community, in large measure because the instrument used to settle those questions—so-called rational debate—leaves no room for what does not meet the criteria for membership in a polis. In this case, what was palpably *absent* in the arguments over who qualifies for membership in a community—Jewish, Palestinian, Israeli, the city of Madison—was the position of the exile, a position into which all parties to the debate, ironically, fell to a significant extent.

Let me explain. The most implacable of the disagreements in the Madison-Rafah sister city debacle had to do with questions of selfhood and belonging. What few if any of the parties to the argument recognized was that their claims for themselves as autonomous and locatable—that is to say, for a nameable position from which to speak, and for a reasonable and stable language with which to make that position clear—were undermined by the visible but *unnamed* and *unnameable* other that haunted the debate from the beginning: the deterritorialized exile. The questions raised most visibly and rancorously by those who participated in the argument—of anti-semitism and racism—can be seen as signs for positions of identification by those who utter the terms. Specifically, the term "anti-semite" is used by those, often Jews but not always, who wished to cordon off the Jewish subject position, insinuating that—in the case of the Rafah sister city proposal—to partner with the city in Gaza is to pose a threat to "the Jew." What is interesting to note, though, is the *territorialization* of the relation of the terms "anti-Semitism" and "Jew" in this case. The danger posed by terrorism (invoked because of the mayor of Rafah's supposed connection to Hamas) and by anti-Semitism (invoked because of Al Mezan's statements about the Holocaust and Israel at the Durban conference) are threats to, in the first case, the United States (and, presumably, Madison and Madison's Jews) and, in the second case, to the nation of Israel. The same thing is true of the charge of racism, which is also meant to cordon off the position of the victim, in this case the Palestinian victim of Israeli (and Jewish) violence. Again, these invocations are territorialized: the immediate charge of racism, made by a member of the Sister City Project, was aimed at the *city's* (Madison's) Jewish Community Council, and a number of those who spoke in favor of the sister city proposal at the various Common Council meetings used the term "racism?" (or invoked it) in describing Palestinian nationhood in the West Bank and particularly in Gaza.

But what's equally interesting about this territorialization of the discourse is its *effect:* it effaces the *deterritorialized*, that is to say exilic, position of *both* the Jewish victim of anti-Semitism *and* the Palestinian victim of racism, positions held by those very individuals speaking at the meetings, and—perhaps most importantly—by those whose names were being invoked by citizens of Madison, Wisconsin, Jews and non-Jews alike, whose ability to speak is granted by statute and by tradition—the forum of the Common Council and its committees, and the homegrown Madison tradition of arguing any proposal or piece of legislation to death. What was forgotten—like Jerusalem as evoked in the 137th Psalm that forms the epigram for this essay—is that those citizens of Madison who were party to the debate, and those who are spoken for in the debate—Israelis and Palestinians, Jews and Muslims—are also not quite at home even in the comfortable confines of Madison, as the graffiti painted on the doors of its synagogues and on the sidewalks in front of Arab students' apartments attest.

By the Rivers of Babylon

I would argue that an exilic—and, as such, a Jewish—rhetorical stance keeps the memory—and the voice—of the exile in mind. Judaism itself is founded on a tension between the homeborn and the exile, who is chosen, apart, and—though a member of a community—is never quite at home. Though a Jewish rhetorical stance is aware of community, belonging, and identity, those terms are always called into question. Adam Zachary Newton sees the foundation of Judaism's exilic stance in Biblical prooftexts and in Jewish history—the expulsion from the Garden, the destructions of the Temple—one of which is the Deuteronomic injunction, "Remember: for once you were slaves in Egypt." For Newton—as for Emmanuel Levinas, the Jewish philosopher whose work Newton sees as important in working out an exilic ethics—a Jewish subject is one that is both comfortably at home at the point of utterance while also dislocated, and unmoored by that very utterance. Levinas presciently writes about the dangers inherent in rhetorics of identification—notions of self and other that ultimately subsume difference to a relation of contiguity or of similarity—as a Jew highly skeptical of systematic thinking and the apotheosis of rationality because he experienced first-hand its historical correlative in the policies of National Socialist Germany.

Levinas writes in *Totality and Infinity* of the obligation of the subject to be hospitable, to welcome. Playing with the double meaning (in French) of the word *hôte* as both "host" and "guest," he writes of the divine law "that would make of the inhabitant a guest [*hôte*] received in his own home, that would make of the owner a tenant, of the welcoming host [*hôte*] a welcomed guest [*hôte*]" (42). When the individual engages the other, she resides in a kind of no-man's land, in which she is both at home and in exile, neither completely apart from, nor completely a part of, the community or the location from which she speaks. The subject, acting as both host and guest—remembering that while he is both a member of a community, or a nation, or is himself a subject who can be named, he was once, and is now also, a stranger to others—he is "a subject put into question [. . . , an] emigrant, exile, stranger, a guest from the very beginning" (Derrida, *Adieu* 56). As *hôte*, both host and guest, there is no place that the subject can comfortably call home, or domicile, or community, or nation. Though she may speak from a location that is home, domicile, or nation, her relation to that place is, like her relation with the other, "thrown out of phase with itself": it isn't "natural," a point of origin from which everything else may be easily understood. In practical terms—and in terms of the Madison-Rafah sister city debacle—it means that anyone who speaks by "taking a position" must bear in mind that she's also taking *another's* position, literally displacing another person by speaking to, and for, that other. Instead of seeing the "Common Council" as a place where the rationality of discourse among free, autonomous individuals may take place, an exilic rhetorical stance would entail understanding that one's place in that community—and any utterance spoken from that location—is temporary at best and carries with it certain risks. One of those risks is that one's insistence on speaking from a discursive location—*as* a Jew, *as* a Madisonian, *as* a member of the Common Council or the Sister City Project—does violence to others. Speaking, then, as a member of the Madison community, or as a Jew, or as one in sympathy with Palestine, not only declares one's membership or affiliation, but it also speaks to one's *dislocation* from the others involved in the conversation. Speaking *as* stands in the way of speaking *to* because the name (identity) forecloses engagement, which is only possible when one is vulnerable, as *hôte*. Speaking *to* recognizes one's vulnerability and the other's vulnerability as well.

This deterritorialized ethical position is related closely to the idea of "chosenness" that has vexed both Israel and Judaism, a notion that is closely related to Levinas's notion of engagement. Levinas writes that the idea of being chosen doesn't involve exceptional rights, but instead involves exceptional duties: "the rabbinic principle by which the just of every nation participate in the future world expresses not only an eschatological view. It affirms the possibility of that ultimate intimacy, beyond the dogma affirmed by the one or the other, an intimacy without reserve" (*Difficult Freedom* 176). The intimacy referred to here is the intimacy of approach, of utterance, of the individual encounter or engagement with the other. If Israel is indeed "chosen," it is because its citizen is "alone in being able to answer the call, [she is] irreplaceable in [her] assumption of responsibility. Being chosen involves a surplus of obligations for which the 'I' of moral consciousness utters" (*Difficult Freedom* 177). Chosenness is related to the notion of sanctity or sanctification—in Hebrew, *kadosh*—which also means apartness. To be chosen is to be radically separate and individual in one's relations to the other: you have to engage with individual others as if your life depended upon it, and you have to do so in the midst of your neighbors and those who are strangers to you as if your life depended upon it.

A model for how to live as both a resident of a community and at the same time as an exile is, in Levinas's estimation, modern Israel. Because Israel was founded essentially by strangers—by those who had arrived from Europe in the generations before the UN Partition Plan and by those who had arrived immediately after the 1947–8 war—and by fellow-Jews, it is Judaism, rather than national community, that establishes the nation. Though it was, in the eyes of its founders, an "ideal community" of sorts, it is no utopia: though its residents may conceive of what he calls a "supernatural order," they see themselves as both hosts and guests, at home and exiled at one and the same time. What Levinas says of the self-other relation in *Otherwise than Being* might also be said of the residents of Israel: that they live in time "out of phase with itself" (*Otherwise than Being* 9). Each of Israel's citizens is both a resident and a usurper, and Israel is a home to aliens and an instigator of exile: "what is signified by the advent of conscience, and even the first spark of spirit, if not the discovery of corpses beside me and my horror of existing by assassination" (*Difficult Freedom* 100)? To act ethically and politically at once is to understand one's actions as both radically individual and, through justice, universal. The citizen "uproot[s himself] from his recent past . . . and seeks his authenticity" (*Difficult Freedom* 164), not by ignoring anti-semitism, race hatred, the language of division, or—for that matter—community norms, traditions, and history. It means instead that the citizen has to act ethically *in the face of* all this—uprooting himself from the context in which he finds himself mired—in order to affect his neighbor, to act justly in his encounters with his fellow citizens one by one. It is only *in* such particularism—such *singularity*, a term I'll return to—that the citizen might also become a member of a broader community.

What all of this suggests is a rhetorical stance that acknowledges the individual's vulnerability, that she is above all else always in the presence of others, and that this presence is as troubling as it is constitutive. In Levinas's terms, the subject is non-coincident with herself as well as non-coincident with the location of her utterance. There is no place that she can comfortably call home, domicile, community, or nation. Though she may speak from a location that is home, domicile, community, or nation, her relation to that place, like her relation with the other, is "thrown out of phase with itself" (*Otherwise than Being* 115). What is especially ironic in the debate over Rafah—a place that is decidedly the place of the exile, in both Israeli and Palestinian terms—is that the very terms of the debate very clearly troubled nearly all of those involved, almost none of whom recognized that it was their double condition, as residents of a domicile they could comfortably call their own and as uncomfortable strangers (as Jews, or as having filial or political relations to Palestine), that caused this displacement. The discourse, in other words, called those involved into question. Such a rhetorical stance is exilic where—in the words of Jean-Luc Nancy—"to exist is a matter of going into exile" (78) because the self is defined by its engagement with others who are never fully known, never (though plural) form a stable "we," and are always close by and proximate.

Following Levinas and Newton, a Jewish and an exilic rhetorical stance—an engagement with others that deterritorializes those involved in the discourse, an engagement that takes place in a kind of no-man's land—involves what Jean-Luc Nancy calls a *singular plurality*, a proximity among individuals that isn't founded on the "us" but the "between" in the phrase *between us*. That is, there will always be people, or a people, in which social engagement takes place, but rather than see that social entity as an end or even a foundation for engagement, Nancy asks "what if each *people* (this would be the revolutionary word), each *singular intersection* [in which engagement takes place] . . . , substituted a wholly other logic for the logic of the sovereign (and always sacrificial) model, not the invention of the multiplication of models—from which wars would immediately follow—but a logic where singularity was absolute and without example at the same time?" (141). A person is always with others—always involved with others, whether socially or simply thrown together—but not "in some general sort of way, but each time according to determined modes that are themselves multiple and simultaneous (people, culture, language, lineage, network, group, couple, band and so on)" (65). Nancy goes on, "this is not to say that the 'group,' whatever it is, is of a higher order; it is a stage that serves as a place of identification. More generally, the question of the 'with' can never be expressed in terms of identity" (66).

The language called for in such an exilic rhetorical stance is far different from the discourse of argument or community or from the reasonable (or even unreasonable) staking of a position; a counter-public discourse would look much more like poetry (or, in Nancy's terms, "literature") than it would look like a rhetorical language. In Nancy's terms, it is "a language stretched out [*en tension*] toward birth and death, exactly because it is, and insofar *as* it is, striving towards address, understanding [*entente*], and conversation" (90). Working between the language of identification and the language of the *between* in the phrase "between us," such a writing places into language the inescapable reality that we can't represent ourselves as autonomous subjects, nor can we represent a point of origin—a self, a community, or a prospective position in discourse or politics or argument—but only *finitude,* "the infinite singularity of meaning" (15) that is, nonetheless, uttered in the presence of others.

To return to where I began, the singer of Psalm 137 sings a song of lament:[5] exiled from his homeland, and living among strangers, he weeps as he thinks of Jerusalem and refuses to sing of home, preferring to hang the lyre from the poplar tree than to "sing us one of the songs of Zion." For "how," he asks, "can we sing a song of the Lord on alien soil?" The 137th Psalm ends with two imprecations, one that the psalmist aims at himself and one that he aims at God. To God, the psalmist begs the recalling of the Edomites' desire to destroy Jerusalem, and in anger he calls for a blessing on anyone who would destroy the Edomites in turn. He also curses himself with the inability to speak or write ("let my right hand wither, let my tongue stick to my palate") should he forget his homeland. It is the tension between these two imprecations—the one at the psalm's conclusion, made in anger, and the one at its center, made in sorrow—that points to the predicament of the Jew in exile, and the ways in which any deterritorialized subject, Jew or non-Jew, finding himself by the rivers of Babylon, can write in a way that marks that exilic and vexed position without succumbing to the language of identity, of the "we" that subsumes all others. That language—of identity, of "we Jews," "we here in Madison," "we of the right-thinking majority"—makes the stranger and the homeborn as one or, perhaps worse, divides the stranger and the homeborn, the Jew and the non-Jew, and places an impassable chasm between them. But the psalmist, outside of his homeland and outside (and quite literally beside) himself in both anger and sorrow, portrays himself as unable to remember Zion, unable to sing, and frozen in his anger against the destroyers of Jerusalem. Yet, the psalm itself stands as a testament to—and as a prayer for—the exile, whose anger and sorrow leads neither to violence nor to argument, but to the voicing of placelessness itself. In that song, the psalmist records the silence that comes of forgetting and the refusal to sing for the stranger, but he also opens up a space—not a civic space of community, a *locus communis* in which he can reside, but the space of finitude, of between-ness—from which something altogether different, unrecognized, and potentially powerful might emerge. It ultimately dashes the silence and impresses upon the reader the position of the exile. It is a song—and a way of speaking—that both indicates the unsettled position of the speaker and deeply unsettles the hearer of the song as well. In being so unsettled, the participants in the conversation—the speaker and the listener of the psalm, the individuals wishing to understand the relation between Israel and Palestine, and (more accurately) those who *live in* and *live without* Israel and Palestine—have no recourse but to start again, without staking a position but by recalling their own exilic position, from a position of vulnerability and with one another

Notes

1. This essay was originally published in *College English* (72.6) as "'By the Rivers of Babylon': Deterritorialization and the Jewish Rhetorical Stance." Copyright 2010 by the National Council of Teachers of English. I am grateful to NCTE and *CCC* for permission to reprint.

2. See Bernard-Donals, "Against Publics (Exilic Writing)." I rehearse the argument in that essay briefly in the following two pages.

3. Diane Davis makes a similar point in her essay, "Identification: Burke and Freud on Who We Are": in order to make sense of identification as the principal aim of rhetoric, Burke had to establish, first, that humans were ineradicably distinct from one another; and yet the problem with this scenario—and what Burke erases from Freud's theory of identification, with which Burke was well familiar—is that such a difference belies a structural *sameness* on which it is in turn founded (which, for Freud, was a sameness based in a kind of horror at one's finitude, mortality, and displacement from oneself, something that, as we'll see, is not unrelated to exile).

4. Chomsky has long taken sometimes-controversial positions on issues of national and international visibility, including on the Israel-Palestine question. Corrie was a member of the International Solidarity Movement, an organization that aimed at non-violent protest of the Israeli military's actions in Palestinian territory, who was killed during a protest in 2003.

5. The psalm reads in full:
By the rivers of Babylon,
>   there we sat,
>   sat and wept,
>   as we thought of Zion.
There on the poplars
>   we hung up our lyres,
>   for our captors asked us there for songs,
>   our tormentors, for amusement,
>   "Sing us one of the songs of Zion."
How can we sing a song of the Lord
>   on alien soil?
If I forget you, O Jerusalem,
>   let my right hand wither;
>   let my tongue stick to my palate
>   if I case to think of you,
>   if I do not keep Jerusalem in memory
>   even at my happiest hour.
Remember, O Lord, against the Edomites
>   the day of Jerusalem's fall;
>   how they cried, "Strip her, strip her
>   to her very foundations!"
Fair Babylon, you predator,
>   a blessing on him who repays you in kind
>   what you have inflicted on us;
>   a blessing on him who seizes your babies
>   and dashes them against the rocks!

Works Cited

Badiou, Alain. *Ethics: An Essay on the Understanding of Evil.* Trans. Peter Hallward. London: Verso, 2001. Print.

Bernard-Donals, Michael. "Against Publics (Exilic Writing)." *JAC* 28.1/2 (2008): 2954.

Davidoff, Judith. "Rafah Debate Anguished, Bruising." *Capital Times.* Madison. com. 7 July 2004. 1C. Web. 28 April 2015.

Davis, Diane. "Identification: Burke and Freud on Who We Are." *Rhetoric Society Quarterly* 38.2 (Spring 2008): 123–47. Print.

Derrida, Jacques. *Adieu: to Emmanuel Levinas.* Trans. Pascale-Anne Brault and Michael Naas. Stanford: Stanford UP, 1999. Print.

Fontana, Benedetto, Cary J. Nederman and Gary Remer, eds. *Talking Democracy:Historical Perspectives on Rhetoric and Democracy.* University Park: Pennsylvania State UP, 2004. Print.

Levinas, Emmanuel. *Otherwise than Being; or Beyond Essence.* Trans. Alphonso Lingis. Pittsburgh, PA: Duquesne U P, 1981/1998. Print.

—. *Totality and Infinity.* Trans. Alphonso Lingis. Pittsburgh, PA: Duquesne UP, 1969. Print.

—. *Difficult Freedom: Essays on Judaism.* Trans. Sean Hand. Baltimore: Johns Hopkins UP, 1990. Print.

"Minutes 5/18/2004." *Amended Minutes of the Common Council Organizational Committee, May 18, 2004.* Web. 1 May 2015.

"Letter." April 22, 2004 Web. 1 May 2015.

Nancy, Jean-Luc. *Being Singular Plural.* Trans. Robert D. Richardson and Anne E. O'Byrne. Stanford: Stanford UP, 2000. Print.

Newton, Adam Z. *The Fence and the Neighbor: Emmanuel Levinas, Yeshayahu Leibowitz, and Israel Among the Nations.* Albany, NY: State U of New York P, 2001. Print.

"Psalm 137." *JPS Hebrew-English Tanakh: The Original Hebrew Text and the New JPS Translation.* Second Edition. David E. Sulomm, ed. Philadelphia: Jewish Publication Society, 1999. Print.

Roberts-Miller, Patricia. *Deliberate Conflict: Argument, Political Theory, and Composition Classes.* Carbondale: Southern Illinois UP, 2004. Print.

6 Feeling the Narrative/s of the Other's Oppression: Toward a Liberatory Mutuality in the Middle East

Michael Kleine

"An enemy is one whose story we have not heard."

—Ms. Gene Knudsen Hoffman[1]

In framing the Palestinian/Israeli conflict, many analysts have noticed that othering narratives need to be transformed if a lasting peace is to be achieved. Noticing narrative rhetoric might help those of a new-rhetorical bent (I include myself in this category) escape from the illusion that argumentative, but mediating writing, presented by a single mediating writer in an arrangement strategy that Young, Becker, and Pike would term "Rogerian" (because it promotes the rhetorical values of Carl Roger's client-centered therapy) might by itself staunch the ongoing blood-letting in the Middle East. My own interest in narrative analysis grows from the work of Walter Fisher, whose work is preeminent among efforts by rhetoricians to consider the relationship of narrative to argument. However, even though Fisher's work is intertextual with the work of Kenneth Burke and evinces new rhetorical impulses, it does not help us understand the kind of deliberate listening and narration that intends to mediate when conflicting narratives collide. The narrative paradigm, as advanced in Fisher's *Human Communication as Narration: Toward a Philosophy of Reason, Value, and Action*, deals with issues that include narrative fidelity, coherence, and probability, through which "good reasons" for maintaining values and acting in the future are supplied; however, extreme Palestinian and Israeli narratives both can be judged as internally consistent stories, accepted as fully valid in their respective discourse communities.

If we examine the arguments made by extremists, perhaps using the perspective offered by Stephen Toulmin, who himself might be considered a new rhetorician, we are forced to conclude that extreme arguments on both sides are "logical." At the risk of over-simplifying the deliberative arguments lurking in extreme narratives, we might lay them out in the following way:

Palestinian Argument

Warrant: We must act decisively to expel those who work to displace us or who keep us from enjoying the statehood that is rightfully ours.

Data: After the Balfour Declaration, Israelis have in fact displaced us, ghettoized us, and politically and economically undermined us.

Claim: We must continue to fight against Israeli statehood and the oppression that has been the result of that statehood.

Israeli Argument

Warrant: We must fight to protect the statehood and security that has been historically and religiously ordained for us and which we now enjoy.

Data: Palestinian extremists and terrorists have continued to threaten our statehood and security.

Claim: We must fight (through military means if necessary) efforts of Palestinian extremists to undermine our statehood and our security.

Both sides, of course, use the backing of competing notions of what would count as a just outcome, and also competing religious texts. If we grant that both sides are being "logical," then we must ask, what good it does, in terms of a peace solution, to simply analyze the arguments and credit them as being "logical." Fisher takes an analytical step that helps us better understand how on-the-ground stories (there are multiple examples on the Internet) work to couple pathetic appeals with logical appeals, but even the narrative paradigm provides not an active step toward reconciling competing narratives, but, again, a way of simply observing the differences.

Listening To and Reading the Narratives of the Other

At this point in time, I see my position in relationship to the Palestinian/Israeli conflict as relatively detached and neutral, while believing, with Martin Luther King, Jr., that "injustice anywhere is a threat to justice everywhere." Sometimes I suffer from the delusion that the conflict only indirectly affects my life, but as a teacher of rhetoric and writing, I am passionately invested in rhetorics that confront injustice and that seek to promote reconciliation of human beings whose lives are undermined by senseless (and ongoing) ethnic and political strife. Also, I have long been deeply influenced by the writing of the Jewish philosopher Martin Buber, particularly *I and Thou*, which offers a powerful remedy for human objectifying discourses. When I started to write this essay, I considered attempting to apply Vladimer Propp's narratological framework (as advanced in *Morphology of the Folktale*) to the contending narratives, but I quickly realized that such a structuralist application would do little good in terms of understanding the perpetuation of othering narratives. Propp proposes that narratives be considered in terms of underlying character roles ("hero" and "villain" for instance) and analyzed in light of their functions (or "*énoncés*"). In fact, Palestinian and Israeli narratives share deep functional and structural proclivities, but they merely reverse the hero/villain binary, largely because they remain confined to completely divided discourse communities. The character roles, then, are not occupied by living human beings but by underlying and dehumanizing narrative types. Thus, the problem that interests me now is how narratives of the other might cross over the deep narrative divide that now exists, in part, because of the narratives themselves. Paulo Freire, in *Pedagogy of the Oppressed*, discusses the pathology of "narration sickness," a monological pathology that exists because of the absence of dialog and turn-taking in oppressive power configurations. What is most needed now, in my opinion, is not the perpetuation of "narration sickness," but a turn toward listening, with mutual regard and respect, to the narratives of the other as they cross the narrative divide. In classical terms, I will be urging here that both sides need to recapitulate the Greek value of *aidos*, or the kind of respect and compassion that ensures not only talking and writing but also listening and reading.

Krista Ratcliffe—in her invaluable essay "Rhetorical Listening: A Trope for Interpretive Invention and a 'Code of Cross-Cultural Conduct'"—advances the claim that listening (an aspect of rhetoric that is often neglected by rhetoricians) can in fact be understood as a means of invention. She writes:

> Defining *rhetorical* listening as a trope of interpretive invention not only emphasizes the discursive nature of rhetorical listening but also plays with the etymology of the term *trope* as a "turning." For rhetorical listening turns hearing (a reception process) into invention (a productive process), thus complicating the reception/production opposition and inviting rhetorical listening into the time-honored tradition of rhetorical invention. (220)

Although Ratcliffe does not discuss Bakhtin's notions of "addressivity" and "dialogism," her work serves to recuperate Bakhtin's views of discourse. Thus, an utterance (or a story) always/already exists in relation to prior and future utterances. Listening, then, can be understood as a factor that is core to the evolution of discourse. Ratcliffe's proposal of a "code of cross-cultural conduct" provides for us a sense of why listening becomes a kind of ethical imperative in any sort of cross-cultural storytelling and communication, especially if such storytelling and communication is undergirded by a condition of *aidos*. The many narratives I have read on the Internet are *written*, and therefore seem detached from the kind of oral "presence" that is valued by Walter Ong in *Orality and Literacy*. But although Ratcliffe's article privileges listening in a journal that is read primarily by theorists and teachers of writing (*College Composition and Communication*), she adds an important caveat: "Rhetorical listening turns the realm of hearing into a larger space, one encompassing all discursive forms, not just oral ones."

I applaud Ratcliffe's "code," believing that such a code can serve as an antidote to the rampant narration sickness that, when confined to self-interested discourses, serves to perpetuate an unnecessary conflict in the Middle East. However, an important question remains: Just how, in terms of delivery and reception, might rhetorical listening be enacted by two parties whose discourses remain so deeply separated?

An interesting answer to this question has been invented by two professors: one is Palestinian (Dr. Sami Adwan, at Bethlehem University) and the other is Israeli (Dr. Dan Bar-on, at Ben Gurion University). In a briefing entitled "Developing a Dual Israeli-Palestinian Historical Narrative" (sponsored by the Task Force on Palestine and held by the Carnegie Endowment for International Peace in Washington, D.C.), the two professors engaged in a dialog having to do with an educational peace initiative the two of them devised with the help of Palestinian and Israeli historians and teachers. At the heart of the initiative is a booklet that they assembled together, *Dual History Narrative*, that has now been translated into multiple languages, including English, Arabic, and Hebrew. The booklet presents two contrasting (and strong) historical narratives, which are juxtaposed in columns but separated by white space. The booklet has been used in progressive Palestinian and Israeli schools and in other schools across the world. Students are asked to read carefully the competing historical narratives and then write in the white space either a kind of mediating historical narrative or, usually, write their own deliberative proposals for a peace solution to the conflict. I am certain that a kind of residue of the home narrative remains, depending on whether a student is Palestinian or Israeli, but follow-up research suggests that students who have engaged in the reading/writing project end up supporting a peace solution rather than one that is either militaristic or terroristic and therefore inevitably violent. The professors reported that a French student, after participating in the booklet-driven activity, asked why French history was not presented in the same way, with one column presenting a French colonial narrative and the other, say, an Algerian narrative having to do with the oppressive effects of colonization.

As an educator, I am deeply attracted to the cooperative work of Adwan and Bar-on, believing that the kind of narrative reception and transformation they have enacted might in fact be a starting point for the rhetorical listening that Ratcliffe privileges and the cross-cultural code she urges as a moral imperative. Could education itself work to ameliorate narration sickness? Might projects disseminating something like the *Dual History Narrative* serve to jump-start a peace process that is long overdue? I am not so naïve as to believe that educative peace projects might lead to immediate reconciliation (through healing, "mourning," and respectful attention to the stories of the other as Adwan suggests), and I know that education itself is a very slow process, but educational transformation might well be requisite if any kind of peace process is to unfold over time.

The Problem of Narrative Residue

Among the many extreme narratives presented in writing on the Internet, there are a few that attempt to mediate—and even to listen to the other's narratives. An extremely interesting (and well-intended) contribution is a short essay by Sylvain Ehrenfeld, an American Jew whose family narrowly escaped the Holocaust, who at one point lived in Israel, and whose writing is advanced under the aegis of the Ethical Culture Society of Bergen, a New Jersey-based group founded on Dr. Felix Adler's motto, "Deed before creed." (See Appendix for the full text of Ehrenfeld's recent contribution.) It is heartening that Ehrenfeld's writing gestures, as he closes, at the Adwan and Bar-on collaboration. He clearly acknowledges the value of their educational initiative, but, like me, acknowledges how difficult it is to enact educational transformation in a short period of time. In his concluding paragraph, he writes, with hope: There have been great difficulties in introducing the booklets into Palestinian and Israeli high schools. However, more and more people in these communities are urging a change in the teaching of history. Understanding the other's narrative is essential for progress, and as well, essential for humanist thinking and ethical action.

Moreover, in his opening paragraphs he underscores the problems that plague extreme narratives: Each side in the Israeli-Palestinian conflict has its own narrative telling some of the truth. What is important for understanding of both sides is to know what they leave out. Each side interprets events in terms of their own story, demonizes the other and omits their own contribution to the conflict. Each side is in a state of denial, ignoring the response to their own actions.

He goes on to write short, reasonable (and critical) summaries of the competing narratives, addressing not only their motivating perspectives, but also their omissions: The Palestinian story focuses on victimhood, their suffering and dispossession and their deep sense of injustice at being punished because of Europe's treatment of Jews. They leave out the history of initiating wars, their violence, their faulty leadership and their constant refusal to take opportunities for accommodation.The Israeli story emphasizes their long-time historic attachment to the land, the legitimacy granted by the UN partition plan, the hostility and constant threat of wars coming from their neighbors, and the rejection of their peace offers. Underlying it all is the ever-present trauma of the holocaust. They leave out their own role. They rationalize and downgrade the cruelties of the occupation. They further aggravate the situation by the historic western attitude of both condescending to and mostly disregarding the local Palestinian population.

I deeply agree with Ehrenfeld's claim that both sides must seek a peaceful political solution, rather than a violent military or terroristic solution, and that a peace solution can only be brokered with the help of the world community and with narrative shifts on the ground. I see his work as a new rhetorical gesture, but here I would like to make a deconstructive turn. The heart of Ehrenfeld's writing still can be read as a narrative that grows primarily from the Israeli perspective and from Israeli security interests. While sympathizing with Palestinian "suffering," his historical *heroes* tend to be

Israeli or American (Ben Gurion and President Clinton, for instance) and the *villains* tend to be Palestinian resistance groups, such as Hamas—and, especially, the Arab world at large. In the following passage, he presents Ben Gurion as a kind of peace hero:

> David Ben Gurion, former Prime Minister, had left politics and moved to a kibbutz in the Negev. He was invited to speak at a Labor Party meeting and arrived late, in traditional kibbutznik style, in shorts. He astounded everyone by saying that if Israel did not immediately return all the territory it had just captured, with the exception of East Jerusalem, it would be heading for a historic disaster.

And although he acknowledges the charitable impulses of Hamas, he goes on to position Hamas as an unsanctioned and villainous entity:

> The election of Hamas was in part a reproach to the corruption of the Palestinian National Authority and in part because of the political ineptness of the Abbas party who ran too many candidates against a well-organized religious fundamentalist party with only a few candidates. Hamas, in spite of its charitable record, since they are responsible for much of the social services Palestinians get, still did not win a majority in the popular vote. However, both Hamas in the West Bank and Gaza, and Hezbollah in Lebanon, are ideologically and religiously opposed to any kind of agreement on a political solution. They believe that Palestine, as stated in their charter, belongs entirely to Moslems. To relinquish any part of the land is forbidden. (Some Orthodox Jews have a similar belief. God promised this land to the Jews and no one can give it up.)

Writing about the Palestinian refugee crisis and what he sees as global Arab indifference, he blames the Arab world as a whole as one of the major villains in his narrative:

> Did the Arab governments help from a humanitarian point of view? Not particularly. The Palestinians have remained unpopular in large parts of the Arab world. When Egypt was in control of Gaza, from 1949 into 1967, Gaza Arabs were rarely allowed to travel into Egypt. After the first Gulf war in 1991, Kuwait expelled 250,000 Palestinians. Only Jordan allows Palestinians to become citizens. Elsewhere in the Arab world they are not permitted to become citizens. Even in Jordan, war broke out, suppressed by the Jordanian government. The Palestinian-Israeli conflict has been a superbly effective scapegoat and distraction for the Arab masses, who rank very poorly in

the UN's human development index in relation to the rest of the world.

In an especially vexing single-sentence paragraph, Ehrenfeld evokes Abba Eban as a kind of hero/pundit, embedding an incendiary remark by Eban in his own essay: "Abba Eban was once quoted as saying, 'Palestinian leadership never misses an opportunity to miss an opportunity for peace.'" In a glaring narrative omission, Ehrenfeld fails to fully contextualize and criticize Eban's remark as one that is clearly not in keeping with the kind of mediating narrative discourse that his concluding paragraph seems to validate. Thus, Ehrenfeld's essay, in the end, leaves us with a post-modern *aporia*, or ironic blockage. On the one hand, he urges us to listen with empathy to narratives concerning the Palestinian condition; on the other hand, his own heroes tend to be Israeli, and his villains tend to be Palestinian or members of the larger Arab world. It is perhaps predictable that someone with Ehrenfeld's particular identity and experience would write an essay advancing what I want to call here "narrative residue," residue that seems to be marked by conventional Israeli narratives and values. Although I commend the gesture that Ehrenfeld endeavors to make, I wonder whether the gesture would be enhanced by an effort to write collaboratively with a Palestinian moderate? Such co-authoring would help address the monological, sometimes totalizing, narrative discourse that Ehrenfeld falls victim to; it would insist on a dialogical text that just might help construct the conditions for the peace that he seeks. No more heroes, no more villains. Just human beings, talking *and* listening with mutual regard and empathy. Palestinian writers, too, might strive to transcend narration sickness by co-authoring with Israeli moderates. We can look to the work of Adwan and Bar-on (as Ehrenfeld does) for a model of how dialogical synthesis might take us all to a better world.

Listening and Feeling to Find Common Ground

Palestinian and Israeli extremists sometimes overlook the common ground that is present in conflicting historical and personal narratives. Although the fact that their different faith traditions are Abrahamic has sometimes been asserted as a basis for reconciliation, shared religious lineage has not proved to provide an effective basis for the resolution of the conflict. Extremists often claim that there is no common ground and that only militaristic or terroristic tactics can advance their respective interests. I believe that, from a narratological point of view, competing stories told in public and on the ground are not only structurally similar (despite the reversing of hero and villain roles), but that they all share the same theme: they are all stories of *oppression*, suffering, and dehumanization. If that commonality is mutually recognized, then the kind of liberatory approach to oppression valued by Paulo Freire in *Pedagogy of the Oppressed* might provide the basis for both listening to and feeling rhetorics that are advanced in narrative form, which inevitably provide not only "good reasons," but also strong emotional appeals.

I will assume that most of my readers are familiar with Freire's work, so I will not summarize it at length. Instead, I will focus on salient features of his writing and teaching that seem to be particularly relevant to my aim, which is not to privilege one side over the other, but to explore the hope for narrative healing. The "oppressed," Freire reminds us, remain oppressed until they are able to pose problems that beset them, and confront those oppressive practices that lead not only to their own suffering, but to the self-objectifying discourses of their oppressors. Moreover, Freire reminds us that oppressed groups, once liberated, often become oppressors themselves. Thus, I read his most important motive as one of breaking the oppressive cycles that dehumanize all involved. The remedy he suggests, of course, is the kind of inter-subjective dialog that refuses to other, while at the same time working relentlessly to undermine oppressive discourses. True liberation, Freire tells us, can only happen when liberatory discourse is advanced by those who are capable of *loving* their oppressors, who are themselves trapped in discourses of objectification and oppression. Othering monological narratives, then, are a kind of discursive trap that are too often devoid of the rhetorical listening valued by Ratcliffe.

I am proposing, then, that the solution to the Palestinian-Israeli conflict must not only be a political one; it must also be a dialogical and emotional one, both publically and on the ground. It must be one that involves listening to and feeling the other's narratives of oppression. Many may question the efficacy of the kind of Freirean action (and reflection) I am valuing here, but common cause (liberation from oppression) may well be the only shared ground available. There needs to be a turn from the demonization of human beings to the demonization of objectifying narratives, the demonization of monological discourse itself. Such demonization of discourse would devalue narratives that lack fidelity (stories told by Holocaust deniers, for instance) and narratives that maintain rigid hero and villain roles, as Zionist narratives often do. But perhaps the best way I can "argue" for what I am suggesting is to tell a story of my own. I will do this as a way of concluding.

An American's Story

At the beginning of this essay, I asserted that my personal stance was both detached and neutral, but this was not the case when I first started teaching rhetoric and writing nearly thirty years ago. As a young professor, the narratives of oppression with which I was familiar were largely Jewish Holocaust narratives and African-American slavery and Jim Crow narratives. I was then convinced that the Balfour Declaration was both legitimate and necessary. I believed that Israel's wars with its neighbors were just wars, and that the Israeli state needed to be protected by both Israeli citizens and by the United States. I was not familiar with Edward Said's book, *Orientalism*, and I had never read or heard a Palestinian narrative of oppression. But in a first-year writing course, an event occurred that began to move me to the middle ground that I now occupy. Demographically, my class consisted mainly of African American students, working-class white students, and one Palestinian student. After providing my students with a brief reading from *Pedagogy of the Oppressed*, I asked them to write about a personal experience of having been oppressed and to add a reflective close in which they discussed both the personal effects of that oppression and whether they were able to transcend the oppressive experience. My African-American students warmed to the assignment at once, as did several of my working-class white students, who tended to write about low-paying and menial jobs they had worked.

In the class, students were asked to compose rough drafts and then read them aloud to three peers. They were also requested to provide affirmation and criticism of each other's drafts. I sat in on the conference groups, not to dominate but to facilitate the readings and conversations. In the group that included the Palestinian student, two of his three peers were working-class white students and one was an African-American student. My Palestinian student, who had grown up in Jerusalem, seemed nervous and somewhat alienated from other group members. When it was his turn, he began to read his narrative. It was about his brother and his family, including himself. As my Palestinian student explained, his family was composed of moderates who were themselves upset by not only Israeli occupation of what they considered to be their home, but also by the terroristic responses of some of their fellow Palestinians. His narrative then recounted an event in which his brother was "in the wrong place at the wrong time." "For no reason whatsoever," his brother was detained and jailed by Israeli police for an indefinite period of time. While in jail he was beaten, and upon his release some time later, the Israeli police refused to give his family either an explanation for the arrest or an apology. As the narrative moved to reflective closure, my Palestinian student was in tears, recounting in the end the injustice and humiliation his family had experienced. The African-American student in the group was also in tears as he listened to the narrative. At first, following the reading, other group members sat silently, reflecting on what they had heard. One of the white students commented that he had no idea such things could happen in a democracy like Israel and expressed sympathy. The African-American student was eager to read next. His narrative had to do with police profiling and his arrest when a small amount of marijuana was found after an unmotivated search of his car. I let the students do most of the talking, but I found myself both moved and indignant after listening to their narrative drafts. (One of my white students wrote about his low-paying job at Walmart, where he was employed for just under forty hours each week so Walmart would be exempt from providing benefits.)

Although I usually resist ideological self-disclosure, at the end of the conference I told my students, briefly, about what I considered to be two years of oppression in my own life. In 1970, even though I had a daughter and was deeply opposed to the war in Vietnam, I was drafted by the US Army while other young men of my age who did not have children were often exempted. In the Army, I quickly discovered that my fellow draftees were largely either African American or from poor working-class white families, such as my own. After basic training, I was unable to see my daughter for over a year. It is difficult to gauge the feelings of others, but during that writing conference I, personally, was able to *feel* narratives of oppression, and I believe my students felt drawn together as they listened and felt together. I *felt* my stance regarding Israel's history and extreme narratives changing. Still deeply sympathetic to Holocaust narratives, I was at last able to empathize with the Palestinian experience, and I began to seek out and read Palestinian narratives.

My journey away from complete acceptance of post-Balfour Israeli narratives had begun. Along the way I read Said's *Orientalism*, and I found a marvelous guide in Matthew Abraham, once my student, now my teacher in matters having to do with Said and oppression in the Middle East. Abraham's career as a professor has not been an easy one, due to his enormous sympathy for Palestinian suffering. So, I was elated when he was awarded the Rachel Corrie award presented for courage in scholarship by the Conference on College Composition and Communication. I was edified and uplifted as his past and future publications evinced deep intertextuality with Jewish scholars and critics of Zionism (including Noam Chomsky and Norman Finkelstein).[2] It became clear to me that Abraham's work was decidedly *not* anti-Semitic; instead, it was deeply anti-oppression.[3]

I am trying to suggest here that, over time, my efforts to both listen to and read differing narratives and theories of rhetoric have changed my ideological stance and my unreflective pro-Israeli sentiments. In concluding, I find myself asking the following question: What, exactly, counts as "oppression"? Clearly, terroristic acts that result in the killings of innocents are oppressive acts, but now I count acts resulting in human displacement and ghettoization and the assertion of a clear power asymmetry in militaristic conflicts as instances of oppression. In addition, I want to conclude by problematizing narratives in which hero and villain roles work to objectify and demonize the very real human beings who suffer the consequences of cycles of oppression. I want to celebrate the kind of rhetorical listening and cross-cultural code valued by Ratcliffe, along with the educational initiatives invented dialogically by rhetorical heroes like Freire, Abraham, Adwan, and Bar-on. For me, now, the real villain that needs to be confronted and resisted is narration sickness, which leads to the perpetuation of dehumanizing discourses. The real hero, the one that provides hope for future conflict resolution and healing, is authentic dialog. Such dialog inevitably involves empathy among all who have experienced oppression but who are, in the spirit of liberation and love, ready to embrace the kind of rhetorical listening that just might lead to the new-rhetorical Burkean conditions for consubstantiatlity, identification, and even transcendence.

Notes:

1. Hoffman's powerful and pithy maxim appeared on an Internet site, *What Storytellers Say About Story*, based on quotes exhibited at the International Storytelling Center in Jonesborough, Tennessee, in affiliation with the California-based Jewish-Palestinian Living Room Dialogue Group (http:/traubman.lgc.org/story.htm).

2. I have only read one of Chomsky's controversial books on the US role in the Palestinian/Israeli conflict, *Fateful Triangle* (often criticized for its strong condemnation of US and Israeli rejection of Palestinian basic national and human rights), and only one of Finkelstein's equally controversial books, *'This Time We Went Too Far'* (in which Finkelstein condemns the Israeli invasion of the Gaza Strip in 2008/9 as a "descent into barbarism"), but Abraham has read many additional books and articles by both of these Jewish critical intellectuals, and he has written and spoken eloquently to defend their work and to supplement it with his own invaluable scholarship.

3. My understanding of Said's work was advanced, especially, by a special issue of *Cultural Critique* (*Edward Said and After: Toward a New Humanism*), which Matthew Abraham co-edited with Andrew Rubin. Although I have read many of Abraham's publications, my chapter here was especially influenced by Abraham's *JAC* essay, which is reproduced in this volume ("Reluctant Rhetoricians: Refusing to Frame the Israel-Palestine Conflict Through Arab-Jewish Antagonism"), where Abraham models outstanding and fair scholarship that includes a personal reflection, one that clearly establishes his own identity in relationship to his critical assessment of the conflict. I have attempted to follow his model in this chapter.

Appendix

The Israel-Palestinian Conflict: Each Side's Contrasting Narratives

Because this is a very difficult and emotional subject, I think it's helpful for you to know something about my background. It is, at least in part, a basis for my point of view. I grew up in Antwerp, Belgium, and lived there until the age of eleven. I came to New York in 1940 in what I think was the last boat before Germany invaded. The reason I'm alive and here is because of my mother. She was organizing a soup kitchen feeding refugees from Germany, and she heard the stories and convinced my father to leave. I was aware of anti-Semitism from my early years.

As a young academic, I spent three years helping to develop a Department of Industrial Engineering at the Technion in Haifa, Israel on a project supported by the Israeli and America governments.

Each side in the Israeli-Palestinian conflict has its own narrative telling some of the truth. What is important for understanding of both sides is to know what they leave out. Each side interprets events in terms of their own story, demonizes the other and omits their own contribution to the conflict. Each side is in a state of denial, ignoring the response to their own actions.

The Palestinian story focuses on victimhood, their suffering, their dispossession, and their deep sense of injustice at being punished because of Europe's treatment of Jews. They leave out the history of initiating wars, their violence, their faulty leadership and their constant refusal to take opportunities for accommodation.

The Israeli story emphasizes their long-time historic attachment to the land, the legitimacy granted by the UN partition plan, the hostility and constant threat of wars coming from their neighbors, and the rejection of their peace offers. Underlying it all is the ever-present trauma of the holocaust. They leave out their own role. They rationalize and downgrade the cruelties of the occupation. They further aggravate the situation by the historic western attitude of both condescending to and mostly disregarding the local Palestinian population.

In order to have some insight into past, present and possible future, we need some history and background. Then we return to the importance of narratives.

A first question—why choose that particular corner of the Middle East as a haven for the Jewish people? Given the long attachment of Judaism to the Holy Land, and the disastrous history of Jewish suffering in Europe, the Jews needed to have a place to go where they would be accepted as Jews. Where would they have gone after World War Two? Chaim Weizmann, the first President of Israel said, "the world seemed to be divided into parts—those places where Jews could not live and those where they could not enter."

At present Jews are the majority in Israel. 5.5 million citizens of Israel are Jews and 1.3 million are Arabs. Arabs compose twenty percent of the Israeli population. They are second class citizens suffering a great deal of discrimination. Most Israelis would not deny this, while allowing for the fact that there are Arabs in the Knesset. The press in Israel is among the freest in the world, and most certainly in the Middle East. The Israeli judiciary is really independent. Still, the large numbers of Arab citizens may become a problem. They have recently become more vocal.

I am concerned about the current situation in Israel and the situation of the Palestinians. It is at a political and military impasse that is becoming increasingly dangerous. Given the attacks by Hezbollah from Lebanon and the steady influx of a complicated mix of weapons that are becoming ever more sophisticated and far reaching, given the fact that these weapons are used by a guerrilla army that mingles with the general population, Israel's military strength is less effective. Hezbollah is generously supported by Iran. Armed Israeli response only increases the anger of Arab populations all over the world.

In my opinion this anger has long been very convenient for autocratic Arab governments, serving as a distraction from the poverty, frustration, and powerlessness of what commentators call the "Arab street." In my view, it is both to Israel's benefit, and an urgent need, to settle the bitter relationship with the Palestinians. The consequences of not doing so are too serious.

Why hasn't this conflict been settled for the past one hundred years? The history of Israel has always been intertwined with the UN. The partition plan of 1947 was the source for the creation of the State of Israel by the UN. The Arabs revolted against partition, a civil war began, the Arab governments joined the war, and the borders were decided by an armistice in 1949.

The struggle between the State of Israel and the Arabs living within the area has always come before world attention within the context of the UN. We need to know this background to see what is possible and where we go from here. When Ben Gurion came to Palestine in 1906, there were about 700,000 inhabitants, of whom 55,000 were Jews. Only about 550 could be defined as Zionist pioneers. The Jewish population was eight percent. Demographically, Palestine was overwhelmingly Arab. In a British census of 1922, the percentage of Jews rose to something like eleven percent. By 1947 it had risen to thirty-three percent. Jerusalem was always mostly Jewish.

Israel Zangwill, a writer and early Zionist, said, "Israel was a land without people, for a people without land." This was clearly not the case. Not all Zionists saw it this way. Asher Ginzberg, better known by his literary name, Ahad Ha'am (One of the People) was a distinguished cultural Zionist. As early as the 1890s he called attention to the presence of the Arabs on the land. He said the relationship would be difficult and enduring. The problem wouldn't go away.

The Arabs saw an increasing number of Jews coming to what they saw as their land—buying up property and becoming more organized—a serious threat that made them feel increasingly dispossessed. Many Jews preferred to ignore the signs, until riots broke out in 1921 and 1929. They attacked Jewish neighborhoods. The Arabs call it a popular uprising, not riots. Some observers began to view the problem as two groups competing for the same land and population dominance.

Chaim Weizmann, First President of Israel, saw the difficulty of the problem in tragic terms, as a conflict between two rights. Even Ben Gurion, at times, acknowledged that the Arabs had legitimate rights. For example, Ben Gurion to the Jewish agency in 1936: "I want you to see things—with Arab eyes—they see immigration on a large scale—they see lands passing into our hands. They see England identifying with Zionism." So did Jabotinsky, the founder of the Herut movement, who was more outspoken. What he said was, "It's them or us." Then came the British Mandate, the Balfour Declaration, giving the Jews a national home, and expanding Zionism. In the late 1930s the feelings of the Arabs boiled over in a revolt that was ruthlessly suppressed by the British, aided by some Jews and some wealthy Arabs. To placate the Arabs, Britain restricted Jewish immigration. This was, of course, strongly opposed by Jewish groups.

Britain organized the Peel Commission to report on this difficult situation. In 1937 the Commission reported: "there is an irrepressible conflict between two national communities within the narrow bounds of one small country . . . there is no common ground between them." The report recommended partition. During World War Two the Grand Mufti of Jerusalem, who was vehemently anti-Semitic, sided with the Nazis. The Jews formed a brigade and fought with the Allies. This brigade was at first opposed by the British who were suspicious of their postwar goals.

After the war the UN organized a commission to study the situation and came to the same conclusion as the Peel Commission. A partition plan won UN approval. Ben Gurion then declared the State of Israel. The Arabs did not accept the plan, and war broke out. The war took place in two phases, firstly a civil war between Jews and Arabs in Israel. As civil wars are, it was fierce and cruel with many deaths. Then, in the second phase, the neighboring Arabs invaded. The war ended in 1949 with an armistice.

In response to the situation, the UN passed the first of many resolutions—194—relating to the right of return of refugees. This constituted about 700,000 Arabs. For several reasons the Israeli state did not accept this resolution. Firstly, accepting so many people of a hostile population would constitute a fifth column. Secondly they pointed out that an equal number of Jews were expelled from Arab countries. Finally, after the end of World War Two, massive immigration of Jews was taking place. After expulsion from both Europe and North Africa, these immigrants were finding a home in Israel. They had no other place to go.

After much discussion and pressure, the Israeli government offered to accept one hundred thousand Arab refugees. But the whole question became moot for an ironic reason. The Arabs rejected the offer of the return of one hundred thousand refugees, and all rejected Resolution 194, because they viewed it as a recognition of Israel's right to exist. From their point of view there was no sharing and no compromise—Jews had no place in Palestine. The refugees and many of their descendants have remained in camps all these years, leading a dislocated life, surviving on UN assistance, virtually ignored by the Arab governments.

In Israel there is much debate as to why and how these refugees were displaced. Benny Morris, the Israeli historian, has studied these brutal times in great detail. Some fled from warfare, some were forcibly kicked out, some were urged by Arab armies to flee with the promise that they could return after victory. How many were kicked out is in contention by Israeli historians. One observation about the partition plan—you have only to look at a map to see how impossible it was for any kind of coexistence. Each state was not a solid block of population. Instead there were little mixed pockets of population. The map was drawn simply to follow the demography. It made no provision for ethnic or political considerations. Two peoples who had been locked in a bitter fight for decades were thrown together.

Did the Arab governments help from a humanitarian point of view? Not particularly. The Palestinians have remained unpopular in large parts of the Arab world. When Egypt was in control of Gaza, from 1949 into 1967, Gaza Arabs were rarely allowed to travel into Egypt. After the first Gulf war in 1991, Kuwait expelled 250,000 Palestinians. Only Jordan allows Palestinians to become citizens. Elsewhere in the Arab world they are not permitted to become citizens. Even in Jordan, war broke out, only to be suppressed by the Jordanian government. The Palestinian-Israeli conflict has been a superbly effective scapegoat and distraction for the Arab masses, who rank very poorly in the UN's human development index in relation to the rest of the world.

The Six-Day War in 1967 created a fundamental change for Israel. Because Israel conquered the territories of the West Bank and Gaza, these lands with their millions of Palestinians came under Israeli occupation. Then followed the much discussed Resolution 242. The UN stipulated that Israel should withdraw essentially to the 1967 borders, as part of an overall agreement and a recognition of Israel's right to live in peace and security. The resolution acknowledges the Arab's rights to these lands, and Israel's right to peace and security. Israel expected to trade land for peace. In June 1967, Moshe Dayan said, "We are waiting for the Arabs' phone call. They know where to find us." The answer was given in Khartoum on September, 1967.

The major Arab states rejected the principles of Resolution 242, and announced their policy towards Israel—the three Nos: No recognition, no peace, and no negotiations. Israel became the occupier of an angry and unhappy population. Living under occupation is terrible for the occupied. It is not a blessing for the occupier.

Arthur Herzberg, former Rabbi in Englewood, and former President of the American Jewish Congress, tells a remarkable story in his book, *The Fate of Zionism*. After Israel's victory, there was great jubilation. David Ben Gurion, former Prime Minister, had left politics and moved to a kibbutz in the Negev. He was invited to speak at a Labor Party meeting and arrived late, in traditional kibbutznik style, in shorts. He astounded everyone by saying that if Israel did not immediately return all the territory it had just captured, with the exception of East Jerusalem, it would be heading for a historic disaster.

Given the consequence all these years later, the loss of Israeli lives, the increasing demonization of Israel in the Arab press and in some parts of the world press, and to some degree in world opinion, in addition to the intifadas, the great suffering and humiliation of the Palestinians, and the damage to the lives of both sides, it is becoming increasingly clear that Ben Gurion was right. He had the foresight to see that time passing only made it more difficult for Israel to protect its citizens and maintain control over a huge angry population. This is a cycle of violence and despair.

For Israel the situation is a trap. Israel cannot stay without creeping annexation that includes more Arabs into Israeli society—the demographic issue—or leave, certainly not easily with all its many settlers. Also, what happens to the millions of Palestinians in the West Bank? Can they become citizens of Israel?

Now, in Israel there is much discussion of the demographic dilemma. Only about fifty percent of the people living between the Jordan River and the Mediterranean are Jews. By the year 2020, the percentage of Jews will be forty-two percent.

Currently, Israeli Prime Minister Ehud Olmert has been heavily criticized for the conduct of the war with Hezbollah. To shore up his faltering government he turned sharply to the right and chose a hard liner, Avigdor Lieberman, for the cabinet. Lieberman is known for his extremely hawkish views. At one time he called for stripping Israeli Arabs of citizenship. This kind of talk makes an impossible situation even more impossible, if that is possible.

A two state solution seems like the way to go. The most detailed attempt was pursued by President Clinton, bringing together Israeli Prime Minister Barak, and Yasser Arafat. The first map outlining borders proposed by Israel has often been cited by the Palestinians as a ridiculous offer—a Bantustan plan of non-contiguous cantons, giving the Palestinians nothing that could be called a state. People have been left with the impression that this was the Israeli position. The final map, reflecting Clinton's final proposal to which Barak agreed, was a contiguous area encompassing most of the West Bank. It was the most reasonable deal to date, but it was rejected by Arafat. There were some weaknesses in the deal—for example—ambiguity over control of the air space over the projected Palestinian state. The real weakness was that the Barak coalition had unraveled and he was now in a minority in the Knesset. However, even if the plan had not been approved by the Knesset, it could have become a signpost for a projected peace and a basis of hopes for the future, the signalling of a willingness to seriously negotiate the peace that both sides really need. Arafat rejected the plan and made no counter-offer. Sharon was elected, and the intifada broke out.

Clinton stated that the plan broke down essentially about the right of return of the refugees. Arafat told Clinton that if he accepted, Clinton could attend his funeral. Perhaps what is most important for the understanding of the conflict is that the plan clearly calls for a final resolution and an end to any further claims. This is the psychological sticking point for the Palestinians. They are interested in their concept of peace and justice—a vindication of their grievance. Unlike Israelis who are very tough negotiators but also pragmatic and interested in solutions. Palestinians and Arab leaders take no responsibility for the disaster they have brought on their own people, both by the ineptness of their leadership and the autocracy and corruption of their governments.

Abba Eban was once quoted as saying, "Palestinian leadership never misses an opportunity to miss an opportunity for peace."

The election of Hamas was in part a reproach to the corruption of the Palestinian National Authority and in part because of the political ineptness of the Abbas party who ran too many candidates against a well-organized religious fundamentalist party with only a few candidates. Hamas, in spite of its charitable record, since they are responsible for much of the social services

Palestinians get, still did not win a majority in the popular vote. However, both Hamas in the West Bank and Gaza, and Hezbollah in Lebanon, are ideologically and religiously opposed to any kind of agreement on a political solution. They believe that Palestine, as stated in their charter, belongs entirely to Moslems. To relinquish any part of the land is forbidden. (Some Orthodox Jews have a similar belief. God promised this land to the Jews and no one can give it up.)

Yet it has become clear that a military solution is impossible. Even worse—ongoing conflict is becoming ever more dangerous. If the nature of the conflict moves from the secular to the religious, we can only expect more bloodletting since it is against God's will to compromise.

At present, given this history, the worst aspect of the problem is that both Palestinians and the leadership of some of the Arab/Moslem states have refused to accept the legitimacy of Israel and realistic negotiations about the right of return of refugees to villages that no longer exist. Whatever the average Israeli and Palestinian thinks about a two-state solution, the constant violence supported and maintained by arms shipments allows extremists to sabotage any deal, even as it begins to take place.

Given the long history of the Arab-Israeli conflict and failure of the many attempts at negotiations, I have come to the reluctant conclusion that both sides cannot come to an agreement by themselves. Arthur Herzberg and Shlomo Ben-Ami, former Foreign Minister of Israel and key participant in the Camp David talks, have come to the same conclusion. There is no military solution. Neither side can impose its will on the other. All further hostilities will only inflict more cruelty on both peoples. Israel's safety has been thought to depend on deterrence, the idea that any attack can be handled by overwhelming force. The Lebanese conflict with Hezbollah's effectiveness in fighting Israel has put the deterrence doctrine in question, making the situation much more dangerous.

A political solution must be found and can only happen with concerted international action. The US, which at one time had the credibility to appear as an honest broker, has lost this power since its entanglement in Iraq. The need for participation by the Arab League is absolutely necessary. Once, in 2002, they proposed a vague initiative. As the situation becomes more and more threatening and dangerous, because of the availability of sophisticated long distance weapons, they may become more willing to participate in negotiations. In fact, they have recently shown renewed interest. Growing Shiite radicalism threatens the Sunni governments. Rage against Israel can rebound against these same governments. Unsettling wars in this area could create economic havoc. From the Israeli point of view, the acknowledgement of the limits of military power could influence Israel if there was a real chance of an agreement.

The outlines of a reasonable agreement are fairly clear from the implementation of Resolution 242 and the Clinton parameters of 2000. Is pressure likely to be more effective now? In the recent hostilities between Israel and Hezbollah in Lebanon, the US was at first reluctant to demand an immediate ceasefire to give Israel time to control Hezbollah. When the situation looked as if it might spiral out of control, the major powers in the Security Council were able to act decisively and effectively to bring peacekeepers into the area. This demonstrates how the major powers in the Security Council can impose solutions if they choose. They may decide to do so in the Arab-Israeli conflict if they think the situation in the region is becoming too unstable and too dangerous. There is some good reason for this. The weapons involved are becoming more and more sophisticated, with potential to ignite a regional war and create chaos. One proposal is to put UN peacekeepers in the West Bank.

Finally, returning to the idea of narratives—Sami Adwan, a Palestinian educator, met with Dan Bar-On, an Israeli social psychologist. They have worked together since 2002 developing three booklets called "Learning the Other's Narrative," to be used in Palestinian and Israeli high schools. Each side is confronted with a contradictory version of history. Each page is divided into three: the Palestinian and Israeli narratives and a third section left blank for the pupil to fill in. The purpose is not to legitimize or accept the other's narrative but to recognize it. The booklets have been translated into English, Spanish, Italian, Catalan, and Basque and will soon appear in German. In France it has sold more than twenty-three thousand copies. It has also been adapted for use for the Macedonian-Albanian narratives.

There have been great difficulties in introducing the booklets into Palestinian and Israeli high schools. However, more and more people in these communities are urging a change in the teaching of history. Understanding the other's narrative is essential for progress, and as well, essential for humanist thinking and ethical action.

(Sylvain Ehrenfeld is a member of the Ethical Culture Society of Bergen County)

Works Cited

Abraham, Matthew. "Recognizing the Effect of the Past in the Present: Theorizing a Way Forward on the Israeli-Palestinian Conflict." *JAC: An Interdisciplinary Journal of Rhetoric, Culture, and Politics* 33.12 (2013). Print.

Adler, Felix. *Creed and Deed*. New York: Published for the Society for Ethical Culture by G.P. Putnam's Sons, 1880. Print.
Adwan, Sami, and Bar-on, Dan. Dialogical Presentation "Developing a Dual Israeli-Palestinian Historical Narrative." Reported by *Washington Report on Middle Eastern Affairs* (May-June 2007).. Web. 15 January, 2013
Bakhtin, Mikhail. *Speech Genres and Other Late Essays*.1979. Trans. Vern W. McGee. Austin, TX: U of Texas P, 1986. Print.
Buber, Martin. *I and Thou*. 1923. Trans. Ronald Gregor Smith. New York: Charles Scribner's Sons, 1958. Print.
Burke, Kenneth. *A Rhetoric of Motives*.1950. Berkeley: U California P, 1969. Print.
Chomsky, Noam. *Fateful Triangle: The United States, Israel and the Palestinians*. London: Pluto Press, 1999. Print.
Edward Said and After: Toward a New Humanism. Eds. Matthew Abraham and Andrew Rubin. Special Issue of *Cultural Critique* 67 (2007): 1-12.Print.
Ehrenfeld, Sylvain. "The Israeli-Palestinian Conflict: Each Side's Contrasting Narratives." *The Ethical Culture Society of Bergen County* (11 Apr. 2012). Web. 5 January, 2013.
Finkelstein, Norman. *'This Time We Went Too Far: Truth and Consequences of the Gaza Invasion.'* New York: OR Books, 2010. Print.
Fisher, Walter. *Human Communication as Narration: Toward a Philosophy of Reason, Value, and Action*. Columbia: U of South Carolina P, 1987. Print.
Freire. Paulo. *Pedagogy of the Oppressed*. Trans. Myra Bergman Ramos. New York: Continuum, 2000. Print.
King, Jr., Martin Luther. "Letter from Birmingham Jail." Published as "The Negro is Your Brother" in the *Atlantic Monthly* 2 (August 1963): 78–88. Print.
Ong, Walter. *Orality and Literacy: The Technologizing of the Word*. Second Edition. New York: Routledge, 2002. Print.
Propp, Vladimer. *Morphology of the Folktale*. 1927. Second ed. Trans. Laurence Scott. Austin: U Texas P, 1968. Print.
Ratcliffe, Krista. "Rhetorical Listening: A Trope for Interpretive Listening and a 'Code of Cross-Cultural Conduct.'" *College Composition and Communication* 51.2 (Dec., 1999): 195–224. Print.
Rogers, Carl. *Client-Centered Therapy: Its Current Practice, Implications and Theory*. London: Constable, 1951. Print.
Said, Edward. *Orientalism: Western Conceptions of the Orient*. London: Penguin Books, 2003. Print.
Toulmin, Stephen. *The Uses of Argument*. Cambridge: U Cambridge P, 2003. Print.
Young, Richard E., Alton L. Becker and Kenneth L. Pike. *Rhetoric: Discovery and Change*. New York: Harcourt, 1970. Print.

7 Dueling Visions of Israel and the World: Netanyahu and Obama at AIPAC

Robert Rowland

In March of 2012, Israeli Prime Minister Benjamin Netanyahu and US President Barack Obama each made major policy speeches to the American-Israel Political Action Committee policy conference focused on ties between Israel and the United States and the threat posed to Israel by the Iranian nuclear program.[1] In many ways, the two speeches functioned as campaign speeches in which the two leaders vied for the support of the American Jewish community. Netanyahu began his speech by praising the "more than a half of the members of Congress [who] are in attendance here tonight" (5), and then spoke of the strong support Israel had received from leaders of both parties. At one point, he asked the audience if there was anyone in attendance from Florida, New York, Wisconsin or California (19), important states in the American election, each with a sizable Jewish population. The strong message was that the Obama administration needed to be unwavering in support of Israel or Jewish Americans might support the Republicans. Obama clearly recognized the potential political danger and focused his appeal to the community on "the unbreakable bond between Israel and the United States," "the partnership between the United States and

Israel," the "more than six decades of friendship between the United States and Israel," the fact that the United States and Israel share "common ideals," and asked to be judged based on "my deeds" as President (2, 3, 5, 12).

In these passages and others, the Prime Minister and the President clearly sought the support of the immediate audience and the larger American Jewish audience by emphasizing commonality between the United States and Israel. If this contest for the support of American Jews was all that was at stake in the two speeches, there would be little to be gained from a detailed consideration of them. However, underneath the surface, the two leaders present very different views about the nature of Israeli society and the continuing threats it must confront.

Underlying the views of the president is a pragmatic assessment of the world situation and the threats to Israel, an assessment that recognizes the genuine danger posed by the Iranian nuclear program for Israeli security, but also recognizes other threats and that all actions have potential risks as well as potential benefits. While the bulk of Obama's speech is aimed at minimizing political risks facing his reelection campaign and persuading Israel that there is no current necessity of attacking Iran's nuclear sites, the underlying worldview is that Israel is a normal state and must pragmatically assess the world situation. Netanyahu's worldview is quite different. Prime Minister Netanyahu sees the world through the lens of the Holocaust, in this way staying true to the ideological roots of the Likud in the Holocaust-centered worldview of Menachem Begin.[2] Netanyahu's focus on the Holocaust provides great power to his message, but at the cost of obscuring differences between the threat posed by Hitler to the Jews of Europe and the dangers posed by Iran to the nation of Israel. For Netanyahu the Holocaust is more than an analogy or historical precedent; it functions as a worldview, driving his message. Kenneth Burke noted that when symbols function as a worldview they "reflect," but also "select" and "deflect" reality.[3] Netanyahu's Holocaust worldview carries with it the very real threat that it will "deflect" his audience from the reality that the threat Israel faces in 2012 is quite dissimilar from what the Jewish community faced in Hitler's Europe during the war.

In the next two sections of this essay, I develop the worldviews present in the two speeches, beginning with the pragmatic perspective evident in the speech of President Obama and then turning to the speech of Prime Minister Netanyahu. I then show that the worldview of Prime Minister Netanyahu provides an epistemically constricted understanding of the world, one that poses immense risks for Israel.

ISRAEL AS A NORMAL STATE: OBAMA'S WORLDVIEW

Three themes dominate President Obama's speech at AIPAC. As noted, the bulk of the speech is focused on minimizing political risks by emphasizing strong support for Israel and shared identity between the United States and Israel. In addition, Obama also argues that Israel should not unilaterally attack Iran, despite recognizing the potential threat posed by Iran. The third theme is the most important; Obama depicts the threats faced by Israel through a pragmatic lens that recognizes multiple threats and costs as well as benefits associated with potential action. In so doing, Obama implicitly argues that Israel is a powerful state that should coldly assess the pragmatic risks and benefits of action and that ultimately the failure to resolve the Palestinian conflict poses every bit as much of a threat to Israel as the Iranian nuclear program.

The first theme dominates the introduction and first half of the speech. Obama begins by recognizing people in the audience who have ties to Israel or the Jewish community in the United States, as well as his administration for the Democratic Party. His message is that his administration and Democrats are strong supporters of Israel. In the third paragraph, he speaks of "my long-time friends on the Chicago delegation" of AIPAC who are here and "the members of Congress" who have "worked hard to maintain the partnership between the United States and Israel," recognizing Debbie Wasserman Schultz in particular. He then emphasizes his relationship with Israeli leaders, mentioning the Israeli Ambassador to the United States, Michael Oren, and adding that "I'm very much looking forward to welcoming Prime Minister Netanyahu and his delegation back to the White House" (4), a statement that at least in the case of Netanyahu was of doubtful veracity.

Obama then focuses on the commonality shared by the United States and Israel, using the example of Israeli President (and former Prime Minister) "my friend Shimon Peres," who Obama announces has been chosen to receive "the Presidential Medal of Freedom" (6, 8). According to Obama, Peres' life and the award he will receive demonstrate that "we also share those human values" including "A commitment to human dignity. A belief that freedom is a right that is given to all of God's children. An experience that shows us that democracy is the one and only form of government that can truly respond to the aspirations of citizens" (8). Here, Obama is emphasizing the values and government principles shared by the United States and Israel, but he is also subtly reminding his audience that Israel faces problems other than the Iranian threat, notably the need for a settlement of the Palestinian problem that Peres had spent literally decades trying to solve. He is reminding his audience that when the Palestinians fail to control their own territory, they are being denied the "freedom" and "democracy" that have been promised "to all of God's children."

Obama then moves from the example of Peres to the shared values manifested in the actions of "America's Founding Fathers" and "Israel's founding generation" by quoting another Democrat, President Harry Truman, who described Israel's future as "'an embodiment of the great ideals of our civilization'" (10). He then moves from shared values to a discussion of "the interests that we share—in security for our communities, prosperity for our people, the new frontiers of science that can light the world," arguing that "our common ideals" undergird the shared interests (11). Here, Obama both argues that the United States and Israel share values and fundamental interests and also that those interests are multiple and should not be reduced to a focus on Iran.

The president then shifts gears from a focus on shared values and interests to a focus on how AIPAC should judge his administration. Recognizing that Republican leaders will strongly state their commitment to Israel, Obama argues that "you don't just have to count on my words. You can look to my deeds," claiming "I have kept my commitments to the state of Israel. At every crucial juncture—at every fork in the road—we have been there for Israel. Every single time" (12). He then reminds them that at the conference during the 2008 campaign he told them "Israel's security is sacrosanct. It is non-negotiable" (13). He then argues that he has followed through on that pledge: "The fact is, my administration's commitment to Israel's security has been unprecedented. Our military and intelligence cooperation has never been closer. Our joint exercises and training have never been more robust" (13). Obama points to the fact that "security assistance has increased every year," and to the fact that the United States is providing Israel "with more advanced technology," including "the Iron Dome system that has intercepted rockets that might have hit homes and hospitals and schools" (13, 14). According to Obama, his administration's commitment to Israel has not been limited to military support, but also "we've been there through our diplomacy" (15). He goes on to cite several instances in which the United States defended Israel against unfair attacks or "one-sided resolutions" (16). Gesturing toward his unwavering support for Israel, he concludes the following: "So there should not be a shred of doubt by now—when the chips are down, I have Israel's back" (16).

The partisan political motive behind these statements should be obvious. It is difficult to imagine any president making a similar speech to demonstrate support for a close ally such as Germany, Japan, or Britain. Obama implicitly recognizes this point when he notes that it is the "political season" and urges his audience that if "you hear some questions regarding my administration's support for Israel, remember that it's not backed up by the facts" (17). To this point, Obama has made an extraordinary effort to develop a sense of commonality between the United States and Israel. He has emphasized that commonality in terms of values, security needs in a dangerous world, and policies, always stating his administration's commitment to Israel.

Later in the speech, he again emphasizes his commitment to Israeli security in his discussion of the threat posed by the Iranian nuclear weapons program to Israeli security. Obama labels the program as "a threat that has the potential to bring together the worst rhetoric about Israel's destruction with the world's most dangerous weapons" (23). Obama then adds:

> Let's begin with a basic truth that you all understand: No Israeli government can tolerate a nuclear weapon in the hands of a regime that denies the Holocaust, threatens to wipe Israel off the map, and sponsors terrorist groups committed to Israel's destruction. (24)

The threat posed by the Iranian nuclear program "is completely counter to Israel's security interests. But it is also counter to the national security interests of the United States" (25). Here, Obama not only emphasizes commonality between US and Israeli policy, but sets the stage for the development of his second theme, that Israel should not preemptively attack Iranian nuclear sites.

In order to credibly develop this theme for an audience focused on Israeli security, Obama begins by discussing the efforts his administration has taken to stop the Iranian nuclear program. Initially, he emphasizes a commitment to "use all elements of American power to pressure Iran and prevent it from acquiring a nuclear program" (27). He then jabs Republican critics by noting, "When I took office, the efforts to apply pressure on Iran were in tatters," adding "In other words, the Iranian leadership was united and on the move, and the international community was divided about how to go forward" (28). Obama had been strongly criticized for a policy of "engagement" with the Iranian government that the administration attempted in 2009.[4] The president argues however that this policy "put forward a very clear choice to the Iranian regime: a path that would allow them to rejoin the community of nations if they meet their international obligations, or a path that leads to an escalating series of consequences if they don't" (29). Although the president admits that this policy was "quickly rebuffed by the Iranian regime," it "allowed us to rally the international community as never before, to expose Iran's intransigence, and to apply pressure that goes far beyond anything that the United States could do on our own" (29). He then notes that the result is that "Iran is under greater pressure than ever before" because he was able to gain the support of Russia and China for "a comprehensive sanctions effort" that is "slowing the Iranian nuclear program and virtually grinding the Iranian economy to a halt in 2011" (30). He then notes that still tougher sanctions will go into effect later this year and as a result "Iran is isolated, its leadership divided and under pressure" (31). Underlying his message is a commitment to pragmatism in two senses: as the basis of policy and as the basis for evaluation of that policy.

It is only after defending his administration's efforts to deal with the Iranian nuclear program that he turns to the key theme that Israel should not preemptively attack Iran. He begins to develop this point in paragraph thirty-two where he observes, "I firmly believe that an opportunity still remains for diplomacy—backed by pressure—to succeed." His point is that there is still time for diplomacy and sanctions to work. He reassures the audience that "we are exceedingly vigilant in monitoring their program" and reminds them that "Sanctions are continuing to increase" (33). As a result of facing "these increasingly dire consequences, Iran's leaders still have the opportunity to make the right decision" and "choose a path that brings them back into the community of nations" (33).

Obama then focuses on the point that attacking Iran will not necessarily resolve the problem and has significant potential costs. He notes that "both Israel and the United States have an interest in seeing this challenge resolved diplomatically. After all, the only way to truly solve this problem is for the Iranian government to make a decision to forsake nuclear weapons" (34). Here, he implicitly makes the point that a military strike is unlikely to permanently prevent Iran from developing a nuclear weapon. Obama then turns to the risks of war, first stating that he has "a deeply held preference for peace over war" (35). He then adds "I will only use force when the time and circumstances demand it. And I know that Israeli leaders also know all too well the costs and consequences of war" (35). Although he says Israeli leaders recognize the costs of war, his real message is to remind them of those costs and also of the unpredictable outcome of war. Again, pragmatic risk assessment trumps ideology.

Obama's goal is clearly to convince Netanyahu and the Israeli government that there is still time for a diplomatic solution and that therefore an attack on Iran is not yet necessary. He also recognizes that this message risks signaling to Iran that the United States will not support military action. Therefore, immediately after arguing that there is still time for diplomacy and sanctions to work, he adds, "Iran's leaders should have no doubt about the resolve of the United States—just as they should not doubt Israel's sovereign right to make its own decisions about what is required to meet its security needs" (36). Here, he signals to Iran that the United States cannot and will not restrain Israel from attacking Iranian nuclear sites if diplomacy fails.

He reiterates this point in the following paragraph, where he promises he has "taken no options off the table" and then defines the options in an ascending series of tough steps:

> That includes all elements of American power: A political effort aimed at isolating Iran; a diplomatic effort to sustain our coalition and to ensure that the Iranian program is monitored; an economic effort that imposes crippling sanctions; and yes, a military effort to be prepared for any contingency. (37)

In the most powerful words of the speech, he then explains, "I do not have a policy of containment; I have a policy to prevent Iran from obtaining a nuclear weapon," a statement he adds punch to by reminding his audience (and the government of Iran), "And as I have made clear time and again during the course of my presidency, I will not hesitate to use force when it is necessary to defend the United States and its interests" (37). Here, he implicitly reminds both Israel and Iran of his escalation of forces in Afghanistan and the raid that killed Osama bin-Laden.

With the tough talk, Obama sought to reassure Israel of his resolve and to send a message to the Iranian government. He clearly hoped that this message would then help in his push for a diplomatic solution and stop the rush toward war. He notes that "there is too much loose talk of war" and argues that "such talk has only benefitted the Iranian government, by driving up the price of oil" (38). Speaking directly to Republican critics who had all but encouraged Israel to attack Iran, he states "now is not the time for bluster. Now is the time to let our increased pressure sink in, and to sustain the broad international coalition we have built" (38). More broadly, for Obama it is always time for a pragmatic assessment of risks and benefits, an analysis focused on the uncertainties of policy action, more than ideological commitment. Obama is often depicted in the conservative media as an extreme knee-jerk liberal. In fact, as this speech indicates, he is a pragmatist who is influenced more by facts on the ground than pre-existing ideology.

Obama develops the third theme, that Israel is a normal state that must pragmatically assess the risks and benefits of action in relation to a world filled with threats and opportunities, in two main ways. First, at almost exactly the mid-point of the speech, he focuses on the Palestinian issue, arguing that a just resolution of the Israeli-Palestinian conflict is not only a moral necessity but would be good for Israeli security. He begins this section by alluding to his administration's failed attempt to persuade Prime Minister Netanyahu to curtail building in West Bank settlements and otherwise make efforts to restart the peace process with the Palestinian Authority.[5] Obama obliquely references these efforts as "my administration's ongoing pursuit of peace" and adds "I make no apologies for pursuing peace" (18). He notes that leaders from across the political spectrum in Israel "understand the necessity of peace," pointing to "Prime Minister Netanyahu, Defense Minister Barak, President Peres—each of them have called for two states, a secure Israel that lives side by side with an independent Palestinian state" (18). The key point according to the president is that "peace is profoundly in Israel's security interest" (18).

Obama notes that there are barriers to achieving peace, including "upheaval and uncertainty" in the region and "division within the Palestinian leadership," but claims that this is no reason "to give in to cynicism or despair" (20, 21). In fact, he argues that "The changes taking place in the region make peace more important, not less" (21). The key point in Obama's message is that ultimately Israel's security and continuation as a democratic Jewish state demands a resolution of the Israeli/Palestinian conflict. He notes that the Iranian threat and other dangers faced by Israel should not obscure "The reality that Israel faces—from shifting demographics, to emerging technologies, to an extremely difficult international environment—demands a resolution of this issue" (19). With these twenty-three words, Obama argues that Israeli security and commitment to democratic values depend on achieving an agreement with the Palestinians. The words "shifting demographics" remind his audience that absent an agreement with the Palestinians, the time is coming when a majority of the citizens in Israel proper and the land Israel seized in the 1967 war will no longer be Jewish. The reference to "emerging technologies" and "an extremely difficult international environment" remind his audience of the long-term dangers facing Israel as a Jewish state surrounded by hostile nations in the Middle East and suggest that achieving peace is essential for Israeli security. Obama is prompting his audience to recognize that the Iranian threat in no way diminishes the need for an ultimate solution to the Palestinian conflict.

At the same time, Obama makes it clear that his support for "a resolution" of the Palestinian issue does not reflect lack of support for Israel. He notes that "there will be no lasting peace unless Israel's security concerns are met" and that "we have continued to insist that any Palestinian partner must recognize Israel's right to exist, and reject violence, and adhere to existing agreements" (21). Obama also points to a speech that he made at the United Nations General Assembly where he "reaffirmed that any lasting peace must acknowledge the fundamental legitimacy of Israel and its security concerns," noting that "No American President has made such a clear statement about our support for Israel at the United Nations at such a difficult time. People usually give those speeches before audiences like this one—not before the General Assembly" (22). Obama then drives the point home that he made clear a commitment to Israel in a very difficult context, when he stated, "And I must say, there was not a lot of applause. But it was the right thing to do" (23).

Obama's focus in the speech to the AIPAC conference is clearly primarily defensive, aimed at reassuring an important constituency that often supports Democrats of his commitment to Israel. For this reason, the president spent far more words expressing a commitment to Israel than he did discussing the peace process. However, his underlying point was still quite clear. Israel faces many threats, and finding a resolution to the Palestinian conflict is central to resolving (or at least minimizing) many of them. Given the context of his administration's efforts to push the Netanyahu government toward greater efforts to make peace with the Palestinians, Obama was implicitly arguing that the policies he supports both more accurately reflected the real situation facing Israel than did the policies of Netanyahu and were better adapted to protecting Israeli security.

He develops this theme in a second way and in a larger frame in the conclusion of the speech, where he begins by returning to the theme of commonality between Israel and the United States, observing that "the United States and Israel have come through" some "challenging times" together in the past (39) and noting all that he has "shared" with Israelis, including President Peres, and Jewish Americans. He then makes the point that Israel and the United States share basic values and have the capacity to defend those values:

> As Harry Truman understood, Israel's story is one of hope. We may not agree on every single issue—no two nations do, and our democracies contain a vibrant diversity of views. But we agree on the big things—the things that matter. And together, we are working to build a better world—one where our people can live free from fear; one where peace is founded upon justice; one where our children can know a future that is more hopeful than the present. (40).

Here, the president explicitly cites the values shared by the United States and Israel and implicitly reminds his audience of the importance of resolving the Palestinian issue in order to create a "peace" that is "founded upon justice." But with the reference to hope and the similarities between "our democracies," he is also reminding the Israeli government of their strength. His point is that Israel is the strongest state in the Middle East. As a state with the most powerful military in the region and as a significant nuclear power, Israel is no longer the isolated and weak state of 1948, or even 1956, or 1967.

In his speech to the AIPAC conference, President Obama walks a rhetorical tightrope, sending messages of strong support for Israel and the American commitment to stopping the Iranian nuclear program from producing nuclear weapons, but also arguing against a unilateral Israeli attack on Iranian nuclear sites. Although the bulk of the speech is spent on the themes of commonalities shared by the United States and Israel and demonstrating the toughness of the American policy on Iran, underlying his message is a pragmatic assessment of the risks facing the United States and Israel. He is quite blunt in his assessment of the dangers posed by the Iranian nuclear program, but he also emphasizes the potential costs of going to war. He makes the point that ultimately peace depends upon "justice," and therefore a fair resolution of the Israeli-Palestinian crisis.

In the next section, I argue that Prime Minister Netanyahu views the Iranian nuclear program through what Kenneth Burke calls a terministic screen[6] based in the Holocaust. He places Israel within what Emil Fackenheim has called the "Commanding Voice" of "Planet Auschwitz."[7] President Obama clearly understands the importance of the Holocaust. He refers to "a great uncle who helped liberate Buchenwald, to [his] memories of returning there with Elie Wiesel," but he also understands that unlike the Holocaust era, Israel is a strong nation with powerful allies and that there are risks as well as potential benefits associated with attacking Iran. His ultimate message is about the importance of weighing risks and benefits in a pragmatic way and also considering the importance of "justice" in securing the peace and protecting the security of Israel. Oddly, the core of Obama's real message is presented in a very small portion of the speech. In order to send the message that Israel is a powerful normal state that must assess risks and benefits of all actions, he had to first establish his commitment to Israel (and commonality between the United States and Israel) and then demonstrate his administration's toughness in confronting Iran. Only after accomplishing those two ends, could he point out that there has been "too much loose talk of war" (38).

The Holocaust-Centered Worldview of Prime Minister Netanyahu

Prime Minister Benjamin Netanyahu addressed the AIPAC conference two days after President Obama spoke, on March 6, 2012. Netanyahu focused on two themes: the political power of AIPAC as a supporter of Israel and the argument that the proper frame for understanding and confronting the Iranian nuclear program was the Holocaust. As noted earlier, Netanyahu was not subtle in highlighting the political power of AIPAC, emphasizing the many members of Congress who were there and that they had "stood up to applaud the State of Israel" and provided "unwavering support to the Jewish state" (6, 7). His message was clearly that any American politician who did not strongly support Israel, which he implicitly defined as supporting the policies of the Netanyahu government, would be politically punished for this failure.

Aside from the quite unsubtle demand of political fealty toward his vision of Israel, Netanyahu builds an argument that the Holocaust provides the proper lens for understanding the Iranian nuclear crisis and implicitly argues that Israel still lives in the Holocaust world. This terministic focus on the Holocaust provides the ideological driver behind Netanyahu's approach to Iran and all other threats to Israel.

He begins to make a point when he pays tribute to Israeli Foreign Minister Yossil Peled, who was in the audience. He retells Peled's story of surviving the Holocaust in hiding "with a Christian family" while "his father and many other members of his family were murdered at Auschwitz" (12). Netanyahu argues that "Yossi's life is the story of the Jewish people—the story of a powerless and stateless people who became a strong and proud nation, able to defend itself" (14). The lesson of this story is that "Israel must always reserve the right to defend itself" (15). With these words, the essential ideological pattern of the speech has been set. Any threat to Israel must be viewed through the lens of the Holocaust and the proper response is for Israel "to defend itself." In this worldview, the ideological equation is quite simple: any threat demands an overwhelming military response. This is precisely the same ideological principle that dominated Begin's Holocaust-centered worldview for thirty-five years from Israel's founding through his service as Prime Minister.[8]

A few paragraphs later, Netanyahu explicitly identifies "Iran" (21) as the subject of the speech. Initially, Netanyahu seems to endorse the approach laid out by President Obama, noting that Obama "stated clearly that all options are on the table, and that American policy is not containment. Well, Israel has exactly the same policy" (24, 25). In the remainder of the speech, he makes it quite clear that Israel and the United States actually have sharply different views of the Iranian threat.

Netanyahu spends the bulk of the speech emphasizing the magnitude of the Iranian threat. Initially, he refutes the Iranian claim that their goal is to develop a program making medical isotopes. Netanyahu responds with withering sarcasm:

> A country that builds underground nuclear facilities, develops intercontinental ballistic missiles, manufactures thousands of centrifuges, and that absorbs crippling sanctions is doing all that in order to advance medical research. So you see, when that Iranian ICBM is flying through the air to a location near you, you've got nothing to worry about. It's only carrying medical isotopes. (30, 31)

Netanyahu then demonstrates his command of American idiom, saying, "If it looks like a duck, walks like a duck, and quacks like a duck, then what is it?" "It's a duck. But this duck is a nuclear duck" (32, 33).

Here, Netanyahu argues that the Iranian nuclear program threatens Israel and the United States equally. The reference to an "Iranian ICBM . . . flying through the air to a location near you" is especially telling. While experts disagree on how close Iran is to developing a nuclear weapon, they agree that Iran is a long way from developing a workable ICBM. Moreover, a missile attack on the United States would be instantly detectable and produce overwhelming retaliation. Such an attack is among the least likely real threats, but by using sarcasm, rather than reasoned argument, Netanyahu is able to claim that the United States and Israel are equally threatened by Iran.

Netanyahu then turns to the idea that even if Iran developed nuclear weapons, it would pose no threat because it could be deterred from using those weapons. He responds: "Responsible leaders should not bet the security of their countries on the belief that the world's most dangerous regimes won't use the world's most dangerous weapons" (37). Of course, "responsible leaders" made precisely that bet in the forty-plus years from the point the Soviet Union developed nuclear weapons to the end of the Cold War. Netanyahu will not make that bet, precisely the same bet made by India and Pakistan today, because of his Holocaust-centered worldview. Netanyahu "will never gamble with the security" (38) of Israel, because the Iranian "regime has broken every international rule and flouted every norm. It has seized embassies, targeted diplomats. It sends its own children through mine fields; it hangs gays and stones women" (39). Netanyahu adds that "Iran's proxies have dispatched hundreds of suicide bombers, planted thousands of roadside bombs and they fired over twenty thousand missiles at civilians" (40). It is not Israelis only who have been killed; "Iran is responsible for the murder of hundreds, if not thousands of Americans" (41) and continues to support terrorism today, including a plot to kill the Saudi Ambassador to the United States that "would have murdered in the process" "several Senators and Congressman" (43). Here, Netanyahu is arguing that Iran is more than a dangerous regime; it threatens Israel today in the way that Hitler threatened the Jewish people.

Netanyahu's point is that Iran is uniquely dangerous and evil. He says, "Iran calls for Israel's destruction, and they work for its destruction—each day, every day, relentlessly" and then adds that "with nuclear weapons" "Iran will be even more reckless and a lot more dangerous" (46). With nuclear weapons, "terror proxies . . . will be emboldened to attack the United States, Israel, and other countries" and "terrorism could grow tenfold" (49). He observes that "A nuclear-armed Iran could choke off the world's oil supply and could make real its threat to close the Straits of Hormuz" (50). A nuclear armed Iran could lead to proliferation as other states in the region started programs to "acquire nuclear weapons," turning "[t]he world's most volatile region" into a "tinderbox waiting to go off" (52). Worst of all, "Iran could threaten all of us with nuclear terrorism" (52). Netanyahu concludes that "for the sake of our prosperity, for the sake of our security, for the sake of our children, Iran must not be allowed to acquire nuclear weapons!" (55).

Netanyahu then systematically explains why any approach other than a military attack on Iran cannot work. He notes, "For the last decade, the international community has tried diplomacy. It hasn't worked. For six years, the international community has applied sanctions. That hasn't worked either" (58, 59). He says "I appreciate President Obama's recent efforts to impose even tougher sanctions," but quickly adds, "Iran's nuclear program continues to march forward" (60). He claims that "Israel has waited patiently for the international community to resolve this issue," but "[n]one of us can afford to wait much longer" (61). Why is it that waiting for tough sanctions to work is no longer an option? The short answer is that Iran is not a normal regime that can be deterred; it is an evil state, the modern equivalent of Hitler's Germany.

Netanyahu then makes it quite clear that his lens for understanding the Iranian nuclear program is a worldview shaped by the Holocaust. When he states that "As Prime Minister of Israel, I will never let my people live in the shadow of annihilation" he makes his Holocaust focus quite clear. It is notable that to this point Netanyahu has not argued for the efficacy of a military strike on Iran. In Netanyahu's worldview, Israel still lives on "Planet Auschwitz." In this Holocaust-centered worldview, any threat to Israel demands an immediate and overwhelming response. In this worldview, issues of effectiveness and a consideration of consequences are secondary. Given the magnitude of the threat he has outlined, it seems quite odd that Israel has not already attacked Iran.

In the conclusion of the speech, he addresses those who claim that "stopping Iran from getting the bomb is more dangerous than letting Iran have the bomb" (63). He says that they claim that "a military confrontation with Iran would undermine the efforts already underway; that it would be ineffective; and that it would provoke an even more vindictive response by Iran" (63). Notably, Netanyahu makes no attempt to refute these arguments, but instead says, "I've heard them before," in, "an exchange of letters between the World Jewish Congress and the United States War Department" (64). Netanyahu reads from the response that the War Department provided in 1944 to a request by the World Jewish Congress to bomb Auschwitz. According to Netanyahu, the response stated: "it would be of such doubtful efficacy that it would not warrant the use of our resources," and, "[s]uch an effort might provoke even more vindictive action by the Germans" (68). He immediately ridicules this view, "Think about that—'even more vindictive action'–than the Holocaust" (69).

There are obvious dissimilarities between the situation facing the Jewish people during the Holocaust and the situation created by the Iranian nuclear weapons program facing Israel and the world today. Contemporary Iran has oppressed its own people and supported terrorism, but it is not Hitler's Germany. Israel is the greatest power in the region, quite dissimilar to the Jewish communities in Hitler's Europe. Unlike the Jewish communities in Hitler's Europe, Israel has the capacity to respond to any attack, conventional or nuclear, with overpowering force. Moreover, the government of Iran faces substantial internal protests and is extremely dependent upon oil revenues that could be threatened by sanctions. Some commentators argue that sanctions "are succeeding as intended" and "are increasingly posing a challenge to its [the regime's] survival."[9] Unlike 1944, the United States has demonstrated a strong commitment to support Israel and prevent a future holocaust.

At this point, Netanyahu seems to recognize these differences, noting "2012 is not 1944. The American government today is different," and, "[t]he Jewish people are also different. Today we have a state of our own. And the purpose of the Jewish state is to defend Jewish lives and to secure the Jewish future" (71). Yet, while appearing to recognize the differences between 1944 and 2012, Netanyahu then makes it clear that the differences are unimportant because he views the Iranian nuclear program through the lens of the Holocaust. He states, "Never again will we not be masters of the fate of our very survival. Never again" (72). He adds a few sentences later, "when it comes to Israel's survival, we must always remain the masters of our fate" (74).

Netanyahu's use of the phrase "never again" is particularly revealing. With these words, he makes it clear that the worldview through which he understands the Iranian threat is that of the Holocaust. Here, he taps into a perspective that dominated the strain of Zionism out of which his party developed, Revisionism. Revisionist Zionism in Israel was shaped for decades by the Holocaust-centered worldview of Menachem Begin, who viewed all threats to Israel through the lens of the Holocaust and consequently "opposed any policy that smacked of weakness or compromise."[10] The similarities to the perspective developed by Netanyahu should be obvious.

Given statements by important figures in Iran calling for the destruction of Israel, Netanyahu's focus on the danger of a future holocaust at first seems understandable. Yet, there are dangers associated with such a focus. While the Prime Minister ridiculed those who argued that an attack on Iran might not work or could make things worse, he did not answer those objections. In 1944, there was little danger that a bombing attack on the railheads leading to the death camps or even on the death camps themselves could make things worse for the Jewish people. After all, the population of Auschwitz was already in a death camp.

In 2012, however, there was both no guarantee that an Israeli attack on Iran would work and a very real danger that the attack could make things worse. It is important to note that an attack on Iran's nuclear sites would be enormously difficult, leading "some analysts to question whether Israel even has the military capacity to carry it off."[11] Moreover, such an attack would not in all likelihood permanently destroy the Iranian program. Mark Landler cites the views of former Under Secretary of Defense, Michèle A. Flournoy, who believes that "[s]uch an attack . . . would set back the Iranian nuclear program, at most, one to three years."[12] There also would be inevitable consequences of an attack. A Pentagon war game of a possible attack predicted disastrous results, including "that the strike would lead to a wider regional war, which could draw in the United States and leave hundreds of Americans dead."[13] Another result that "many fear" is "a new Middle East war."[14] As a result of such forecasts, Ethan Bronner has observed that "many . . . fear a catastrophe if Israel strikes at Iran."[15] Notably, Iran already has the capacity to close the Straits of Hormuz, use proxies to launch terror attacks, or attack Israel or others with conventional missiles. Moreover, an attack might convince the Iranians that they never would be safe until they had nuclear weapons. This seems to be the lesson sent by North Korea, which faced threat of military intervention or air strikes until it demonstrated possession of nuclear weapons. There is also a danger that an attack could "create a nationalist backlash that would cement this regime in place for years" at a time when "discontent appears to be growing with the entire political system."[16]

In fact, there is a consensus that an attack on Iran, even if successful, would only delay the successful building of nuclear weapons by a limited amount of time and would shore up internal support for the current regime. For all of these reasons, many defense and nuclear experts, including major figures from the Israeli military, have concluded that Israel and the West should not attack Iran. Perhaps the most telling comment comes from the former head of the Mossad, Meir Dagan, who says "a strike on Iran's nuclear installations would be 'a stupid idea,' adding that military action might not achieve all of its goals and could lead to a long war."[17]. Netanyahu's Holocaust-worldview leads him to ignore the facts that Iran is not Nazi Germany and that there is no easy or riskless military solution to the crisis.

The other danger of a Holocaust-centered worldview is that by focusing on dangers similar to the Holocaust, the worldview may obscure other issues, producing a kind of terministic blindness. In such a situation, the terminology "blinds" someone to aspects of the world not within the terministic focus. In this case, the Holocaust-fixation both blinds one to the differences between the contemporary era and that of the Holocaust and obscures dangers different from the Holocaust. This danger is on display in the conclusion of Netanyahu's address where he discusses "Israel's fate." According to Netanyahu:

> Israel's fate is to continue to be the forward position of freedom in the Middle East. The only place in the Middle East where minorities enjoy full civil rights; the only place in the Middle East where Arabs enjoy full civil rights; the only place in the Middle East where Christians are free to practice their faith; the only place in the Middle East where real judges protect the rule of law. (75)

Notably missing in Netanyahu's description of Israel as "the forward position of freedom in the Middle East" is any mention of the fate of the Palestinians, who certainly do not enjoy the "full civil rights" of Israelis.[18]

Absent a resolution of the conflict with the Palestinians, Israel will have to choose between continuing to deny rights to Palestinians or becoming a state with a minority Jewish population. The head of the Kadima party, Shaul Mofaz argues that "'The greatest threat to the state of Israel is not nuclear Iran, but that Israel might one day cease to be a Jewish state because it would have as many Palestinians as Jews."[19] Moreover, many believe as former Prime Minister Ehud Olmert stated that "a two-state solution is the only way to ensure a more stable Middle East and to grant Israel the security and well-being it desires."[20] There is also a very real risk that "[w]ithout a deal," there could be renewed conflict between Israelis and Palestinians. Bernard Avishai argues that without final resolution of the conflict through a peace agreement:

> Jerusalem and the West Bank will almost certainly explode again, this time perhaps igniting the kind of local war we saw in Bosnia: violence spreading to Israeli Arab towns and drawing in both Syrian-backed Hezbollah from Lebanon and Hamas from Gaza, each armed with thousands of missiles.[21]

Of course, Israel cannot be held solely responsible for the failure to achieve peace with the Palestinians. During the ten months in which the Netanyahu government froze settlement activities, Palestinians "refused to join talks" for almost all of the period.[22] There is blame enough for all parties in the peace process. Still, it is immensely troubling that in Netanyahu's Holocaust-focused worldview, the plight of the Palestinians did not even merit mentioning.

Netanyahu's Holocaust reductionism leads him to magnify the threat posed by Iran (and ignore the potential risks of military action) and blinds him to the threat to Israel posed by the failure to resolve the Palestinian problem. It also blinds him to the true situation in Israel, where not only Palestinians living in territory seized by Israel in the 1967 war but also Israeli Arabs fail to receive "full civil rights."[23]

Ideology and Pragmatism in two days in March at AIPAC

At first glance, the underlying principles in the speeches by the President and the Prime Minister were traditional Revisionist ideology in the case of Netanyahu and simple pragmatism in the case of Obama. The benefits and risks of each approach are well-known. An ideology centered worldview provides a firm grounding for understanding the world as demonstrated in the steadfast way that President Ronald Reagan dealt with the Soviet Union. Yet, an ideological approach also risks disaster if it misstates the facts on the ground or fails to keep pace with a shifting scene.[24] For example, it is now widely believed that the neoconservative worldview of key aides to President George W. Bush led them to vastly underestimate the risk of war with Iraq, leading to the quagmire that ensued.

On the other hand, ungrounded pragmatism may lead to passivity and inaction. President Reagan's criticism of the pragmatic Soviet policy known as détente was based in this view. Reagan famously observed that he had been "amazed that our national leaders had not philosophically and intellectually taken on the principles of Marxist-Leninism. We were always too worried we would offend the Soviets if we struck at anything so basic. Well so what? Marxist-Leninist thought is an empty cupboard. Everyone knew it by the 1980s, but no one was saying it." He added that consequently he decided, "to do some things differently, like speaking the truth about them for a change."[25] As the examples of Reagan and George W. Bush demonstrate, ideologically driven worldviews have great power, but there is always a risk that the ideological worldview will as Burke argued "deflect" attention from key aspects of the world.

It would seem that there are risks to both pure pragmatism and to a worldview rooted in an unquestioned ideology. From this perspective, one might view the speeches of Obama and Netanyahu as each representing strengths and weaknesses for conceptualizing the proper policy toward Iran. That is not the conclusion I draw. In fact, Obama's perspective is not rooted in pragmatism alone, but in a set of values closely tied to the democratic tradition that emerged out of the Enlightenment. In this tradition, values such as peace, protection of basic human rights, the opportunity to participate in democratic elections, and justice, are the proper goals of any just society. Obama is not a pure pragmatist; he makes clear his commitment to protecting these values. Rather, he is a pragmatist about means, not ends. In that way, the approach he develops bears an odd similarity to that of the Soviet policy of President Reagan, who combined a commitment to core values with pragmatic adaptation to the particular situation. It was this combination of principle and pragmatism that allowed President Reagan to boldly confront the Soviet leadership with an arms buildup and very tough words and also to negotiate quite substantive arms limitation treaties.[26] Similarly, Obama defended a pragmatic evaluation of risks and benefits as a method of evaluating how well policies could fulfill the principles he supported. As he demonstrated with the decision to send American special forces into Pakistan to kill Osama bin-Laden, he was not averse to using force if the pragmatic evaluation and the principle at stake coincided. Obama's pragmatic worldview was grounded in basic principles undergirding democratic liberalism.

The difficulty with the Holocaust-centered approach of Prime Minister Netanyahu was not that it was based in ideology, but that it was based in "calcified" ideology.[27] By viewing the contemporary Iranian threat, which is quite real and very dangerous, through the lens of the Holocaust, he both ignored the many differences between the two situations and specified an inappropriate standard for judging policy. If threatened by a true holocaust, there is no option but to strike at the party threatening mass-murder. There was no downside to bombing the railheads to Auschwitz for the Jews at Auschwitz or to bombing Auschwitz itself, but there are many risks associated with attacking Iranian nuclear sites and the result could be a much more dangerous world. The calcified worldview present in Netanyahu's speech has immense rhetorical power. The Holocaust is widely viewed as the defining moral event of our time, tragically repeated on a smaller scale in Bosnia, Kosovo, Rwanda, and elsewhere. By viewing the Iranian threat through the lens of the Holocaust, Netanyahu taps into the terror of the event and also to the guilt that Americans quite rightly feel for failing to bomb Auschwitz and take other actions to end the mass slaughter. But as an ideological map for policy, a calcified ideological worldview is immensely dangerous.

The power of a principled ideological worldview and the danger of ideological calcification were both evident in events at the very end of the tenure of Menachem Begin as Prime Minister of Israel. In March of 1982, Begin confronted groups who protested the Israeli withdrawal from Sinai that was occurring as part of the Israeli-Egyptian peace process. The protesters demonstrated their anger at the policy by wearing yellow patches, equating the withdrawal with the Nazis who had forced Jews to wear such patches. In reaction, Begin said, "You wear a yellow badge in Eretz Yisrael [the Land of

Israel], where there is an elected government—one elected democratically—and a democratically elected Knesset." He went on to "urge all the people in Israel to unite around its elected government, which is treading the path toward peace, for the prevention of war and bloodshed—and at all costs for the prevention of the spilling of Jewish blood."[28] Begin understood that achieving peace with Egypt was worth the sacrifice of the Sinai settlements and that Sadat's Egypt was not Hitler's Germany.

A few months later, Israel attacked sanctuaries in Lebanon occupied by supporters of the Palestinian Liberation Organization (PLO). In Begin's mind, the PLO and Yasser Arafat were the same as the Nazis and Hitler. The Holocaust-centered worldview was obvious in many statements, perhaps most notably when he sent a telegram to President Reagan saying, "I feel as a Prime Minister empowered to instruct a valiant army facing 'Berlin' where amongst innocent civilians, Hitler and his henchmen hide in a bunker."[29] Of course, Arafat was not Hitler and the PLO, a group that Israel would sign an agreement with a little more than a decade later, was not the Nazi state. In pulling Israel out of the Sinai, Begin rejected ideological calcification in favor of a pragmatic evaluation of how to achieve a just peace. A few months later in Lebanon, a fully calcified worldview based in the Holocaust led to disaster.

It is possible that Prime Minister Netanyahu's use of the Holocaust was purely tactical, designed to maximize support for Israel. It is even possible that Netanyahu's perspective is coldly calculated to convince the Iranian regime that they must compromise or Israel will in fact strike. Yet, there is a very real danger that Netanyahu's speech to AIPAC represents a calcified worldview no longer based in a pragmatic evaluation of real threats and real opportunities. Calcification is one of the primary causes of heart disease and ideological calcification similarly risks producing disastrous policy miscalculation.

Notes

1. See Barack Obama, "Remarks by the President at AIPAC Policy Conference," March 4, 2012, http://www.whitehouse.gove/the-press-office/2012/03/04/remarks-president-aipact-policy.conf . . . Benjamin Netanyahu, "Prime Minister Netanyahu's Speech at AIPAC Policy Conference, 2012," The Prime Minister's Office. Future references to both speeches will be made in the text by paragraph number.

2. See Robert C. Rowland, *The Rhetoric of Menachem Begin: The Myth of Redemption Through Return* (Lanham, MD.: University Press of American, 1985); Robert C. Rowland and David A. Frank, *Shared Land/Conflicting Identity: Trajec-*

tories of Israeli and Palestinian Symbol Use (East Lansing: Michigan State University Press, 2002).

3. Kenneth Burke, "Terministic Screens," in *Language as Symbolic Action: Essays on Life, Literature and Method* (Berkley: University of California Press, 1966), pp. 44–62, especially 44.

4. See David E. Sanger, "Despite Crisis, Policy on Iran is Engagement," *New York Times,* July 5, 2009, http://www.nytimes.com/2009/07/06/world/middleeast/06policy.html.

5. See Leon Wieseltier, "That Nebo Feeling," *The New Republic*, June 9, 2011, 40.

6. See Burke, "Terministic Screens," 44–47.

7. See Emil Fackenheim, *God's Presence In History: Jewish Affirmations and Philosophical Reflections* (New York: Harper and Row, 1970) 67–79. Tom Segev, *The Seventh Million: The Israelis and the Holocaust*, Trans. Haim Watzman (New York: Hill and Wang, 1993), 393.

8. See Rowland and Frank, *Shared Land*, 48–67 and 105–115, especially the chart on p. 67.

9. Nicholas D. Kristof, "Pinched and Griping in Iran," *New York Time*, June 17, 2012, WK 11.

10. Rowland and Frank, *Shared Land*, 106. Rowland also develops this perspective in *The Rhetoric of Menachem Begin*.

11. Elisabeth Bumiller, "Iran Raid Seen as Huge Task for Israeli Jets," *New York Times,* February 19, 2012, http://www.nytimes.com/2012/02/20/world/middleeast/iran-raid-seen-as-complex-task-for-israeli-military.html?pagewanted=all.

12. Mark Landler, "U.S. Aides In Israel Give Assurances about Iran," *New York Times*, June 7, 2012, A7.

13. Mark Mazzetti and Thom Shanker, "U.S. War Game Sees Peril of Israeli Strike Against Iran," *New York Times*, March 19, 2012, http://www.nytimes.com/2012/03/20/world/middleeast/united-states-war-game-sees-dire-results-of-an-israeli-attack-on-iran.html?pagewanted=all.

14. Ellen Barry and Rick Gladstone, "Setback in Talks on Iran's Nuclear Program in a 'Gulf of Mistrust,'" *New York Times*.

15. Ethan Bronner, "2 Israeli Leaders Make the Iran Issue Their Own," *New York Times*, March 27, 2012, http:www.nytimes.com/2012/03/28/world/middleeast/Netanyahu-and- . . . Also see Thomas L. Friedman, "Israel's Best Friend," *New York Times*, 7 March 2012, A27.

16. Kristof, "Pinched and Griping in Iran," WK11.

17. Isabel Kershner, "Israeli Strike on Iran Would be 'Stupid' Ex Spy Chief Says," *New York Times*, May 8, 2011, http://www.nytimes.com/2011/05/09/world/middleeast/09israel.html.

18. It should be obvious that living under Israeli military control inherently means that basic human rights are restricted. See David Shulman, "Israel and Palestine: Breaking the Silence," *New York Review of Books*, February 24, 2011, 42–44.

19. Mofaz is quoted in Ethan Bronner, "Defying an Image With at Tilt to the Left," *New York Times*, April 2, 2012, A9.

20. Ehud Olmert, Peace Now, or Never," *New York Times*, September 22, 2011, A27.

21. Bernard Avishai, "A Separate Peace," *New York Times Magazine*, February 13, 2011, 50. Also see Nathan Thrall, "The Third Intifada Is Inevitable," *New York Times,* June 24, 2012, WK10.

22. Ben Birnbaum, "The Visionary: A Palestinian reformer's downfall," *The New Republic,* Mary 24, 2012 , 16.

23. There is a widespread "sense of alienation from the state felt by many Arab citizens, who make up 20 percent of Israel's population," largely based in the feeling that they do not possess all the same rights as Jewish Israelis and also face discrimination. See Isabel Kershner, "Israeli Cabinet's Draft of New Citizenship Pledge Faces Wave of Criticism, *New York Times,* October 11, 2010, A4. Also see Shulman, "Israel and Palestine: Breaking the Silence," 42–44.

24. See Rowland and Frank, 30.

25. *Ronald Reagan, Speaking My Mind: Selected Speeches (New York: Simon and Schuster, 1989),* 107, *108.*

26. This argument is developed in detail in Robert C. Rowland, "Principle, Pragmatism, and Authenticity in Reagan's Rhetoric," paper presented at the Ronald Reagan Centennial an Academic Symposium, the University of Southern California and the Reagan Presidential Library, February 2, 2011; Robert C. Rowland and John M. Jones, *Reagan at Westminster: Foreshadowing the End of the Cold War* (College Station: Texas A & M University Press, 2010).

27. See Rowland and Frank, 105–110.

28. Menachem Begin: We Will Fulfill Commitment To The End," *FBIS* 3 March 1982, I6-I10.

29. See Begin is qtd. in Colin Shindler, *Israel, Likud and the Zionist Dream: Power Politcs and Ideology from Begin to Netanyahu* (London: I.B. Tauris, 1995), 149–150. Begin made a very similar statement in a meeting with the Knesset Foreign Affairs Committee on June 13, 1982. See "Begin Cites Historical Examples of Cities Bombed," *FBIS* 15 June 1982: I2. Also Rowland and Frank, 151–154.

8 Traumatic Myth, the Middle Voice, and Genuine Argumentation in the Israeli-Palestinian Civil War

David Frank

Consider two horrific historical events: Deir Yassin and the Holocaust (European Shoah). Deir Yassin is the name of a small village on the outskirts of Jerusalem that was the site of a massacre of 120 Palestinians, many women and children, on Friday, April 9, 1948 by Irgun irregular forces.[1] The Deir Yassin massacre is one tragic event illustrative of the *Nakba,* or catastrophe, in which over 800,000 Palestinians were expelled from their homes and land in 1948.[2] The European *Shoah* represents the murder of seven million Jews between 1933 and 1945, a result of European anti-Semitism, Adolf Hitler's rhetoric, the betrayal of European cosmopolitan values, and the industrialization of genocide.[3] Many have learned about the Shoah through Anne Frank's diary[4] and the movie *Schindler's List,* making concrete the tragedy with the image of a little girl in the red coat fleeing the Nazis during the Warsaw uprising.[5] Deir Yassin and the little girl in the red coat capture the historic suffering of Palestinians and Israelis with the illustrations needed for humans to understand catastrophe, but the larger traumatic myths they inform, the *Nakba* and the *Shoah,* can become in argumentative encounters sublime, beyond the pale of reasonable argument.

Jeff Goldberg in *Prisoners: A Muslim and a Jew Across the Middle East Divide* writes that he came to understand that Deir Yassin is translated into the "argumentum ad Yassinum, the Katyusha rocket in the arsenal of Palestinian rhetoric" (36). Goldberg reports he is "never surprised, in debates, to hear a Palestinian immediately invoke Deir Yassin as the truth that trumps all Jewish truths" (36). Similarly, the introduction of the Holocaust into the arguments about the Israeli-Palestinian conflict can, as Philip Lopate in his *Portrait of My Body* writes, dead-end "all intelligent discourse by intruding a stridently shrill note that forces the mind to withdraw. . . . The image of the Holocaust is too overbearing, too hot to tolerate distinctions. In its life as a rhetorical figure, the Holocaust is a bully" (92). The Israeli-Palestinian conflict reveals that genuine argument is often sidetracked by traumas expressed in transhistoric terms.

Deir Yassin, the Nakba, and the European Shoah are historical traumas that have historical contexts (Palestine 1948; Europe 1933–1945) and an indeterminacy resisting reduction to a simple explanation and ultimate purpose. They constitute horrific events nested in a particular time and place. However, these traumas are often cast in transcendental mythic terms, offering some of the central symbolic forms used by Israelis and Palestinians to justify their own identities and violent action.[6] In this chapter, I seek to examine how genuine argument can take place between Israelis and Palestinians when historic traumas do not rule.[7]

To accomplish this aim, I study Carolin Emcke's account in *Echoes of Violence* of an argumentative exchange she had with an Arab photographer who, as they surveyed Palestinian suffering in Lebanon, declared he wished Hitler had killed all the Jews.[8] I then consider the Geneva initiative, which offers a number of compromises most reasonable Palestinians and Israelis would grudgingly accept. I conclude by reviewing the riparian model of conflict management and illustrate it with a brief discussion of an Israeli, Jordanian, and Palestinian collaboration intended to save the Jordan River, efforts to share Jerusalem and Hebron, and ongoing pragmatic arrangements that make life easier in Palestine/Israel. I fully acknowledge the profoundly dysfunctional larger pattern of rhetoric at play in the conflict, but I can point to more productive displays of Israeli-Palestinian argumentation as well. To better understand how genuine argumentation can be used to work through trauma, I provide a brief overview of trauma theory through the work of Dominick LaCapra.

Working through Trauma with Argument

Dominick LaCapra, in a series of articles and books, has explained how trauma is acted out and can be worked through.[9] Trauma is acted out when the patterns of the original trauma are rehearsed in an inalterable pattern. The difference between the past and present is collapsed, and no critical space is allowed between the historic trauma and the present. LaCapra is always quick to challenge those who argue that a traumatic past should be interned and its evil put to rest. Rather, he argues that trauma involves some acting out, but that it becomes pathologic when traumas become structural, transhistorical, metaphysical, and expressed in ideological myth.

An ideological myth is immune to questioning and experience and takes the form of a deduction.[10] Both Deir Yassin and the Holocaust can be used by advocates to reduce the world to a single explanation based on historical trauma. For Palestinians, Deir Yassin represents the total evil of Zionism, and in some cases, Judaism, as forces of genocide. The myth of Deir Yassin neglects the role played by Palestinian leaders in their own demise and, when taken as the representative anecdote of the Nakba, it neglects the desperate state of many Jews in the wake of World War II, a historical account provided by the most important scholar of Palestinian politics and history, Rashid Khalidi.[11] I must, of course, rush to state that Khalidi is not "blaming the victims," nor does he absolve Zionists of their responsibility for the Nakba; he does insist on placing the Palestinian trauma in its context. Similarly, the European Shoah is used by some Israelis to depict the world as essentially anti-Semitic. Israel, working from this premise, becomes, in Thomas Friedman's terms, a "Yad Vashem [the Israeli Holocaust museum] with an air force" (281).

Ideological myths are beyond the pale of questioning and interrogation, and argumentation controlled by these myths becomes less a process of testing reasons and evidence than a compulsive repetition of claims. Acting out trauma may be necessary at a given moment, but when it is compulsive, unthinking, and resistant to experience and the passage of time, it becomes pathological. LaCapra identifies working through trauma as an alternative to pathological acting out. Working through trauma is, essentially, an act of genuine argument. According to LaCapra,

> Working-through implies the possibility of judgment that is not apodictic or ad hominem but argumentative, self-questioning, and related in mediated ways to action. In this sense, it is bound up with the role of distinctions that are not purely binary oppositions but marked by varying and contestable degrees of strength or weakness (*Representing the Holocaust* 210).

To work through trauma, one must engage in an argumentative act of self-questioning, a testing of the degrees to which a claim is strong or weak. The historicity of trauma is granted; in the case of the Palestinian-Israeli conflict,

Deir Yassin is vested with the status of historical fact as is the Holocaust, but the meaning of both remains open to interrogation, ethical inquiry, and an understanding that may unfold over time. For example, Deir Yassin remains a great tragedy in Rashid Khalidi's history, but it does not prevent him from both blaming the Zionists for their role in the Palestinian dispersion and Palestinian leaders for their pre-1948 failures of strategy and tactics.[12] Similarly, Saul Friedlander, the well-regarded historian of the Holocaust, has insisted that the meaning of the Holocaust is not fixed, that we should continue to ask questions about its history and ethical meaning (3–15). Again, both Khalidi and Friedlander do not deny or question the basic or essential historicity of Deir Yassin and the Holocaust; rather, they insist that the two events remain within the realms of lived history and argument. In these realms, there are stronger and weaker versions of truth, ethics, and history dependent on the proof offered in support of claims.

Genuine argument can and does break out when historical traumas are not fully absorbed by structural assumptions (LaCapra, *Writing History Writing Trauma* 82). As an expression of genuine argument, "working through" seeks a future that acknowledges and confronts historic trauma but is not held hostage by it. What is lost must be mourned. Without mourning, melancholy can break out, locking in a permanent state of grief. Accordingly, one of the more effective linguistic approaches to genuine argument in response to trauma is use of the middle voice (White 179–80). There are, of course, a host of other voices that should be heard when working through trauma, but the middle voice offers a strong glide path to genuine argument.

The middle voice is modulated, giving agency to history, victims, survivors, bystanders, and those living in the present. In contrast, the passive voice offers little agency, and the active voice vests actors with determinative freedom, beyond constraints. The middle voice navigates between the passive and active voices to provide the space necessary to consider and reconsider the implications of trauma (Crownshaw 12–14). Those who use the middle voice seek to interrogate their own traumas and those of their enemies for illumination. Scholars note the middle voice lends an aporetic openness to argument and a reflexivity inviting the possibility that those working through trauma can achieve a better contextualization of their traumatic myths. The characteristics of the middle voice can be summarized as follows: It allows for some indeterminacy, is reflexive, invites reconsideration of subject positions (victim, aggressor, bystander, etc.), and can challenge or rectify efforts to engage in an unmediated transfer of traumatic myths to new generations.

When, in contemporary arguments between Israelis and Palestinians, Deir Yassin is introduced as a symbol intended to "trump all Jewish truths" and the Holocaust is used to create analogies transforming Palestinians into

Nazis, then Palestinian and Israeli traumatic myths are transferred from their original contexts without recontextualization, making genuine argument impossible. To illustrate how the use of the middle voice can escape the toxic grips of ideological myth, consider the 1988 Palestinian Declaration of Independence and how it frames the Nakba. Between 1948 and 1988, Palestinians acted out the trauma of the Nakba by denying the existential reality of Israel; by 1988, Palestinians had regained their pride as a result of the intifada, and they began the process of working through their trauma by acknowledging their new realities—there would be no return to a Palestine before the establishment of the State of Israel.[13]

The Palestinian Declaration of Independence, Francis Boyle explains, "created a remarkable opportunity for peace with Israel."[14] Mahmud Darwish, the distinguished Palestinian poet, wrote the document in Arabic, which was then cast into English by Edward Said (Khalidi 194). It is this sentence in the declaration that illustrates the adoption of the middle voice:

> Despite the historical injustice inflicted on the Palestinian Arab people resulting in their dispersion and depriving them of their right to self-determination, following upon U.N. General Assembly Resolution 181 (1947), which partitioned Palestine into two states, one Arab, one Jewish, yet it is this Resolution that still provides those conditions of international legitimacy that ensure the right of the Palestinian Arab people to sovereignty.

As Boyle notes, until the Declaration of Independence, Resolution 181 "had been deemed to be a criminal act," and the "acceptance of the Partition Resolution in their actual Declaration of Independence signaled the genuine desire by the Palestinian people to transcend the bitter conflict with the Jewish people. . . ."[14] This passage effectively placed a wedge between the 1948 Nakba and the political realities faced by Palestinians in 1988, affected as they were by the first intifada, effectively refusing to transfer the original Palestinian trauma myth into the present without modification.

Similarly, the Israeli peace movement, led by Shalom Aschav (Peace Now), has articulated, using the middle voice, an Israeli vision operating within the limits of the green line, a two-state solution, a shared Jerusalem, and a severe critique of West Bank and Gaza Jewish settlements (Frank 165–182). Formed by Israelis celebrated for their military experience, the movement drew from a new generation of Israelis who saw themselves as self-reliant, and they did not conflate their identities with those of the Holocaust generation (Harman 45–46, 53). Most of the larger and smaller groups operating under the larger Israeli peace movement constellation hold true to the purpose of Zionism and the need for Israel to be a Jewish state. The Israeli peace movement seeks to limit territorial expansion precisely because it threatens the Jewish character of Israel.

The Palestinian Declaration of Independence and the rise of the Israeli peace movement were results of genuine argument that took place within the Palestinian and Israeli nations. Genuine argumentation, I suggest, is most often engaged in the middle voice. The middle voice can serve the cause of genuine argumentation, which can provoke attitude changes, putting at risk the status of trauma myths held by those who live by and through them.

To summarize, genuine argumentation can be a vehicle for working through trauma. Henry W. Johnstone's observation that genuine argumentation, compared to other forms of reasoning, entails risk of self and identity is informative here, as argumentation questions the evidence offered in support of traumatic claims; it does not treat them as sublime or beyond the realm of reason.[15] However, those engaged in genuine argument about trauma and its meaning fully acknowledge how traumatic suffering informs identity. Similarly, Chaïm Perelman and Lucie Olbrechts-Tyteca's *New Rhetoric: A Treatise on Argumentation* outlines a theory of argumentation intended to work through the traumas of World War II and beyond. They identify *argument* and *argumentation* as the vehicle that can be used to work with and through trauma.[16] In the three illustrations I provide below of genuine argumentation, the theories of Johnstone, Perelman, and Olbrechts-Tyteca are in play.

Emcke's Argument with B

Emcke is a German national and a *Der Spiegel* war correspondent; her *Echoes of Violence* is a collection of letters to friends in which she struggles with the meaning of the cruelty she witnessed in Iraq, Lebanon, Afghanistan, and New York City on September 11. The chapter on her experience in Lebanon turns on her journey through the land of the Hezbollah and her exposure to Palestinian suffering. She employed an Arab driver and a photographer she calls B. As a German national, she responded by placing Hitler and National Socialism in its context, demonstrating empathy for the Palestinians and Israelis and inviting the photographer to consider how "the experience of injustice all too often immunizes against the suffering of others" (Emcke 67). Her response, I believe, is an exemplary illustration of genuine argument that helps to work through trauma.

"Never before" Emcke writes, "have I been confronted with so many people who admire Hitler. Unfortunately, one of them was our photographer" (65). She remained silent in the face of his "occasional anti-Semitic rants, his occasional praise for the Nazis, and his pronouncements of sympathy for Hitler" (65) Her confrontation with a crude display of anti-Semitism invited her to reflect on her childhood as a girl in postwar Germany. "When I was a child, it was a normal phenomenon that when we were on class trips to the Netherlands or Denmark, other children would throw stones at us, cursing us as Nazi kids." Before opening her mouth to confront B, she engages in an interrogation of her personal history and that of her home country. In so doing, she found "outrageous" that Germany was the subject of B's praise for its treatment of Jews. In a telling statement, Emcke observed:

> It seemed difficult to explain my rejection of Nazism and my relationship with Jews or with Israel to our photographer, B, and others without losing their confidence in me as a fair-minded journalist, as someone who could report just as critically about Israel and its human rights violations as about the terrorist activities of Hezbollah and authoritarian Syria (65).

At this moment in her exchange with B, she adroitly positions herself, situating Israel's human rights abuses and those of Palestinian resistance movements and Syria in the context of her own connection to Germany and the Third Reich. In so doing, she defined German, Jewish, and Palestinian trauma in historic rather than transhistorical terms.

Emcke, however, kept these introspections to herself for two days. Upon return from the village Khiam, the site of terrible violence and bloodshed, the result of a battle between the Israeli defense force and Hezbollah, B declared:

I would preferred it if Hitler had killed them all, the Jews (65).

Emcke knew she could not remain silent, asked the driver to stop the car, and directly engaged the claim made by B.

Emcke meditated on the conditions she thought would be necessary to "set the historical facts straight" and to "explain the significance" of the Holocaust to B. How was she to get these facts straight for B and others "directly affected by the displacement and exodus of European Jews?" (65). She lamented the potential for dialogue "about such irreconcilable experiences" that, for her, would take place in a car, on a highway, and for a limited moment in time. It seemed, to her, a "hopeless" prospect.

Emcke recognized that a major barrier to dialogue and argument with B was the transhistorical assumptions about Jews and Israelis held by many Arabs:

> Jews have always been Israelis, and Israelis have always been perpetrators, not victims—this was the distorted formula of many in the Middle East. Those who subscribed to it ignored Jewish or German history, the immeasurable suffering the Jews experienced (65).

Those who subscribe to this conflation of Judaism with Israel, and Israeli human rights violations as a function of an eternal and essential evil, smack of an anti-Semitism that is profoundly mythic in its character. The trauma suffered by Palestinians, in this narrative, is cast in ahistoric terms, elevating both the Palestinian victim and the Israeli oppressor beyond the context of time.

Emcke's acute rhetorical intuitions led her to understand that B needed to be "coaxed into a story" requiring him and others to "imagine Jews as defenseless, marginalized, displaced, and finally murdered victims" (67). Here, Emcke's view of the discourse and rhetoric needed to work through trauma is Baconian. Francis Bacon argued that reason alone, raw logical appeals, could not move the will of humans to action. In Bacon's rhetoric, imagination is a power of the mind and soul to which reason is applied for the purposes of right action.[17] Emcke realizes a simple rehearsal of the historical facts would be insufficient, that as "accustomed as they were to fear and rejection of Jews, it took a slow, careful telling of the story of the Holocaust to open up their minds to understanding and compassion" (67). The story she told was the abbreviated version, and she reports she "talked for a long time" (67).

Emcke told B he could "curse her as a German, for the wars we have forced on the world, for the destruction of Jewish life in Eastern Europe, for the disgusting, unbelievable industrial extermination of millions of people, and for the Holocaust—and rightly so." However, she insisted, B "should never again dare to praise Hitler and his unprecedented crimes in my presence" (67). In so doing, Emcke created a wedge between that episode of German history and her current understanding of German identity, one that has changed dramatically in the wake of World War II and the Holocaust.[18] She insisted, in her resistance to B, that B not assume, because she was German, that she would agree with his celebration of Hitler and his claims.

The conversation continued:

> And then all of us, one after another, began talking about our pasts, about the real and imagined experiences of each of our societies.
>
> We talked about how difficult it is to free oneself from the special treatment of these roles of victims—and not to become indifferent to others (67).

Her arguments against B seemed to open up the possibility of talking about their pasts and histories with a context, that there are both real and imagined experiences of trauma that invite a working-through with argumentation.

On reflection, Emcke noted, the "experience of injustice all too often immunizes against the suffering of others" (67). It may be that her invitation to B that he imagine the story of Jewish suffering in Europe prompted him to have more empathy for Israelis, a feeling that would not absolve the Jewish state of human rights violations; rather, it would put them in their context.

Emcke concludes the story with a reference to the twentieth-century painter Francis Bacon and his famous oil paintings of *Heads*. These paintings, Emcke observes, capture the agony of twentieth-century suffering with "disembodied figures and distorted faces" that "hover in an almost depthless space, imbued with agony" (68). She notes that what "is missing in Bacon's images—and I am reminded of this on our journey through Lebanon—are the eyes. These mistreated figures are no longer capable of gazing outward. Their agony absorbs everything; displacing their perceptions into their inner selves—and the outside world becomes invisible" (68). Although she does not make her reference explicit, she may have seen that B, because of the agony he may have suffered, was not able to look beyond his inner self. Her argument with him may have allowed him to extend his imagination, empathy, and understanding beyond his own trauma.

Her argument begins with recognition of her subject position, one she interrogates with an interior monologue. Using the middle voice, she insists on fidelity to historical facts while engaging Germans, Palestinians, and Israelis with empathy and an invitation to imagination. She also recognizes the problems of transference and holds that rapprochement is possible when the structural and historical traumas of the self and others are understood with the use of critical reason and argument.

My reflection on Emcke's argument with B suggests that genuine argument is often undermined by trauma, expressed in its transhistoric and metaphysical fashion. Indeed, what often passes as argument in traumatic contexts are expressions of acting out.

To work through trauma, one must engage in argumentative encounters that allow for the participants to work through the issues they face. LaCapra does not hold that working through is always better than acting out; nor does he deny the role of hyperbole, anger, and the rehearsal of tragic events in ultimately living with or through trauma. He does suggest that acting out should not be a state of being, and that working through trauma with argumentation can cultivate better recognition of the other. The Geneva Initiative established a communicative process that allowed Palestinians and Israelis to argue with each other, doing so to produce a reasonable set of compromises.

The Geneva Initiative

Amos Oz, a founder of the Peace Now movement, observed in his *Land of Israel* that he preferred a Chekhovian rather than a Shakespearean resolution to the Israeli-Palestinian conflict (260). A Shakespearean resolution leaves the stage "strewn with dead bodies, and maybe there's some justice hovering high above." In contrast, a Chekhovian resolution "ends with everyone disillusioned, embittered, heartbroken, disappointed, absolutely shattered, but still alive." The Geneva initiative sets forth a Chekhovian resolution. The process used by Palestinians and Israelis in the Geneva Initiative involved a series of secret negotiations, assisted by mediators, between experienced and knowledgeable Israelis and Palestinians. The negotiations produced a host of rational compromises, suggesting it is possible to work through Israeli and Palestinian traumas with reasoned discourse. These compromises included:

- A declaration of an end to the conflict and future claims by both Israelis and Palestinians.
- A mutual recognition of both nations and their right to an independent state.
- Almost complete Israeli withdrawal to the 1967 borders, with a limited number of settlement blocs on the basis of a 1:1 land swap.
- A comprehensive solution to the issue of the Palestinian refugees based on the Clinton Parameters (2000), of which the main component will be compensation and a return to an independent Palestinian state.
- Jewish Jerusalem as Israel's capital and Arab Jerusalem as Palestine's capital, with Jewish areas under Israeli sovereignty and Arab areas under Palestinian sovereignty.
- A nonmilitarized Palestinian state and detailed security arrangements.

Many Palestinians and Israelis agree that these compromises are reasonable. The Palestinians and Israelis responsible for these compromises accomplished them through a process of genuine argumentation.

Menachem Klein, in his book *A Possible Peace Between Israel and Palestine*, details how Palestinians and Israelis argued to these compromises.[18] With the assistance of President Thabo Mbeki of South Africa, a group of Palestinians and Israelis met to establish the conditions necessary for genuine argument on the issues dividing the two peoples. Klein reports:

> At the request of President Mbeki, we [Israelis] and the Palestinians both engaged in self-criticism alongside criticism of each other.... [The Israeli] critical stance toward [its] own government impelled [the] Palestinian counterparts to address not just the injustices committed by Israel but also their own errors (23).

The Palestinians and Israelis who engaged the Geneva process did so by turning the critical light of argumentative reason in all directions, including the collective self.

According to Klein, the Palestinian delegation acknowledged the need for the Palestinians to better frame the 1948 trauma for the Israeli audience, the disadvantages of the armed militias, and the failure of Palestinian leadership to advance the cause of peace. The Israeli delegation, including Klein were clear they believed Israeli settlements were a major mistake, and they focused significant criticism toward their government (23). In so doing, both Israelis and Palestinians created the context necessary for genuine argument. Palestinians and Israelis, in their arguments, engaged a strategy of "mutual gain;" the function of argumentation during the Geneva process was less to impose a claim on the audience than to seek out how Israeli and Palestinian claims might be reconciled (Schechet 128). This strategy invited use of the middle voice.

The Nakba and the Holocaust served as historic backdrops of the Geneva initiative, but the negotiators did not treat them as tragedies that would prevent them from dealing with the present and the future. With the 1988 Palestinian Declaration of Independence reframing of the 1948 Palestinian traumatic myth, the Israeli endorsement of the Oslo accords and the recognition of a Palestinian people, the Geneva negotiators found commonplaces they could use in their argumentation. However, they went beyond mutual recognition to developing a truly pragmatic set of compromises. In the third illustration, I highlight the power of the riparian model of conflict management, one that places an emphasis on mutual gain and survival.

The Riparian Illustration

In a 2002 article in *Political Geography*, the geographer Shaul Cohen and I introduced what we call the "riparian model" of conflict management.[19] We discovered that very few, if any, wars or major conflicts have been waged over water resources, a discovery backed by significant scholarship.[20] We sought to identify the reasons why. Riparian negotiation, we discovered, encourages movement from rights to needs, the utilization of time as a variable, a focus on how water might be shared for mutual benefit, and the "creation of language recognizing local contingencies (Cohen and Frank 745). We then, as a thought experiment, applied the lessons gained from riparian negotiations to the conflict between Israelis and Palestinians over the city of Jerusalem. Although the city is not literally in a body of water, it is nested within a historic basin.

We suggested, and were certainly not the first, that Jerusalem should be treated as a problem of human geography, not simply as a sacred and sublime city, resisting the reach of reason and compromise. If rivers and water, which are often deemed "sacred," yield to sharing, why, we asked, couldn't the riparian principles of negotiation help with the problem of Jerusalem? In the last decade, some efforts to mediate the problem of Jerusalem framed it as a basin open to reconfiguration. The arrangement in Hebron, in which Jews and Arabs share the same building but during different days of the week is yet another illustration of accommodation in the Israeli-Palestinian conflict, although one undermined by the occupation by Jewish settlers.[21]

By broadening the frame used to define the space of Jerusalem, then the sacred sites within the city could be considered part of a larger more cosmopolitan whole. All parties would have access and a claim on their sacred space, but both would operate within the limits of time. The needs of Jews, Muslims, and Christians could be better balanced with identity rights and claims by enlarging the basin of the city to include the western slope, the Old City, Mount Zion, Christian sites, the Mount of Olives, and the carefully constructed boundaries identified by Lapidoth and her workgroup.[22] Even the sacred space, within the larger basin, could be shared by religious groups at different times. Lifting Jerusalem out of its abstract and mythic status can liberate those who wish to engage in genuine argument about how the city might be shared. As an illustration of the riparian model's potential, consider the recent negotiations between Israeli Prime Minister Ehud Olmert and Palestinian President Mahmoud Abbas.

According to Bernard Avishai's account, Olmert and Abbas met thirty-six times between 2006 and 2008. They argued about all the issues dividing them and their two peoples. However, as Avishai writes, "Olmert and Abbas departed from transcendental claims to holy space and decided to base a solution on the practical challenge of governing the holy sites—so as to maximize access for all pilgrims from the three Abrahamic religions . . ." (MM 26). The two treated Jerusalem as a "basin," and in the context of the larger negotiations.

The really creative ideas were about the disposition of the Old City and holy places—the Islamic sites of the Haram Al-Sharif (or Temple Mount), the Western Wall, the Church of the Holy Sepulcher and so forth, which both sides agreed were indeed part of the "holy basin." Olmert suggested that it be governed by a kind of custodial committee, made up of five countries: Palestine, Jordan, Saudi Arabia, the US and Israel. (Abbas was under the impression that as many as seven trustees might be involved, including Egypt and the Vatican.) Itamar Rabinovich writes that the Jerusalem problem was addressed by Olmert and Abbas "with comparative ease" (179). Although the negotiations were not brought to a close because Abbas and Olmert disagreed on the inclusion of Abu Tor and the nearby City of David in the holy basin, the reframing of the city as constituting a larger basin and their willingness to challenge the existing political definition of Jerusalem's character by their respective communities was courageous, reflecting genuine argument.

Palestinians and Israelis have reached accommodations at the local level, "driven by practical exigencies rather than conflicting ideologies" (Cohen 733–43). Cohen details a rich history of territorial pragmatism often ignored in the more global accounts of the Israeli-Palestinian conflict. In his research on the West Bank, Cohen has witnessed multiple instances of "accommodations . . . in contests over specific parcels of disputed land, and that civilians, government workers, security forces, and PLO operatives were able to navigate in ways that belied the zero-sum rhetoric generated by politicians and uncritically replicated by academics" (743). These accommodations were "off the books," a result of informal discussion and argument. Certainly in the context of a brutal occupation by the Israelis Defense Force, it is hard to imagine the possibility of genuine argument. However, Cohen documents communicative exchanges between the IDF and local Palestinian leaders that reduced tension and kept the peace, demonstrating that "people are able to peruse specific accommodations without abandoning their claims to rights or a nationalist agenda" (743).

A third illustration is the effort made by the Jordanians, Israelis, and Palestinians concert to clean up the Jordan River. According to an October 2, 2012 account in *Haaretz*.[22] Palestinian, Israeli, and Jordanian activists have pressured their respective governments to collaborate in an effort to save a river the three nations share. Purification plants are under construction, and there are ongoing discussions concerning water quantity and quality. The "Friends of the Earth-Middle East," a group with members from the three nations, "has successfully pressured their governments into acting to save the river."[23] This "pressure" is that of argumentation.

Of course, my central claim, that genuine argument can assist Israelis and Palestinians in their efforts to achieve a rapprochement is challenged by the ongoing occupation, which keeps Palestinians in what Khalidi calls an "Iron Cage" of agony and despair.[24] However, as Sari Nusseibeh notes, the answer to the occupation and the Palestinian liberation from the Iron Cage is not violence and force, but the use of universally shared values to ground the use of reason to deal with difference and disagreement (167). Nusseibeh shifts the burden to those who advocate violence, recognizing they have good reason to condemn the violence of the occupation, to demonstrate the physical force will do more good than harm. In the place of violence, Nusseibeh suggests a realism tempered with moral dialogue.

Conclusion

The Palestinian-Israeli conflict is a civil war rooted in historic trauma, not an eternal and immutable "clash of civilizations."[25] Violence and war have not improved the standard of living or workable settlements. Eventually, the conflict will yield to accommodations that look much like the Geneva initiative, which will be the result of interpersonal arguments similar to those between Emcke and B, the local accommodations reached by Israelis and Palestinians on the ground, and the negotiations between leaders of the two countries that move to pragmatic arguments that allow both peoples to maintain what is sacred and central to their respective identities. The shards of trauma—the Holocaust and the Nakba—inform and warp how Palestinians and Israelis argue. Emcke's confrontation with B, one in which she demonstrates empathy for Palestinian suffering while confronting B's symbolic acting out, offers a vivid illustration of how argumentation can be used to work through trauma. In adopting the middle voice, Emcke reframed how B depicted Germans, Israelis, and Palestinians, suggesting they all had agency in their fates.

Reflecting Pinker's global claim that humans are less violent in this century than in the last, and that a flexible system of reason is more often in use than in the past, leading Palestinian and Israeli politicians and intellectuals, as evidenced by the Geneva initiative, are insisting on the use of argumentative reason rather than physical force to reach a settlement in their civil war.[26] Refusing the lure of framing the conflict primarily through the lens of Deir Yassin and the Holocaust, these Israelis and Palestinians draw lessons from these traumas that invite them to work through their differences through hard negotiations and third party mediations. In so doing, they make a powerful claim that physical force does not raise the dead, liberate land, or do more than create spirals of violence. The alternative to acting out is genuine argument, using among other techniques, the middle voice, to work through trauma toward a reasonable but contested settlement.

Notes:

1. See Walid Khalidi, *All That Remains: The Palestininan Villages Occupied and Destroyed by Israel in 1948* (Washington: Institute for Palestinian Studies, 1992), Daniel A. McGowan and Marc H. Ellis, *Remembering Deir Yassin: The Future of Israel and Palestine, Voices & Visions.* (New York: Olive Branch Press, 1998).

2. Ahmad H. Sa'di and Lila Abu-Lughod, *Nakba: Palestine, 1948, and the Claims of Memory, Cultures of History.* (New York: Columbia University Press, 2007).

3. Peter Hayes and John K. Roth, *The Oxford Handbook of Holocaust Studies* (New York: Oxford University Press, 2010).

4. "Ann Frank," *The Holocaust Encyclopedia,* eds. Walter Laqueur and Judith Tydor Baumel (New Haven: Yale University Press, 2001).

5. See Caroline Joan Picart and David A. Frank, *Frames of Evil: The Holocaust as Horror in American Film* (Carbondale: Southern Illinois University Press, 2006).

6. For a recent exploration of the role played by the Holocaust and the Nakba, see Yair Auron, *Israeli Identities: Jews and Arabs Facing the Self and the Other* (New York: Berghahn Books, 2012).

7. For a study of the trajectories of argument in the Israeli/Palestinian civil war, see Robert C. Rowland and David A. Frank, *Shared Land/Conflicting Identity: Trajectories of Israeli and Palestinian Symbol Use*, Rhetoric and Public Affairs Series. (East Lansing: Michigan State University Press, 2002).

8. Carolin Emcke, *Echoes of Violence: Letters from a War Reporter*, Human Rights and Crimes against Humanity (Princeton: Princeton University Press, 2007).

9. Dominic LaCapra, "Personal, the Political and the Textual: Paul De Man as Object of Transference," *History & Memory* 4 (1992), Dominick LaCapra, *Representing the Holocaust: History, Theory, Trauma* (Ithaca: Cornell University Press, 1994), Dominick LaCapra, *History and Memory after Auschwitz* (Ithaca, NY: Cornell University Press, 1998), Dominick LaCapra, *Writing History, Writing Trauma* (Baltimore: Johns Hopkins University Press, 2001), Dominick LaCapra, *History in Transit: Experience, Identity, Critical Theory* (Ithaca, N.Y.: Cornell University Press, 2004).

10. See Hannah Arendt, *The Origins of Totalitarianism* (Cleveland: World, 1958).

11. Rashid Khalidi, "The Palestininians and 1948: The Underlying Causes of Failure," *The War for Palestine: Rewriting the History of 1948*, eds. Eugene L. Rogan and Avi Shlaim (Cambridge; New York: Cambridge University Press, 2001). See as well Rashid Khalidi. *Palestinian Identity* New York: Columbia University Press, 1997).

12. Khalidi, "The Palestininians and 1948: The Underlying Causes of Failure."

13. See my work and collaboration with Robert Rowland on this point: David A. Frank, "The Mutability of Rhetoric: Haydar 'Abd AlShafi's Madrid Speech and Vision of PalestinianIsraeli Rapprochement," *Quarterly Journal of Speech* 86.3 (2000): 334–53, David A. Frank, "My Enemy's Enemy Is My Friend: A Close Reading of the Palestinian Response to the Gulf Crisis," *Communication Studies* 45.3–4 (1994): 309–24, R.C. Rowland and D.A. Frank, "Mythic Rhetoric and Rectification in the Israeli-Palestinian Conflict," *Communication Studies* 62.1 (2011): 41–57, Rowland and Frank, *Shared Land/Conflicting Identity: Trajectories of Israeli and Palestinian Symbol Use.*

14. Francis Anthony Boyle, *The Palestinian Right of Return under International Law* (Atlanta: Clairty Press, 2009).

15. Henry W. Johnstone, *Philosophy and Argument* (University Park: Pennsylvania State University Press, 1959).

16. Chaïm Perelman and Lucie Olbrechts-Tyteca, *The New Rhetoric: A Treatise on Argumentation* (Notre Dame: [Ind.] University of Notre Dame Press, 1969). For an elaboration on Perelman and Olbrechts-Tyteca's new rhetoric as a response to trauma, see David A. Frank, "A Traumatic Reading of Twentieth-Century Rhetorical Theory: The Belgian Holocaust, Malines, Perelman, and De Man " *Quarterly Journal of Speech* 93 (2007): 308–43.

17. See Karl Richards Wallace, *Francis Bacon on Communication & Rhetoric; Or: The Art of Applying Reason to Imagination for the Better Moving of the Will* (Chapel Hill: The University of North Carolina Press, 1943), Karl Richards Wallace, *Francis Bacon on the Nature of Man; the Faculties of Man's Soul: Understanding, Reason, Imagination, Memory, Will, and Appetite* (Urbana: University of Illinois Press, 1967).

18. Menachem Klein, *A Possible Peace between Israel and Palestine: An Insider's Account of the Geneva Initiative (*New York: Columbia University Press, 2007).

19. Shaul Cohen and David A. Frank, "Jerusalem and the Riparian Simile," *Political Geography* 21 (2002): 745–60.

20. Aaron Wolf, "Spiritual Understandings of Conflict and Transformation and Their Contribution to Water Dialogue," *Water Policy* 14 (2012): 73–88, H.A. Amery and A.T. Wolf, *Water in the Middle East: A Geography of Peace*, vol. 200 (University of Texas Press Austin, Texas, USA, 2000). Also, see Cohen and Frank, "Jerusalem and the Riparian Simile."

21. 21. Shaul Cohen and David A. Frank, "Innovative Approaches to Territorial Disputes: Using Principles of Riparian Conflict Management," *Annals of the Association of American Geographers* 99.5 (2009): 948–55.

22. Ruth Lapidoth, *The Historic Basin—Problems and Possible Solutions*. Ed. Amnon Ramon (Jerusalem: The Jerusalem Institute for Israel Studies, 2010).

23. Zafrir Rinat, "Israel, Jordan Taking Steps to Clean up Jordan River Water," *Haaretz* October 2 2012, <http://www.haaretz.com/news/national/israel-jordan-taking-steps-to-clean-up-jordan-river-water-1.467711>.

24. Rashid Khalidi, *The Iron Cage: The Story of the Palestinian Struggle for Statehood,* 1st ed. (Boston: Beacon Press, 2006).

25. Samuel P. Huntington, *The Clash of Civilizations and the Remaking of World Order,* Simon & Schuster hardcover ed. (New York: Simon & Schuster, 2011).

26. Steven Pinker, *The Better Angels of Our Nature: Why Violence Has Declined* (New York: Viking, 2011).

Works Cited

Amery, H.A. and A.T. Wolf, *Water in the Middle East: A Geography of Peace*, Vol. 200 Austin: U of Texas P, 2000. Print.
"Ann Frank," *The Holocaust Encyclopedia*. Ed. Walter Laqueur and Judith Tydor Baumel. New Haven: Yale UP, 2001.
Arendt, Hannah. *The Origins of Totalitarianism*. Cleveland: World, 1958. Print.
Auron, Yair. *Israeli Identities: Jews and Arabs Facing the Self and the Other*. New York: Berghahn Books, 2012. Print.

Avishai, Bernard. "A Plan for Peace That Still Could Be," *New York Times Sunday Magazine*. February 7 2011. Print.
Boyle, Francis. *The Palestinian Right of Return under International Law*. Atlanta: Clarity Press, 2011. Print.
Cohen, Shaul. "Revisiting Territorial Pragmatism in the Palestinian-Israeli Conflict." *Eurasian Geography and Economics* 51.6 (2010): 733–43. Print.
Cohen, Shaul and David A. Frank, "Jerusalem and the Riparian Simile," *Political Geography* 21 (2002): 745–60. Print.
Crownshaw, Richard, Jane Kilby and Antony Rowland. *The Future of Memory*. New York: Berghahn Books, 2010. Print.
Emcke, Carol. *Echoes of Violence: Letters from a War Reporter*. Princeton: Princeton UP, 2007. Print.
Frank, David A. "My Enemy's Enemy Is My Friend: A Close Reading of the Palestinian Response to the Gulf Crisis." *Communication Studies* 45.3–4 (1994): 309–24. Print.
—. "'Shalom Achshav'—Rituals of the Israeli Peace Movement." *Communications Monographs* 48.3 (1981): 165–82. Print.
—. "The Mutability of Rhetoric: Haydar 'Abd Al-Shafi's Madrid Speech and Vision of Palestinian-Israeli Rapprochement." *Quarterly Journal of Speech* 86.3 (2000): 334–53. Print.
—. "A Traumatic Reading of Twentieth-Century Rhetorical Theory: The Belgian Holocaust, Malines, Perelman, and De Man" *Quarterly Journal of Speech* 93 (2007): 308–43. Print.
Rowland, Robert C. and David A. Frank. *Shared Land/Conflicting Identity: Trajectories of Israeli and Palestinian Symbol Use*. Rhetoric and Public Affairs Series. East Lansing: Michigan State UP, 2002). Print.
—. "Mythic Rhetoric and Rectification in the Israeli-Palestinian Conflict." *Communication Studies* 62.1 (2011): 41–57. Print.
Friedlander, Saul. "History, Memory and the Historian: Dilemmas and Responsibilities." *New German Critique*, 80 (2000): 3–15. Print.
Friedman, Thomas L. *From Beirut to Jerusalem: Updated with a New Chapter*. New York: Anchor Books Doubleday, 1995. 281. Print.
Goldberg, Jeffrey. *Prisoners: A Muslim and a Jew across the Middle East Divide*. New York: Knopf, 2006. Print.
Perelman, Chaïm, and Lucie Olbrechts-Tyteca, *The New Rhetoric: A Treatise on Argumentation* Notre Dame: U of Notre Dame P, 1969. Print.
Hayes, Peter, and John K. Roth. *The Oxford Handbook of Holocaust Studies*. New York: Oxford UP, 2010. Print.
Hermann, Tamar S. *The Israeli Peace Movement: A Shattered Dream*. Leiden: Cambridge UP, 2009. Print.
Huntington, Samuel P. *The Clash of Civilizations and the Remaking of World Order*. New York: Simon & Schuster, 2011. Print.
Henry W. Johnstone. *Philosophy and Argument*. University Park: Penn State UP, 1959). Print.

Judt, Tony. *Postwar: A History of Europe since 1945.* New York: Penguin Press, 2005. Print.
Khalidi, Rashid. *The Iron Cage: The Story of the Palestinian Struggle for Statehood.* Boston: Beacon Press, 2006. Print.
—. *Palestinian Identity.* New York: Columbia UP, 1997. Print.
—. "The Palestininians and 1948: The Underlying Causes of Failure." *The War for Palestine: Rewriting the History of 1948.* Ed. Eugene L. Rogan and Avi Shlaim. Cambridge: Cambridge UP, 2001. Print.
Khalidi, Walid. *All That Remains: The Palestininan Villages Occupied and Destroyed by Israel in 1948.* Washington: Institute for Palestinian Studies, 1992. Print.
Klein, Menachem. *A Possible Peace between Israel and Palestine: An Insider's Account of the Geneva Initiative.* New York: Columbia UP, 2007. Print.
LaCapra, Dominick. *History and Memory after Auschwitz.* Ithaca, NY: Cornell UP, 1998. Print.
—. *History in Transit: Experience, Identity, Critical Theory.* Ithaca, NY: Cornell UP, 2004. Print.
—. *Representing the Holocaust: History, Theory, Trauma.* Ithaca, NY: Cornell UP, 1994. Print.
—. *Writing History, Writing Trauma.* Baltimore: Johns Hopkins UP, 2001. Print.
—"Personal, the Political and the Textual: Paul De Man as Object of Transference." *History & Memory* 4 (1992): 538. Print.
Lapidoth, Ruth. *The Historic Basin of Jerusalem Problems and Possible Solutions.* Ed. Amnon Ramon. Jerusalem: The Jerusalem Institute for Israel Studies, 2010. Print.
Lopate, Phillip. *Portrait of My Body.* New York: Anchor Books, 1996. Print.
McGowan, Daniel A., and Marc H. Ellis. *Remembering Deir Yassin: The Future of Israel and Palestine.* New York: Olive Branch Press, 1998. Print.
Nusseibeh, Sari. *What Is a Palestinian State Worth?* Cambridge, MA: Harvard UP, 2011 167. Print.
Oz, Amos. *In the Land of Israel.* New York: Vintage Books, 1984.
Picart, Caroline Joan, and David A. Frank, *Frames of Evil: The Holocaust as Horror in American Film.* Carbondale: Southern Illinois UP, 2006. Print.
Pinker, Steven. *The Better Angels of Our Nature: Why Violence Has Declined.* New York: Viking, 2011. Print.
Rabinovich, Itamar. *The Lingering Conflict: Israel, the Arabs, and the Middle East, 1948–2011.* Washington, DC: Brookings Institution Press, 2011. Print.
Rinat, Zafir. "Israel, Jordan Taking Steps to Clean up Jordan River Water," *Haaretz. com*. October 2 2012. Web.. 1 May 2015.
Sa'di, Ahmad H., and Lila Abu-Lughod, *Nakba: Palestine, 1948, and the Claims of Memory, Cultures of History.* New York: Columbia UP, 2007. Print.
Schechet, Nita. *Disenthralling Ourselves: Rhetoric of Revenge and Reconciliation in Contemporary Israel.* Madison, NJ: Fairleigh Dickinson UP, 2009.
Wallace, Karl Richards. *Francis Bacon on Communication & Rhetoric; Or: The Art of Applying Reason to Imagination for the Better Moving of the Will.* Chapel Hill: U of North Carolina P, 1943. Print.

—. *Francis Bacon on the Nature of Man; the Faculties of Man's Soul: Understanding, Reason, Imagination, Memory, Will, and Appetite*. Urbana: U of Illinois P, 1967. Print.

White, Hayden. "Writing in the Middle Voice " *Stanford Literature Review* 9 (1992): 17987. Print.

Wolf, Aaron. "Spiritual Understandings of Conflict and Transformation and Their Contribution to Water Dialogue." *Water Policy* 14 (2012): 73–88. Print.

9 Poetry and Conflict: on Civility, Citizenship and Criticism

Shai Ginsburg

To think of critical rhetoric—the theme of the present volume—to think critically of rhetoric vis-à-vis poetry in the context of the Israeli-Palestinian conflict—this is my task in what follows. Poetry—inasmuch as it simultaneously establishes a community of interlocutors and challenges it—raises questions of civility and citizenship that are central to the consideration of the Israeli-Palestinian conflict. Inasmuch, that is, as it affirms the identity of that community in and of language even as it provokes its language, poetry opens up a space in which one can read rhetoric—and the rhetoric that is immersed in the conflict between two ethno-national communities all the more so—critically.

These questions are paradigmatically broached by the poetry of Yehuda Amichai (1924–2000), in his poetic corpus as well as in the critical endeavor to account for that corpus. Commonly noted as Israel's most renowned poet, both locally and internationally, critics have hailed his poetry as path breaking. Marked by its use of seemingly (and, perhaps, misleadingly) simple syntax and vocabulary, it was received by the general public as communicative and accessible and gained popularity unmatched by any other Hebrew poet.[1] More than any other poet, then, Amichai is central to the Israeli-Hebrew community of language.

Endeavoring to account for the place of Amichai's corpus in Israeli poetry, critics vacillate between two poles. Some would like to anoint him as Israel's poet laureate, a "post" unmanned since the 1934 death—prior to the establishment of the State—of Hayyim Nachman Bialik. Nili Scharf Gold accordingly titles her recent biographical study of Amichai *The Making of Israel's National Poet*.[2] On the other hand, however, Amichai is often portrayed as *meshorer ezrachi*, that is, as what could be translated as a *civil poet*. In a recent interview, Agi Mishol, a prominent Israeli poet in her own right, says so of her poetry:

> Here and there, I hear that I am called "a national poet," but I associate this expression with the authority of leadership, from which I am far removed. I am truly not made up of the cloth of the preacher at the gate, and I even recoil from people who are unequivocally opinionated about everything. I know how to observe, I am good at looking. Since Uri Zvi Greenberg, Nathan Alterman and Haim Gouri [the poets most identified as giving expression to the national sentiment in the 1940s and 1950s, S. G.], the establishment of national poets, so it seems, had demised. A new poetic establishment, whose founder is Amichai, has emerged in its stead—a civil poet, whose poetry is by and large personal, not submerged in 'big' issues but, rather, gives expression to the mood of Israelis. So in this sense, I am a civil poet.[3]

Mishal posits an opposition between national poets and civil poets. The distinction is, in effect, between two types of poetics: public poetics of decisive expressions, lofty political and moral ideals, and authority and dominion, versus personal poetics of observation and mood, which gives expression to the Israeli human condition.[4] This poetic distinction corresponds to the distinction between two poetico-political visions, between the poet as a lawgiver,[5] and the poet as "one of the people"[6] as subject to state laws, i.e. as a citizen. Amichai, then, is credited, with the poetic-political supersession of the former by the latter. In what follows I would like interrogate his poetics as an act of civil-citizenship: In what sense is Amichai a civil-citizen poet? And how is this civil-citizenship articulated in the context of the Israeli-Palestinian ethno-national conflict?

Dictionary

It is worthwhile pausing here for a moment to consider the field of signification of *ezrachi*—and all the more so since poetry determines a linguistic community. The Even-Shoshan New Hebrew Dictionary, arguably the foremost Hebrew dictionary, defines the noun *ezrach* as follows:

> 1. A native born or a permanent resident in the state, who has full rights, in distinction to the *ger* [the stranger, foreigner, non-permanent resident, one who resides, *gar*]: "One law shall be to him that is homeborn [*ezrach*], and unto the stranger that sojourneth among you" (*Exodus* 12:49). 2. [loan] A well-rooted plant: "spreading himself like a green bay tree [*ezrach*]" (Psalms 37:35). 3. [loan] A deeply-rooted and firmly established man in a particular place or society: so-and so is a citizen [*ezrach*] of the Zionist movement.

The adjective *ezrachi* also denotes the following:

> 1. Of the common civilian, in distinction from the military, the religious, etc. 2. Of the middle class, the bourgeoisie, not of the working class. 3. [Law] adjective for an action pertaining to monetary disputes between person and person and is not within the scope of the criminal.

The comparison with the English definition is revealing. The *OED* thus notes on the etymology of "civil":

> <Anglo-Norman and Middle French *civil* (French *civil*) (in legal use, of a case, law code, etc.) not belonging to criminal law, not belonging to canon law, relating to the relations between ordinary citizens (1290 in Old French), that concerns the citizen or his life, rights, etc. (1330), (of war) occurring within a society (a1413 in *guerre civile*), polite, courteous (c1460), not belonging to the military or religious spheres (1835) and its etymon classical Latin *cīvīlis* of or relating to citizens, (of war) occurring between citizens, of or connected with such war, (of law) for citizens, of or according to such law, forensic, legal, determined by law, (of divisions of time) legally recognized, of or connected with the running of the state, political, relating to the citizen as distinct from the soldier, of or suited to one's status as a citizen, suitable for a private citizen, unassuming, unpretentious. <*cīvis* citizen + -īlis -il suffix. Compare Catalan *civil* (14th cent.), Spanish *civil* (12th cent.), Portuguese *civil* (14th cent.), Italian *civile* (13th cent.); also Middle Dutch *civil* (15th cent.; Dutch *civiel*), German *zivil* (17th cent.). With the semantic development compare SOCIAL adj., and also later CIVIC adj.[7]

Both the Hebrew and the English entries contrast the civil on the one hand, and the military, religious and criminal, on the other. Yet, the distinctions between the English term and the Hebrew one, which are commonly employed as equivalents, are striking. Derived from the "Latin *cīvīl-is* of or pertaining to citizens," that is, "an inhabitant of a city or (often) of a town,"[8] the English term has as its foundation an urban (and, by extension, the body politics of the state as a city writ large) setting. Within this setting, it marks a public realm, legally defined, of interaction and culpability beyond the pale of warfare or faith, on the one hand, and of bodily harm, on the other.

The character of the Hebrew *ezrachi* is very different. Derived from the radix *z/r/ch*, that which is clear, bright, and pure, it suggests an essence, a state or a condition of being that applies to the human as well as to the natural realms, blurring the boundaries between the two. The legal contrast between the citizen and the stranger (a contrast that the insistence that there should be no legal distinction between the two merely accentuates) could thus be interpreted not only as the contrast between the local and the outsider, but also between the embedded and the impermanent, the inborn and the acquired, the pure and the impure, the clear and the obscure.

More explicitly than the English *civil*, the Hebrew *ezrachi* designates a class affiliation. Whereas the English term obscures the relationship between the legal, economic, social and political formations, the Hebrew term conflates these: the *ezrach* is a member of the middle class. His identity is construed (particularly in pre-State Hebrew rhetoric) in opposition (political and economic) to the worker and his interests as represented by labor parties. The *ezrach* signifies, it seems, a polarized political field.

In the context of our discussion, of import is that the Hebrew *ezrach* does not pertain to one of the central aspects of *civil*, namely, conduct. The realm of manners and of the social demands made on individuals—to be polite and considerate, not to mention kind and benevolent—the realm of judgment of what is befitting or appropriate (to the citizen), and so, by extension, of cultivation and refinement, of mastery of high culture and the admiration of cultural achievements—is absent from the Hebrew word.[9] Many considerations of the Israeli-Palestinian conflict seek to put into relief the linkage between modes of conduct and of political engagement. Yet, it should be underscored that this linkage, so clear in English—and I take the latter to be representative in that respect of other Romance and Germanic languages—is not operative in Semitic languages, the primary languages of the Israeli-Palestinian conflict. In other words, the linkage is external to the languages in conflict and is part of a rhetoric that is often conceived in the region as foreign, if not outright hostile.

Moreover, the endeavor to think constructively of civil discourse tends to suppress the violent dimension of the English definition, the potential and threat the civil realm contains for its own disruption and undoing. It is telling that it is the first definition the *OED* provides for *civil*: "Of warfare, conflict, etc.; occurring within a society or community; taking place between inhabitants of the same country or state, or between the populace and the ruling power; of or relating to such conflict." The question is, of course, how to address this violence, and what is the relationship between the violence of English civility and the Hebrew lack of civility within the civil.

The Hebrew dictionary marks once again the difference between English rhetoric and Hebrew rhetoric. It notes indeed an equivalent term to *civil war*, namely, *milchemet ezrachim*, literally "a war of citizens." Still, tellingly enough, it does so not in the discussion of the noun *ezrach* or the adjective *ezrachi* and their special uses but, rather, in the discussion of the noun *milchama*, that is, war; and the brief entry *milchemet ezrachim* is followed by a more extensive entry of its equivalent, *milchemet achim*, literally, a war of brothers. In Hebrew usage, the former term is reserved for conflicts elsewhere, such as the American Civil War or the Spanish Civil War, whereas the latter is used to designate intra-Jewish conflicts. In other words, within the Hebrew-Jewish-context, the Hebrew dictionary dissociates the civil and the citizen from the threat of violence, transposing the latter into the question of kinship. What is endangered, then, in the Hebrew "civil conflict" is not so much the political association but, rather, the family.[10]

BAD MANNERS AND CIVIL SOCIETY

I linger at length on these dictionary definitions, because they seem to inform Amichai's designation as a civil poet. Amichai's poetry, so it seems, has little to do with questions of manners and decorum; in fact, Amichai's language has often been conceived as irreverent, challenging the sexual and religious mores of its readers (and, at least initially, also their poetic mores).[11] If, as George Mosse suggests, manners and morality lie at the heart of the modern nation, if, in truth, "concepts of sexuality haunted bourgeois society and nationalism, to be acknowledged yet curbed, deflected from the physical onto an ideal stereotype of male and female beauty";[12] then Amichai's explicit language could easily be construed as subverting the nation state. Yet, this is not how Amichai's poetry was and is being read. Rather, it is hailed as an endeavor to carve a realm of human interaction well distinct from the demands of official Israeli-Hebrew rhetoric—political, religious and military. As Amos Oz writes in his eulogy for Amichai:

> More than forty years ago, Amichai—a young poet whose poem spoke in an everyday voice—made his appearance and enacted a "civil revolution." He changed a whole system of values. [. . .] In this revolution, he led his poetry from the public, the historical, the

combative, and the general, into the intimate, homely, prosaic, quotidian. [. . .] This man [. . .] was a religious poet and also an anti-religious poet. The truth of the matter is that Amichai was not a secular man [. . .] God was for him an intimate member of the household, and Amichai held a personal dialogue with Him and spoke to Him harshly. And at one and the same time, Amichai is an anti-religious poet because he hated established religion, nationalist religion, messianic religion, religion that is turned into a means at the hand of the legions that march to conquer.[13]

Oz makes clear that Amichai's emphasis on "the intimate, homely, prosaic, quotidian" should not be mistaken for a withdrawal from public life into an apolitical, hermitic realm. On the contrary, in this emphasis Amichai's readers saw an endeavor to refashion a civil sphere of resistance to the oppression of the apparatuses of the nation state. At the heart of Amichai's civil resistance lies what his translators Chana Bloch and Chana Kronfeld call his unwavering faith in "the human capacity for language."[14]

Amichai's civil sphere is indeed *ezrachi*. For one, it is one of class. Repeated elisions and omissions clearly reveal its class affiliation: elisions and omissions not only and most obviously of the economic foundation of the human interaction enabled within this sphere, but also and as importantly, of social and ethnic markers (which are at the heart of class conflict in Israel). The easy exchange between the public and the homely, the general and the quotidian—the very claim to the universal validity of the personal—mark Amichai's "human capacity for language" as a faculty of the middle class.

More importantly in the context of our discussion here, however, is the interdependence of the figural and the political that lie at the core of such capacity. Intimate, homely, prosaic, and quotidian as Amichai's language may be, it aims to undo the conflation of state proclamations and the language of its subjects, enacting a possible hiatus between the two, a hiatus that reveals a gap or a breach between them. Reading figures of speech literally and literal speech figuratively—his core poetic strategy—Amichai points at the uncertainty—or indeterminacy—of signifier as well as signified and, with it, at the fundamental figurality of language. As such figurality introduces poetry—as a loaded term here—into the language of decrees and promulgations, it defines a space in which, as official pronouncements are tested, the poet can assert himself over and against them as a citizen—as one "possessing civic rights and privileges"[15] and, most importantly, a voice to speak back (and differently) to power as it were—rather than as a mere subject to power. Poetically man becomes a citizen, if you will.

Poetry and Return

Yet, what happens when such figural civility and citizenship encounter its Other—the Palestinian Arab in the context of an ethno-national conflict? To address this question let us read more closely Amichai's poetry. Here I can consider only one example of Amichai's rich poetic corpus. In January 1969, Amichai published his fourth book of poetry, *'Akhshav be-Ra'ash* [*Now with Clamor*]. Divided into four *she'arim*—sections or gates—the book opens with the Gate of Jerusalem, which opens in turn with a cycle of poems entitled "Jerusalem 1967." The twenty-two poems that make up the cycle were written in the aftermath of the 1967 War (June 5–10), within months of the Israeli capture of Jordanian Jerusalem and the villages in its vicinity (which were later incorporated into the municipal area of the city), and appeared in print shortly afterwards. The cycle thus articulates the very early experience of the "unified" city and encounters with its Palestinian residents, and is among the first canonical works of literature to address these. Whereas these were by no means the first poems Amichai dedicated to Jerusalem, they no doubt presented his most extensive and intensive treatment of the city to date, marking its turn into a focal *topos* of his poetic corpus at large. As such, they seem to me to form a foundational moment of Amichai's poetics, from the late 1960s on.

The Hebrew readers of the cycle at the time did not fail to note its subdued tone,[16] a stark contrast with the ecstatic euphoria that informed, with only isolated exceptions, the rhetoric of the "liberation" of Jerusalem.[17] Some readers could not but feel uneasy at the reservation of his poetic *I* in the face of the public celebration over the "unification" of the city. Avraham Blatt thus notes, "The poet views and probes the transformation of Jerusalem 1967 with seething hatred from every side and, on the other hand, blind love."[18]

Others, on the contrary, indeed most of the critics who commented on Amichai's Jerusalem poetry, saw in his reserved rhetoric a source of strength. For them, it manifests his "fierce resistance," as Omer-Sherman puts it, "to dogmatic absolutes in that abiding spirit of skepticism [. . .] uncompromising affirmations of the moral individual, often imagined as a citizen of Jerusalem, struggling under the weighty travesties of history, war, and nationalisms." Commenting on "Jerusalem 1967," Omer-Sherman perceives "an acute awareness of the poet's . . . struggle not only to transform the mute stones that have witnessed death, destruction, and God into a vernacular Hebrew that must serve the present, but also to issue a quixotic insistence that the timeless city acknowledge the human lives it encases."[19] In a characteristic manner to Amichai's critical reception, Omer-Sherman notes a tension, or even a conflict: not between political, ethnic, national, or religious collectives, nor between human beings but, rather, between Jerusalem in its materiality and its human residents, between the city's stones and the "pervasive sense of shared fate with all the other hapless inhabitants."[20] It is this tension that I wish to test in what follows.

"Jerusalem 1967" is bracketed between departure and return. The first poem charts the movement in space that frames the cycle as a whole:

> This year I traveled far away
> to view the silence of my city.
> A baby is calmed by rocking, a city is calmed
> in the distance. I dwelled in longing. I played the game
> of the four strict squares of Yehuda Halevi:
> *My heart. Myself. East. West.*
> I heard the bells ringing in the religions of time,
> but the wailing that I heard inside me
> has always been of my desert Judean [Yehuda].
> Now that I've come back, I'm screaming again.
> And at night, stars rise like the bubbles of the drowned,
> every morning I scream the scream of a newborn baby
> out of the confusion of houses and all this great light.[21]

Between departure and return, the poem designates two perspectives from which Jerusalem is observed, the distant and the near at hand. It thus poetically addresses one of the main concerns of the present volume, namely, the value of the discourse from a distance on the encounter between Israelis, Palestinians, and the violence that appears to be inherent to that encounter. From afar, the city can certainly be probed, calmly and cerebrally as it were; yet, calm and cerebration also mystify the city, the poem seems to suggest.[22] For from afar, poetry is revealed to be a scholastic game of verbal hopscotch, triangulated between the poet's body and self, language and geography.[23] In part, it is a game of names and, more particularly, of the name of the poet himself—Yehuda, as in Yehuda Amichai (whose name haunts, but is not spelled out in the poem), Yehuda Halevi and the Judean Desert (*midbar yehuda*)—that is divergently, perhaps even incommensurably inscribed into the first two stanzas of the poem. At first glance, Yehuda Halevi—the twelfth century Jewish poet and philosopher who was made into the prime figure of Hebrew poesy by the nineteenth century Heinrich Heine[24]—appears to be but Amichai's double or, rather, the mold into which Amichai seeks to cast himself. Yet Amichai's endeavor to find solace in Halevi's famous lines of longing for Jerusalem, "My heart is in the East and I am at the edge of the West" comes to little as the poetic lines break down into their constitutive elements, and Amichai finds himself playing a game whose significance and meaning is uncertain.[25] Surprisingly, it is the other Yehuda, the desert—which marks the eastern boundaries of Jerusalem—that is claimed by the poet as his true possession: *midbari, my* desert, but also *my* word. Over and against Yehuda Halevi's articulateness, Amichai sets the inarticulateness of the Judean Desert as well as his own inarticulateness, a mere wordless howl. It is the desert rather than the medieval poet that echoes the poet's experience of Jerusalem, recaptured in his return to the city. In the inarticulate and anxious cry of return, one finds the origin for the cycle as a whole,[26] in-between birth and death, in-between the hushed drowned, whose muted scream is materialized in bubbles, and the scream of the baby who—overwhelmed by his perceptions—fails to apprehend and comprehend what it is that he sees. "Jerusalem 1967" is thus framed by these two inadequate perspectives, the distant articulates mystification and the near at hand articulates incomprehension.

Still, what is to be made of Jerusalem from near at hand, within the moment of return?

> I've come back to this city where names
> are given to distances like to human beings
> and numbers not of bus routes
> but 70: After, 1917, five hundred
> before the common area, forty-eight. These are the routes
> you truly travel.
> And already the demons of the past are meeting
> with the demons of the future and sentence me above me,
> give-and-take, don't give and don't take,
> in high arches of shell-orbits above my head.
> A man who comes back to Jerusalem senses that the places
> that used to hurt don't hurt anymore.
> But a light warning remains in everything,
> like a light veil swaying: warning (no. 2).

Amichai's departure and return are not merely personal but municipal (and, in fact, national and even universal) as well. He departs from the divided pre-1967 Jerusalem, often described as wounded and desolated. His return is to the seemingly healed "city that is compact together" (*Psalms* 122:3), a verse repeated ad-nausea in Israeli official parlance in reference to post-1967 Jerusalem. Amichai's departure and return, however, reveals to him what remains concealed, so it seems, from those who have stayed put: the danger lurks beneath the "restored" surface of the city.

This may explain what seems to be the main axis of the cycle of poems: Amichai's ambivalence towards the city in its new guise. That ambivalence is embodied in the transition from the first sentence of the first poem to the first sentence of the second poem: Amichai had left *his* city, but has come back to *this* city. Indeed, the first poem is the only place in the cycle in which the *city* appears in the possessive form. Whereas the poet initially allows himself to claim possession of the city, he feels barred from continuing doing so afterwards. It appears, then, that Amichai feels alienated from Jerusalem in its new guise, alienated from the city that has now captured its history or, rather, has been captured by it. For the poem articulates a protest against history or, rather more precisely, against the subjugation of mundane human space, cut and crossed as it is by public transportation, to history perceived as a chain of cataclysmic events: 70 AD for the destruction of the Second Temple; 1917 AD for the British conquest of Jerusalem; 500 BCE or, rather, 586 BCE and 538 BCE for the destruction of the First Temple and Cyrus's Edict to repatriate the Babylonian captives and restore the Temple respectively; and (19)48 for the first Israeli-Arab War and the division of Jerusalem. Such a perception of history, framed in-between past and future, in-between visions of destruction and deliverance, does not allow the poet to claim the city as his, for its contradicting moments negate and annul each other. Such a perception can only chart the path for yet another catastrophe, which would necessarily condemn him.

Law

Amichai's return is not merely personal, nor is its significance only poetic, for it explicitly echoes the Israeli Book of Law, and one of its foundational pieces of legislation at that, namely, the Law of Return. The law, passed unanimously by the Israel parliament on July 5, 1950, is perceived by many to be the key legal expression to the Jewish character of the State of Israel. Indeed, it is one of the main legal tools to the establishment of a Jewish hegemony in the State of Israel. As such, it has generated both political and academic debates and a rich literature[27]. Presenting the law to the Israeli Parliament, David Ben-Gurion, the founding father of the State of Israel and its first Prime Minister, says:

> The Law of Return is one of the Foundation Laws of the State of Israel. It contains a main mission of our state, the mission of the Ingathering of the Exiles. This law determines that it is not the state that grants the Jews of other lands to settle in the state but, rather, that that right is inherent to him as a Jew, if only he wishes to join in the settlement of the land.

[. . .]
The Law of Return has nothing to do with immigration laws; it is the law of the persistence of Israeli history; it determines the state principle, by the power of which the State of Israel was established.[28]

The Law of Return, at least in Ben-Gurion's interpretation, merely spells out the foundational principle of the State of Israel, a principle that logically and historically precedes the actual establishment of the State. The law states as follows:

1. Every Jew has the right to come to this country as an *oleh* [a Jew immigrating to Israel, SG].

    a. *Aliyah* [Jewish immigration to Israel, SG] shall be by *oleh's* visa.

    b. An *oleh's* visa shall be granted to every Jew who has expressed his desire to settle in Israel, unless the Minister of Immigration is satisfied that the applicant

       i. is engaged in an activity directed against the Jewish people; or

       ii. is likely to endanger public health or the security of the State.

    c. A Jew who has come to Israel and subsequent to his arrival has express his desire to settle in Israel may, while still in Israel, receive an *oleh's* certificate.

    d. The restrictions specified in section 2.b shall apply also to the grant an *oleh's* certificate, but a person shall not be regarded as endangering public health on account of an illness contracted after his arrival in Israel.

2. Every Jew who has immigrated into this country before the coming into force of this Law, and every Jew who was born in this country, whether before or after the coming into force of this Law, shall be deemed to be a person, who has come to this country as an *oleh* under this Law.

3. The Minister of Immigration is charged with the implementation of this Law and may make regulations as to any matter relating to such implementation and also as to the grant of *oleh's* visas and *oleh's* certificates to minors up to age of 18 years.[29]

As its name suggest, the Law of Return was perceived as restitutive, as the reinstatement of Jews in the land of their ancient homeland. Accordingly, the law distinguishes between Jewish and non-Jewish immigrants to the State of Israel, establishing in effect a special category of Jewish immigration to Israel, *Aliya*, which is paradoxically defined as *non*-immigration but, rather, as restoration.[30] Proclaiming that, "Every Jew has the right to come to this country," the articles of the law merely determines the subject to this law (that is, who is a Jew)[31] and the restrictions to this law. The Law of Return *does not* deal with the acquisition of citizenship, which is the subject of the Israeli Nationality Law, passed on April 1, 1952. Here I quote only the articles relevant to our discussion:

    a. Israel nationality is acquired—by return (section 2),

    b. by residence in Israel (section 3),

    c. by birth (section 4) or

    d. by naturalization (section 5 to 9).

    e. There shall be no Israeli nationality save under this Law.

    f. Every *oleh* under the Law of Return, 5710–1950, shall become an Israel national.

        i. A person who, immediately before the establishment of the State, was a Palestinian citizen and who does not become an Israeli national under section 2, shall become an Israeli national with effect from the day of the establishment of the State if—he was registered on the 4th Adar, 5712 (1st March 1952) as an inhabitant under the Registration of Inhabitants Ordinance, 5709–1949(2); and

        ii. he is an inhabitant of Israel on the day of the coming into force of this Law; and

        iii. he was in Israel, or in an area which became Israeli territory after the establishment of the State, from the day of the establishment of the State to the day of the coming into force of this Law, or entered Israel legally during that period.

    g. A person born after the establishment of the State who is an inhabitant of Israel on the day of the coming into force of this Law, and whose father or mother becomes an Israel national under subsection (a), shall become an Israel national with effect from the day of his birth.

4. A person born while his father or mother is an Israel national shall be an Israel national from birth.

    a. A person of full age, not being an Israel national, may obtain Israel nationality by naturalization.[32]

Conjointly, the two laws determine membership—i.e. citizenship—in the political community of the State of Israel and chart the boundaries of this community. These boundaries, however, are not merely civil, but of language as well, and moral ones at that. For only within these boundaries does one have an inalienable right to address the State and its apparatuses and demand justice from them.[33] What lies outside the boundaries of this community belongs to a different order (of language and justice) altogether.

It is therefore crucial that in their initial form, these two laws together distinguished between two types of citizenship: ethnic citizenship (*ius sanguinis*) versus territorial citizenship (*ius soli*). Whereas Jews—inasmuch as they are Jews by birth or by conversion—acquire citizenship by virtue of their return (and immediately upon their return), non-Jews (including Palestinians) acquire citizenship by virtue of their presence, birth, naturalization, or grant.[34] In this context, article four of the Law of Return is of particular interest. It does not merely extend the force of the law retroactively, to a time not only prior to its legislation, but also prior to the establishment of the State. It also, more strikingly, designates Jews who were actually born in the country as indigenous only by and through the power of this law. That is, those Jews who were born in the country become its citizens *not* by virtue of their birth but, rather, *by* the power of their figurative return to it. Establishing thus common fate among all Jews in Israel, the two laws also serve to clearly tell them apart from the non-Jewish citizens of the State.

Jewish citizenship is defined by the right of Jews to traverse space, to come and go (or, rather, to go away and come back). The Law of Return and the Nationality Law thus serve as symbolic redress to the recent history of Jews, which was characterized by restrictions and bans on Jewish immigration and mass internment, which resulted in turn in extermination. Palestinian citizenship is defined, on the contrary, by its immobility, by its permanent presence. By determining that only those Palestinians present in Israel on March 1, 1952 could claim Israeli citizenship, the Nationality Law prevented citizenship from the Palestinians who were expelled or fled the areas under Israeli control during the Israeli War of Independence-Nakba and its aftermath—at least eighty percent of the original non-Jewish population in these areas, even according to the official conservative Israeli numbers.[35] Indeed, the Israeli Book of Law used the principle of Palestinian presence to spurn the Palestinian insistence on the Right of Return of refugees.

Poetics between Jews and Palestinians

Amichai's return, then, in "Jerusalem 1967" is not merely poetic, but bears full political significance. It cannot but be marked by the Law of Return and the Nationality Law, by granting Israeli Jews the liberty to cross space, to go away and, most importantly, to return, to turn poetic longing into political belonging—the liberty, that is, to speak poetically as well as politically.[36] Nowhere is this clearer than in the fifth poem of the cycle, one of most-often quoted poems in Amichai's oeuvre as a whole:

> On Yom Kippur in 1967, the year of Forgetting, I put on
> my dark holiday clothes and walked to the Old City of Jerusalem.
> For a long time I stood in front of an Arab's hall-in-the-wall shop,
> not far from the Damascus Gate, a shop of
> buttons and zippers and spools of thread
> in every color and snaps and buckles.
> A rare light and many colors, like an open Ark.
> I told him in my heart that my father too
> had a shop like this, of thread and buttons.
> I explained to him in my heart about all the decades
> and the causes and the accidents, that I am now here
> and my father's shop is burned there and he is buried here.
> When I finished, it was time for Closing the Gates of prayer.
> He too lowered the shutters and locked the gate
> and I returned, with all the worshippers, home.

This poem features the only encounter in this cycle between Amichai and a Palestinian (whom he call Arab and not Palestinian). The encounter is marked by the juxtaposition of time and place. The time is the Day of Atonement, a time of mercy and pity, but also of Judgment, in which one is to ask for forgiveness from God and Human beings. The place is the Old City of Jerusalem, defined by the Damascus Gate on the one hand and, on the other hand, by the Western Wall, which is alluded to but not explicitly named. Or, rather, the poem is framed by the projected movement of the Israeli Jew who crosses the city—now his dominion. Much as the poet would have liked to downplay it, his movement through space cannot be dissociated from its military and political significance. Yet, the movement is interrupted, and rather than join the other Jewish worshipers at the Western Wall— where they are able to pray for the first time in nineteen years—the poet stops where he should not have stopped, not far from where he started, by a small shop. There he poetically performs a private ceremony of asking for forgiveness from the new subject of the Jewish state. The encounter revolves around Amichai's articulation of a shared humanity or, to be more precise, of the shared material experience of Amichai's father and the Palestinian as merchants of dry goods. In other words, at the center of this poem lies a process of identification, of Amichai, through his father, with the Palestinian shopkeeper.

But this disruption of the Israeli-Jewish projected movement is on the surface only. Amichai does not speak to the Palestinian, nor does he engage him in a dialogue. He simply stands on the other side of the street, gazing at the Palestinian merchant, thinking his thoughts to himself. The poem as a whole thus forms a soliloquy, in which the Israeli-Jewish subject speaks merely to himself and to his poetic-political community. The Palestinian, on his part, remains voicelessand unable to articulate his own position or even to return the gaze. He remains outside the political and moral purview of Israeli citizenship. At the end of the prayer, at the time of closing, each returns to his assigned place. Nothing, it seems, was removed from its place. The poem indeed allows for an interruption and a humanist poetic of identification that for a brief moment raises the possibility of co-habitation (at least from a Jewish perspective). Still, it does not necessarily yield a dialogue, civil or otherwise.

Architecture and Citizenship

Whereas Amichai seems unable to liberate himself from the Israeli civil poetic-political logic, his treatment of Jerusalem nevertheless bears the promise of other kinds of encounters, of other modes of civility and citizenship beyond the Israeli one. Indeed, it is a mode of civility and citizenship that is more akin to the Latin radix of these words than to the Hebrew one, a mode grounded in the shared urban experience of Jerusalem. One may begin with the conclusion to the poem upon which I have just commented. Ultimately, the poem seems to suggest a route different from the official Israeli one: for the poet does *not* make it to the Israeli-Jewish destination—the Western Wall—but rather only to the said shop that in the poem, rivals the national-religious site. The poem, that is, charts another route of leaving and returning, an alternative to the official Israeli route.

In an endeavor to escape the beaten track, Amichai turns to the materiality of Jerusalem, that is, to the architecture of the city—its structures architectural elements, building materials, urban layout, topography, and more—the key *topos* of the cycle. Consider, for instance, poem no. 13:

> Always beside ruined houses and iron girders
> twisted like the arms of the slain, you find
> someone who is sweeping the paved path
> or tending the little garden, sensitive
> paths, square flower-beds.

> Large desires for a strange death are well-nurtured
> as in the monastery of the White Brothers next to the Lions Gate.
> But farther on, in the courtyard, the earth is gaped:
> columns and arches supporting vain land
> and negotiating with one another: crusaders and guardian angels,
> a sultan and rabbi Yehuda the Pious. Arch vaults with a
> column, ransom for prisoners, and strange conditions in rolled-up
> contracts, and sealing stones. Curved hooks holding air.
> Capitals and broken pieces of columns scattered like chessmen
> in a game that was interrupted in anger,
> and Herod, who already, two thousand years ago, wailed
> like mortar shells. He knew.

The poem betrays Amichai's fascination with the architecture of the Old City of Jerusalem, and more than that, with its shattered state. The ruins bear testimony not simply to the ravages of time, but also to the horror of war, including the very recent one that raged just a few short months before the cycle was put to print.

In the context of our discussion, one cannot but think here of Naomi Shemer's "Jerusalem of Gold." Written by one of Israel's most popular songwriters at the time, this song was first performed mere weeks before the 1967 Israeli-Arab War. At the conclusion of the battle over the Old City of Jerusalem on June 7, 1967, Israeli paratroopers gathered by the Western Wall. There, as can be heard in the radio broadcast of the battle, the Chief Military Rabbi Shlomo Goren recited a prayer and blew the shofar, which was immediately followed by the soldiers who spontaneously began singing "Jerusalem of Gold." The immense popularity of the song in the aftermath of the war has led to repeated calls to replace Israel's official anthem *ha-Ttikva* with it.[37]

> The mountain air is clear as wine and the scent of pines
> Is carried on the breeze of twilight with the sound of bells.
> And in the slumber of tree and stone captured in her dream
> The city that sits solitary and in its midst is a wall.
> Chorus: Jerusalem of gold, and of bronze, and of light
> Behold I am a violin for all your songs.
> How the cisterns have dried, the market-place is empty
> and no one frequents the Temple Mount in the Old City.
> And in the caves in the mountain winds are howling
> and no one descends to the Dead Sea by way of Jericho.
> But as I come to sing to you today, and to adorn crowns to you
> I am the smallest of the youngest of your children and of the last poet.

For your name scorches the lips like the kiss of a seraph
If I forget thee, Jerusalem, which is all gold . . .
We have returned to the cisterns, to the market and to the market-place
a ram's horn calls out on the Temple Mount in the Old City.
And in the caves in the mountain thousands of suns shine—
we will once again descend to the Dead Sea by way of Jericho!.[38]

Originally, Shemer wrote only the first three stanzas, adding the fourth in the aftermath of the war. Like Amichai, Shemer's "Jerusalem of Gold" centers on the architecture of the Old City of Jerusalem. More blatantly than him, she contrasts the pre-war' divided city with the post-war unified city. The first three stanzas clearly allude to the opening verses of the Book of Lamentations: "How doth the city sit solitary, that was full of people! How is she become as a widow! She that was great among the nations, and princess among the provinces, how is she become tributary!" Accordingly, Shemer's divided city is a dream-like place, desolated and emptied of all human presence. The final stanza marks a radical change: once again the city is peopled and, once more, the market and the Temple Mount are crowded. The transformation in the city—or, rather, of the city—is brought about by *return*, which reunites the city and its citizens, all Israeli-Jews. No mention is made or space reserved for Palestinian citizenship (a position for which Shemer was harshly censured over the years). As the public reception of the song evinces, this "return" to the city was (and still is) perceived as the ultimate realization of the Jewish national vision, the ultimate realization of Jewish national citizenship.

Like Shemer's song, Amichai's cycle as a whole is not so much about "Jerusalem" as about the Israeli-Jewish initial encounter with it, but to a different effect. As in Shemer's song, Amichai takes his reader on a guided tour to a haunted city, eerily emptied of its residence but for one man—surely a Palestinian—who continues his mundane chores, sweeping the path or tending the garden amidst the architecture of ruins and the ghosts that peopled them. In contradistinction to Shemer's poem, this haunted city is not the pre-war one but, rather, the post-war one. Emptied of the living, Amichai's ruined, haunted city may be captured in her dream, but the dream is a far cry from Shemer's vision of bleak desolation. Indeed, it is a dream that wishes away the movement of Israeli *return*. Amichai's city is one of ruins as markers of the divergent faiths who struck *presence* in the city throughout the ages in close proximity to each other. In this space of a dreamt city, crusaders, sultans and rabbis, the human embodiments of the ruins, amicably converse with each other, amicably compete with each other, as they jointly bemoan the destruction and carnage brought by war. The architecture of the city thus offers a civil vision beyond the failure of flesh and blood Jews and Palestinians to speak to each other.

Amichai's Jerusalem, very much unlike Shemer's city (with which so many Israeli-Jews have and still identify), is not petrified under the weight of its history and religious investment. Anything but static, his Jerusalem is elastic. Responding to multiple and diffused powers rather than a single power source, its architecture cannot be understood as the material embodiment of a unified political will or as the product of a single ideology. Rather, its organization should be seen as a kind of 'political plastic,' or as a map of the relation between all the forces that shaped it.[39] The resilience of architecture in the face of the destructive powers of history—even if buildings are not completely immune to them—its apparent permanence allows Amichai to imagine human co-habitation of the city.

Doom

And yet the cycle as a whole marks the failure to escape doom, which is not in and of the future but of the very present. For the divine pronouncement of doom is inextricably woven into the poems of the cycle and is repeatedly engraved in the architecture of the city. The last poem of the cycle thus reads:

> Jerusalem is Sodom's sister-city,
> but the merciful salt didn't have mercy on her
> and didn't cover her with silent whiteness.
> Jerusalem is an unwilling Pompeii.
> History books thrown into the fire,
> their pages strewn about, stiffening in red.
> An eye too light, blind,
> always shattered in a sieve of veins.
> Many births gaping below,
> a womb with numberless teeth,
> a double-edged mouthed woman and the holy beasts.
> The sun thought that Jerusalem was a sea
> and set in her: a terrible mistake.
> Sky fish were caught in a net of alleys,
> tearing one another to pieces.
> Jerusalem. An operation left open.
> The surgeons went to sleep in faraway skies,
> but her dead gradually
> form a circle all around her,
> like quiet petals.

My God!
My stamen! (No. 22)

Untypically difficult (and rich in allusions to Christian imagery, as we shall presently see), the poem nevertheless—or perhaps by virtue of its difficulty—imparts a sense of impending destruction and annihilation, eerily suspended for some unfathomable reason. Held in abeyance between Sodom's divine judgment and Pompeii's natural disaster, Jerusalem cannot congratulate herself on the temporary stay of the promised doom, for its current life is deemed more horrific than death. As the fourth stanza suggests, in this state the city is like a surgery interrupted. Undercutting the Jewish prayer, "Heal me, o Lord, and I shall be healed; save me, and I shall be saved: for thou art my praise" (Jeremiah 17:14), the authority in charge in the poem, God the surgeon—God the healer—has withdrawn Himself, leaving the patient on the operating table unsewn and untended. Alluding perhaps to the Book of Revelation, the poem goes on to list apocalyptical images of a collapsed world in quick succession. The second stanza weaves together images of threatening sexuality and motherhood: a blind eye (cataract?), a teethed womb, a woman of multiple cutting mouths, and holy beasts. Portraying a threatening woman, to her sexual partners as well as to her offspring, Amichai picks up a tradition that has identified Jerusalem with the deadly mother.[40] The third stanza suggests that the sky has fallen on the city, now consumed by the sun as simultaneously the sky, captured by the city, consumes itself. In light of these menacing images, the final image of the dead who arrange themselves round about in the form of petals around God the stamen, in a clear allusion to Dante's vision of bliss at the Empyrean in Canto XXX of the *Paradiso*, brings little comfort. Like Jesus on the cross, the poet can only call up to his God in despair, "My God, my God, why hast thou forsaken me?" (Matthew 27:46).

Amichai's "Jerusalem 1967" ends on a bleak note. As I have suggested, in light of the failure to establish civil dialogue between Israeli Jews and Palestinians, the poem turns from the human encounter to architectural encounters as a way to imagine human co-habitation and civil interaction. For the poet, the city's architecture seems to bear a promise of undoing the Israeli return and for granting a voice for those silenced, that is, the promise to imagine other forms of citizenship. The final poem appears to quash this promise: forsaken by its God, the city is left incapacitated, unable to fend off its nightmares. All the reader can do is watch with horror at its protracted, suffering demise.

Notes

1. See, for instance, "Mi-hu ha-meshorer ha-nimkar be-yisra'el li-shnat 2009?" Walla http://e.walla.co.il/?w=/6/1611857, retrieved Nov. 21, 2012. For a useful survey of the criticism of Amichai's work see Yehudit Tzvik (ed), *Yehuda Amichai: Mivchar ma'amrey beikoret 'al yetsirato* (Tel Aviv: ha-Kibbutz ha-Me'uchad, 1988), and in particular, Tzvik's intoriduction (pp. 7–60). On Amichai's Language see, for instance, Shimon Sandbank, "Shirav ha-mekubatsim shel yehuda 'amichai," *Amot* 1.5 (1963): 93–95; Boaz Arpaly, "On the Political Significance of Amichai's Poetry," in *The Experienced Soul: Studies in Amichai*, edited by Glenda Abramson (Boulder, CO.: Westview Press, 1997), 27.

2. Nili Scharf Gold, *Yehuda Amichai: The Making of Israel's National Poet* (Waltham, Mass. Hanover, Brandeis University Press; University Press of New England, 2008).

3. Agi Mishol, "Kmo litpos parpar bi-me'ufo," interview with Vered Lee, *Haaretz* May 3, 2012.

4. Hamutal Tsamir contends, however, that the opposition between national and civil poetics set by the poets of the so-called "State Generation" is fictitious. Indeed, the very negation of the figure of the preacher at the gate—the central figure of pre-State Hebrew national poetry—is not merely retained in state poetry, but actually serves these poets to produce the universal subject as a citizen of the nation state. See Hamutal Tsamir, "ha-Meshorer-ha-Navi ke-met chay be-shirat do ha-medina," *'Itot shel shinuy: sifruyot yehudiyot ba-tkufa ha-modernit: kovets ma'amarim li-khvodo shel dan meron*, edited by Gidi Nevo, Michal Arbel, and Michael Gluzman (Sde-Boker: Makhon ben-guryon le-'heker yisra'el veha-tsiyonut; oniversitat be-gurion ba-negev, 2008): 282–316; "Jewish-Israeli Poetry, Dahlia Ravikovitch, and the Gender of Representation," Jewish Social Studies: History, Culture, Society n.s. 14. 3 (2008): 85–125.

5. This is how the critic Yehoshua Heschel Yeivin has depicted Uri Tsvi Greenberg, see Yeivin, *Uri tsvi grinberg: meshorer me'hokek* (Tel Aviv: Sadan, 1937).

6. One of the people, or *A'had ha-'Am* is the acronym of on eo fthe most important early ideologues of modern Jewish nationalism.

7. "civil, adj., n., and adv.." OED Online. March 2013. Oxford University Press. http://www.oed.com.proxy.lib.duke.edu/view/Entry/33575?rskey=SpdRnB& result=1 (accessed March 13, 2013).

8. "citizen, n.." OED Online. March 2013. Oxford University Press. http://www.oed.com.proxy.lib.duke.edu/view/Entry/33513?rskey=rX5Adt&result=1&isAdvanced=false (accessed March 13, 2013).

9. Norbert Elias has written extensively on the emergence of *civility* in European cultures and in its relation to political formations; see Norbert Elias, *The Civilizing Process: Sociogenetic and Psychogenetic Investigations* (Oxford, UK; Malden, Mass., Blackwell Publishers, 2000). The primary Hebrew adjective for civil conduct would be *adiv*, that is, polite, courteous, obliging, well mannered, designates civil in the context of decorum. Arabic is similar to Hebrew in distinguishing politics from manners. Thus whereas *madani* designates the civil in the context of cities and

civilization, *adab* designates the civil in the context of manners and how to acquire them. I thank Miriam Cooke for her comments in this context.

10. This has far reaching implications for both the historiographical and the political discourses in Israel. In their struggle against the Oslo accord, Jewish settlers continuously raised the specter of *milchemet achim* (war between brothers); on the other hand, Israeli historians still have great difficulties in portraying the conflict between Jews and non-Jews, first in pre-State Palestine and then in areas under the rule of the State of Israel as *michemet ezrachim*. They would rather turn to the more comfortable vocabulary of ethnic and national conflict.

11. Amichai's third book of poetry *ba-Gina ha-Tsiburit* (*In the Public Garden*, 1959) thus elicited complaints about his explicit sexual descriptions, which were often perceived as pornography. See, for instance, Binyamin Yizhak Michali, *Pri ha-aretz: havayot ve-yotsrim be-sifrutenu ha-tseʿira* (Tel Aviv: Agudat ha-sofrim leyad hotsa'at masada, 1966): 97; Emanuel Katz, "*ha-Tseʿirim ha-zoʿamim*," *Heruth*, Sep. 4, 1959. See likewise the recent attempt to revise one of his poems on the *shironet* website, apparently because it challenges religious sensibilities (Ido Kenan, "kshe-Yehuda amichai mekabel tipul mi-golesh tsadik," *Haaretz Weekend Magazine* Mar. 2, 2013).

12. George Mosse, *Nationalism and Sexuality Respectability and Abnormal Sexuality in Modern Europe* (New York: H. Fertig, 1985) 2.

13. Amoz Oz, *be-ʿEtsem yesh kan shtey milchamot* (Jerusalem: Keter, 2000): 79–80. Similarly, see Boaz Arpali, "Yerushalayim chatranit: yerushalayim ke-tsomet mefarek mitosim be-shirat yehuda ʿamiʿhay," *Dapim le-mechkar be-sifrut*, 14–15 (2006):293–320; Boaz Arpali, *ha-Prachim veha-agartal: shirat ʿamichai 1948–1968 (mivne, mashmaʿut, poʾetika)* (Tel Aviv: ha-Kibbutz ha-meʾuchad, 1986), chapter 10.

14. Chana Bloch and Chana Kronfeld, "Amichai's counter-theology: opening *Open Closed Open*," *Judaism* 49.2, 157.

15. "citizen, n. and adj.." *OED* Online. September 2014. Oxford University Press. http://www.oed.com.proxy.lib.duke.edu/view/Entry/33513?rskey=gLgCCO&result=1&isAdvanced=false (accessed December 03, 2014).

16, See, for instance, the decision to award Amichai's volume *Now with Clamour* the Brenner Literary Prize, "Pras brener Ta.Sh.Ka.T," *Davar* 21 Nov. 1969.

17. Naomi Shemer's poem *"Yerushalayim shel zahav"* ("Jerusalem of Gold") is arguably the best-known expression of the Israeli public sentiment in the aftermath of the 1967 War. The song, which was written and first performed shortly before the war was revised in its aftermath and amended to reflect the new political reality that Shemer renders in spiritual, not to say messianic terms. On the song, see Dan Almagor, "Eych nolad ha-shir yerushalayim shel zahav," *Hadoʾar* 75.7 (1996).

18. Abraham Blatt, *Tchumum ve-chotam* (Tel Aviv: Sigalit 1974), 120. (pp. for the whole essay 117–127). .

19. Renan Omer-Sherman. "Yehuda Amichai's exilic Jerusalem." *Prooftexts* 26.1–2 (2006): 221.

20. Omer-Sherman 222.

21. Throughout my discussion, I am relying on two English translations of the cycle: *The Selected Poetry Of Yehuda Amichai*, revised and expanded edition,

translated by Chana Bloch and Stephen Mitchell (Berkeley: University of California Press, 1996), 47–55; and *Yehuda Amichai: A Life of Poetry, 1948–1994*, translated by Benjamin Harshav and Barbara Harshav (New York: HarperCollins Publishers, 1990), 79–87. I have combined and modified, however, these translations to render them closer to the literality of the Hebrew original. For the Hebrew original, see Yehuda Amichai, *Shirey Yehuda 'amichai*, vol. 2 (Jerusalem: Schocken, 2002), 11–22. In what follows, I will merely cite in brackets the number of the poem in the cycle.

22. The cycle indeed suggests an identity between Amichai the poet and the poetic *I*, who remains unnamed throughout the cycle. The conflation of poet and poetic *I* has, in fact, become the critical norm in the interpretation of Amichai's poetry in general. For the sake of clarity, I shall likewise follow this norm, though a more thorough discussion of the cycle would have to question this conflation.

23. On the centrality of play to Amichai's poetics see Shimon Sandbank, "Amichai: ha-mischak veha-shefa,'" in Yehudit Tzvik (ed), *Yehuda Amichai: Mivchar ma'amrey beikoret 'al yetsirato*, edited by in Yehudit Tzvik (Tel Aviv: ha-Kibbutz ha-Me'uchad, 1988), pp. 105–114.

24. Central to the modern conception of Yehuda Halevi is Heine's long ballad "Jehuda ben Halevy," which was first published in Heine's *Romanzero* (1851). On Heine and Halevi see, for instance, Hillel Halkin's recent book *Yehuda Halevi* (New York: Knopf Doubleday Publishing Group, 2010).

25. For translation of the poem, see Peter Cole (trans. And ed.), *The Dream of the Poem: Hebrew Poetry from Muslim and Christian Spain, 950–1492* (Princeton: Princeton University Press, 2007), 164. As Cole notes, "this is one of the most famous poems in all of Hebrew literature, and its theme and lyric concision have spoken to Jews throughout the Diaspora for centuries. On the whole, it is a song of antithesis, contrasting East and West, ease and hardship, waste and worth, and material and spiritual planes of existence. Cole, *The Dream of the Poem*, 450.

26. See also Stephane Moses' discussion of Benjamin's notion of origin in *The Angel of History: Rosenzweig, Benjamin, Scholem* (Stanford: Stanford University Press, 2009), 65–83.

27. See, for instance, Ruth Gavison, *The Law of Return at Sixty: Years: History, Ideology, Justification* (Jerusalem: The Metzilah Center for Zionist, Jewish, Liberal and Humanist Thought, 2010); Alexander Yakobson and Amnon Rubinstein, *Israel and the Family of Nations* (London: Routledge, 2009); Chaim Gans, *me-Rikhard vagner 'ad zkhut ha-shiva: nita'u'h filosopfi shel be'ayot tsibur yisre'eliyot* (Tel Aviv: 'Am 'oved: ha-Mikhlalah ha-akademit Sapir, 2006), pp. 165–285; Na'ama Carmi, *'Hok ha-shvut: zkhuyot hagira u-gvuloteyhen* (Tel Aviv: Tel Aviv University Press, 2003).

28. *Divrey ha-kneset* 6(30), 2035–2037 (my translation from the Hebrew)

29. *Laws of the State of Israel*, vol. 4 (Jerusalem: Government Printer, 1948–1987), p. 114. The law was amended on October 3, 1970. Here I only address the original version of the law. For the history of the law and its amendments, as well as its relationship to the nationality law see, for instance, Gavison, Ch. 1, 3; Yfaat Weiss, "The Golem and its creator, or how the Jewish nation-state became multi-ethnic," in *Challenging Ethnic Citizenship: German and Israeli Perspectives on Im-*

migration, edited by Daniel Levy and Yfaat Weiss (New York: Berghahn Books, 2002); see also the responses to Weiss's argument, Zeev Rosenhek, "ha_politika shel 'hok ha-shvut," *Te'orya u-vikoret* 19 (2001), 75–78; Ian S. Lustick, "ha-Kasta ha-republikanit be-medina ha-lo 'arvit," *Te'orya u-vikoret* 19 (2001), 71–74.

30. See also Carmi 21–23.

31. Subsequently, a heated debate erupted in Israel over the question of who is a Jew and on the pertinence of the religious definition of Jewishness to the secular legal system and, consequently, to the body politics of the State of Israel. This has been the main focus of the debates over the law in Israel.

32. *Laws of the State of Israel*, vol. 6 (Jerusalem: Government Printer, 1948–1987), p. 50–3. The law was amended on March 3, 1958; August 7, 1968; May 17, 1971; July 29, 1980; November 30, 1987; May 1, 1996; July 28; 1998; August 4, 2004. Here I only address the original law and the first amendment.

33. I cannot address here the distinction between liberal and republican conceptions of citizenship. For a discussion of Israeli citizenship vis-à-vis these two conceptions, see Lustick; Yoav Peled, "Zarim be-utopya: ma'amadam ha-ezra'hi shel ha-falastinim be-yisra'el," *Te'orya u-vikoret* 3 (1993), 21–35.

34. Carmi 24–25. Carmi argues that whereas the Law of Return clearly privileges Jews over Palestinians, the Nationality Law treat all as equal. It should be noted, however, that even for the Nationality Law, *return* is still the primary category of nationality.

35. For a discussion of the question of citizenship vis-à-vis Israel Palestinians, see Peled. The assignation of two divergent principles to the Jewish National Character versus the national Palestinian character is not an innovation of the Israeli Book of Law, and the association of the former with movement and the latter with intransience is one of the fundamentals of the Hebrew discourse of the nation. See Shai P. Ginsburg, *Rhetoric and Nation: The Formation of Hebrew National Culture, 1880–1990* (Syracuse: Syracuse University Press, 2014), Ch. 4.

36. Sidra DeKoven Ezrahi suggests that at the heart of modern Jewish literature lies the poetics of exile and Return, closely linked to the rise of modern Jewish nationalism in the late nineteenth century (Sidra DeKoven Ezrahi, *Booking passage: exile and homecoming in the modern Jewish imagination* [Berkeley: University of California Press, 2000]). Her argument suggests not only that we have to explore the close ties between Jewish poetic and political visions, but also have to ask ourselves more specifically how is the Israeli Book of Law frames Israeli poetics—my task in this article.

37. Dan Almagor, "Eikh nolad ha-shir 'yerushalayim shel zahav,'" *Ha-doar* 75 (7), 1996.

38. http://en.wikipedia.org/wiki/Jerusalem_of_Gold#Lyrics retrieved March 17, 2013.

39. I am paraphrasing here Eyal Weizman, *Hollow land: Israel's Architecture of Occupation* (London: Verso, 2007), 5. Weizman discusses the notion of elastic architecture in the context of the aftermath of the Israeli occupation of Palestinian territories during the 1967 War. Yet, Amichai's poetics suggest that this has little to

do with the particular character of Israeli occupation and is much more universal than Weizman seems to suggest.

40. See Shai Ginsburg, "The City and the Body: Jerusalem in Uri Tsvi Greenberg's Vision of One of the Legions." *Jerusalem: Conflict and Cooperation in a Contested City*. Eds. Miriam Elman and Madelaine Adelman. Syracuse: Syracuse University Press, 2014. 143–171.

10 The Point Is to Change It

James Crosswhite

In the United States, the discussion of the Israeli-Palestinian conflict slips quickly into dogmatism, antagonistic personal attack, and the predictable playing out of an identity-politics. The result is an inability to debate American policy and a refusal of many even to enter the discussion. The conviction that informed the original roundtable that led to this book was that the way to move forward would be to find the best way to examine the discursive powers that prevent us from clarifying complex realities, developing a hospitable hearing of all sides, and opening up a productive agonistic conflict. However, I will maintain that the point is not simply to examine this distorted discourse; the point is to change it. A productive examination will be practical and experimental. It will not only establish once more what we already know about what has gone wrong and what we already know about the goals we seek, but will also express this knowledge in the design of public discursive spaces while experimenting with discursive practices.

My own instinct has usually been to step out of these discussions. The 2008–2009 violence in Gaza and its aftermath have served only to reinforce this feeling. From a distance, the killing looked like nothing so much as repetition compulsion, and all the shouting about it seemed just as helpless and automatic. What could one say about the discourse, here in the US or around the world? And how could one be heard, anyway? The point seemed to be to stop the killing and to care for the wounded. There seemed to be nothing new to say about Israel or the Palestinians or the way Americans talk about them. What good is accomplished by talking about the way people talk about a repetition compulsion?

Yet, this reaction is obviously unsatisfactory, a simple refusal to take responsibility, what Stanley Cavell would call skepticism or what Emmanuel Levinas would call indifference.[1] Whatever knowledge and informed action arises will arise from our acknowledging one another and taking responsibility for one another, or at least trying to. It is impossible to escape this call of responsibility. In the simple act of buying my lunch, I am forced into this responsibility. At lunches over the years, I have had regular conversations with Alex, who owns the falafel stand near my office. He was wounded while serving in the Israeli army during the Yom Kippur war. He moved his family to Oregon and has raised his children there. One of his daughters moved back to Israel to live. Over the last fifteen years, our conversations have often drifted through the conflict and its history. It will be a sunny summer day in our city of Eugene, about as distant from the conflict as one can imagine, and we will sit there in the sun, and talk about the wars and even about the way people talk about them. Alex believes that the root of the conflict is religion and that there is no solution to the religious conflict.

Then, on my daily drive home to Southeast Eugene, in the rolling hills covered with Douglas Firs, on the shoulder of 2500-feet-high Spencer Butte, I will round a curve near the city limit sign, and there in the woods, in a clearing, I will come to a church. In front of the church, three enormous stainless steel flagpoles soar up nearly level with the treetops. Nothing could appear more out of place, until one looks up at the flags—the US flag, the Christian flag, and the flag of the State of Israel, flying over the forested hills of South Eugene where deer and raccoons nearly outnumber the people. There is no escape unless one shuts one's eyes and ears. The conflict between Israelis and Palestinians is a persistent presence, not only in the Middle East but also in American culture.

However, admitting the responsibility to speak does not make it any easier to speak, and it does nothing to increase my own confidence in the idea that talking about the way we talk will necessarily improve the way we talk. As I was pondering why I tend so strongly in this direction, an event in a course I was teaching shed new light on my doubts. The course was a training seminar that qualifies graduate students to teach written composition to undergraduates. It draws students from several departments: English, Creative Writing, Comparative Literature, Philosophy, Folklore, and Journalism. We had just read Chris Anson's article on "Reflective Reading," and it had led us into a deeper awareness of why we respond to student writing the way we do. The graduate students had had a vigorous and very smart discussion about the forces that influenced the way they responded to student writing, disciplinary influences among them. This was a very self-aware group, highly cognizant of the way our responses are shaped by our particular situations. It was one of the best discussions of the term.

Then the students looked at a particular paper and the way they had graded it, and there was quite a spread of opinion, which I displayed in a graphic in the front of the room. In the discussion that followed, people became defensive and aggressive and quite heated when explaining why they had graded the way they did. The disagreements developed very fast, and it was only as time was running out that I realized that the Creative Writing MFA and the PhD students as groups had split in their judgments—the Creative Writing students using the word "craft" frequently, and complaining strongly about the sentences and the opacity of the language, the PhD students speaking out for the "complexity" of the ideas, the ambition of the paper, and its close engagement with the reading. That is, immediately after reading and thinking and talking in a very sophisticated way about why we respond the way we do, the students stepped forth and unconsciously and passionately performed as if the reading and discussion had accomplished nothing. It was very tricky for me to find a way that would help us move forward and come closer in our responses for the sake of the students. In the end, it required abandoning our discussion and our initial judgments, and my leading a close reading of the student paper, walking through each part very slowly, all of us helping each other to see what we saw, and responding for the sake of the student.

Perhaps you can see where this is going. It is one thing to know what is happening, or what happens, when people respond the way they do. It is one thing to know why people produce the particular discourse they do. That is hard enough. It is another thing for this knowledge to make a practical difference. It is not simply a matter of learning to perceive the discursive formations in our own thought and speech. That would be helpful, but the problem is not simply what we believe or do not believe, rightly or wrongly. It is not simply the content of our speech that causes difficulties. It is also that we are ruled by discursive practices that have managed to get control over us. The point is also to change these practices.

We already know a great deal about what has gone wrong, but this knowledge by itself is not a guide to action. Matthew Abraham identified some of the problems very clearly in his original invitation to a roundtable on this issue: dogmatic position-taking, seeking to shame the other side, engaging in ad hominem attacks and one-sided brinkmanship, and refusing to acknowledge the complex realities of the conflict. Anis Bawarshi has spoken of the rhetorical patterns and uptakes and the ways discussions of the conflict trigger habitual responses. Michael Bernard Donals has considered the idea that speaking of community, inclusion, and filiation will in fact simply trigger these responses. Robert Jensen has spoken of the way basic narratives tend to take over and lead to their own ends. My colleague David Frank and Robert Rowland have written about the way mythic and symbolic discourse function in the conflict and the way mythic discourse, unchecked by pragmatism, produces violence. If I were to go forward and write about what is wrong in my own way, I would try to show that discourse concerning the Israeli-Palestinian conflict is incoherent because there are so many different conflicts hidden in that phrase, with many different parties to those conflicts, many different degrees of intensity and levels of conflict, carried out by many different means or instruments, and engaged in for many different purposes, and I believe that this is at least as true in the United States as it is in the Middle East.

However, I think we know enough. No matter how much more we knew about what was wrong with the way we talk about the conflict, it would not be enough to change it. This is true not only because there is a vast distance to go between knowing what is wrong with the way people talk and getting them to change the way they talk, especially in the complicated ways we are discussing here, though that is difficult enough. Think back to my graduate students. The PhD students valued conceptualization, complexity, logic, unity, and ambition because they were writing dissertations. The creative writers valued craft and style and sentences because they were writing poetry and fiction. To upend their hierarchies of judgment would be to upend the grounds on which they chose to pursue their degrees and their careers. They did not simply speak out of an unconscious formation that could be brought to light for them to examine dispassionately. They spoke out of hierarchies to which they had staked the next several years of their lives. In fact, they spoke as a way of practicing their disciplines according to their training. How much more so can this apply for many of the parties who speak with such volume and certainty concerning the conflicts wrapped up in what we call the Israeli-Palestinian conflict. Their speech is constituted by the practices that define them as belonging to the groups they belong to. When they abandon those practices, others may call their identities and loyalties into question.

The conviction that informed our roundtable was that the way to move forward was to find the best way to examine the discursive forces that prevent us from clarifying complex realities, developing a hospitable hearing of all sides, and opening up a productive agonistic conflict. My response is, in part, that we already know enough, even though I also believe that we should go forward with this academic work. Times change, and so does language and its use. However, the point is not simply to examine this distorted discourse; the point is to change it. In addition to strictly scholarly work, we also need a productive examination that will be practical and experimental, one that will not only establish what we already know about what has gone wrong, and what we already know about the goals we seek, but one that will express this knowledge in the design of public discursive spaces and in discursive experiments. In addition to our knowledge and our disciplinary methods, we have resources in our institutions and in the positions we hold to create new forums, new sites and structures that allow us to put our learning into practice—perhaps to invite *different* people to speak, saying different things, in different frameworks from the ones that have been producing the impasses with which we are familiar. Taking action of this kind will raise interesting questions about how these experiments in democracy are to be judged, but the move to that practical discussion will be a step forward.

Permit me one more story. Last May, my colleagues and I hosted a public event called the contrarian forum. The name was chosen by a donor who had said that his most valuable experiences in college were when he heard strong arguments on opposing sides of an issue, and learned to see from both sides. I won't go into the details of how, but we ended up hosting a debate on academic freedom between Carey Nelson, president of the American Association of University Professors, and David Horowitz, founder of the David Horowitz Freedom Center. Knowing that the debate could go wrong, we wanted to experiment with the debate format, so we invited Michael Leff and Barbara Warnick to intervene in the debate after the opening arguments. They described what the debaters were doing and tried to evaluate the quality of the debate, pointing out where the contest of ideas lapsed into personal attack and so forth. We did this to raise audience awareness and, we hoped, to have an influence on the following arguments. Unfortunately, the intervention seemed to influence neither the debate nor the question and answer session at the end. However it did offer a little more support for some beliefs I had been developing: that the debate format has serious limitations, that staging public spectacles of this kind puts the wrong kind of pressure on the discourse, and that leaders of organizations are probably the wrong people to invite as debaters. After all, they are expected to advocate for their side and even raise money for it—not to risk having their perceptions of the other side altered in public.

It was, for me, an instructive failure. Traditional debate is constituted by specific practices. We tried to intervene or even contravene with additional practices, but all this seemed to accomplish was an interruption in the sequence of practices specified by the debate. The question and answer session followed the ethos of the practices specified by the debate format, especially advocating and refuting, along with exaggerating the strengths of one's own position and weaknesses of one's opponents. Some of the problems already noted in American discourse concerning the Israeli-Palestinian conflict were evident here as well. The debate format also generated certain expectations for what kind of practices were indicated for both speakers and audience, as did the venue—in this case, a sports /events facility whose center was a basketball court. It was a spectacle, a kind of entertainment. It delivered a kind of political-aesthetico-emotional product: a contest in which one could re-experience strong identification with one's group by means of familiar practices.

However, it was not only the debate format and our weak attempt to experiment with it that led to this failure. It was also the fact that we had invited the heads of two organizations to speak about a topic on which their organizations had already set forth developed positions. As leaders, they were expected to advocate for them and even raise money for their furtherance. That is the practice of leaders of organizations. If David Horowitz suddenly discovered common ground with the President of the AAUP and engaged in new discursive practices that led to new cooperation between their organizations, he would very likely no longer be able to raise the funds on which his organization and his office depend. The same is true of Carey Nelson, although he must be credited with trying to discover some common ground with Horowitz.

So, in this very practical and personal way, I have become more suspicious of so-called agonistic conflicts that are spectacles, of traditional debates, and of forums in which the participants are leaders of organizations or fundraisers. They seem pitched toward reproducing the very kinds of discursive practices we want to avoid, but that is negative learning.

To move forward in a more creative way, I would want to study not just those features of American discourse about the Israeli-Palestinian issues that seem to prevent us from having productive discursive conflict, but also to seek out communicative situations where people are already practicing genuine cooperative conflict. I would want not only to study this communication, I would want to support and amplify it. I would want to invite these people to speak on our campuses. I would want to see whether their communicative practices could be reproduced through design. So, let me return to the question that the original roundtable was charged to answer: "How can a productive examination of the social, political, and rhetorical forces within the public sphere—that seem to prevent people of good will from talking to one another about the conflict—take place?"

I have already said that an examination of the discursive forces that *prevent* people of good will from talking to each other may not be as productive as we would hope. What I believe *might* be productive is an examination of the rhetorics and frameworks that *allow* people of good will to talk to each other. This would be productive for two purposes. First, we could begin to experiment with using those rhetorics and frameworks as models to design our own forums and discursive spaces that might be hospitable to conflict and productive of more mutual understanding. Second, we might find people whose discursive practices had been shaped by those better discursive environments, and then perhaps we could put *them* in front of cameras and microphones instead of all the usual suspects saying the usual things.

I am not an expert on the Middle East conflict, so others will know of better places to look than I would, but, to give some examples, the first place I would look might be the organization Seeds of Peace, which aims to provide young people from regions of conflict with the leadership skills required to advance reconciliation and coexistence.[2] Seeds is focused on the *next* generation, and it is especially focused on equipping it with communication and negotiation skills. The organization began this work in 1993 with forty-six Israeli, Palestinian, and Egyptian young people. It has trained approximately four thousand young people since then. The organization conducts international camps in Maine. Here is how it describes what happens there: "Worlds away from the daily scenes of bloodshed, the International Camp provides an escape from the explosive rage and violence spilling over in the Middle East and South Asia. This neutral, supportive setting makes it possible for hundreds of young leaders from both sides of major conflicts to meet their enemies face-to-face, often for the first time in their lives. Here they confront their hatreds and deep-seated fears and tackle the issues that fuel the conflict back at home." They have designed an interesting forum! Naturally, I would want to know what that communication looks like, especially since the outcome is said to be "a new threshold for tolerating ideas and understanding perspectives that were once beyond comprehension." However, the organization tells us only a little about the structure. The "seeds," as they are called, bunk with each other; share athletic, cultural, and artistic activities; and the center of their day is occupied with dialogues, led by facilitators, in which the campers confront their differences.

I thought it would be interesting to get a transcript or account of some of these sessions, so I wrote to the organization and got this reply: "The dialogue sessions we have at camp with the kids are closed and confidential, and no official records or transcripts are kept or available." I was, however, pointed toward other sources of information. Is this not remarkable? We are concerned with civic discourse in the public sphere, but this organization finds it necessary to *protect* young people from the public sphere in order to provide an environment in which it is possible for them to work through their conflicts and reach mutual understanding. Wouldn't it be interesting to study this a little more, perhaps to invite veterans of these camps to speak on our campuses, to amplify their speech, to study their discursive practices, or perhaps to model an available alternative? It would be a kind of experiment.

The Seeds of Peace website does provide video interviews with graduates of the camps. Videos are also available on YouTube. Some of the graduates are now Israeli Channel Two journalists, occupational health workers, workers in international development agencies, financial analysts, *Al Jazeera* programmers, international lawyers, and civil engineers. Here are some of the things they say:

> "I, as a Jew, was offended by the Arabs saying they lived in Palestine. I believe in Israel, and Palestine does not exist."

> "I always met Israelis as settlers, as soldiers, as occupiers. I always met them killing Palestinians, shooting Palestinians, and I've never met an Israeli who is just like me."

> "We have fought for four decades. OK? What did we get? The peace process is the only way. We have to coexist"

> "I am thinking about the children of the children of the people I am working with. Slowly but surely more and more of us will be in key positions to influence others. If we are the poor children of idealism, we are going to get people to change slightly in the direction we are looking for."

> "One major difference we all made is that there is no point of winning discussions with the other side. The only thing we can do is learn about what the other side thinks, and that's how I try to see things now."

> "It's enormous gaps between us and them, but I still believe that we can close those gaps."

> "I talked to the other side. It's hard. When I say that it's possible to have peace in the future, I'm not talking out of a dream or out of ignorance."

Here is a possible line of research into some communication as well as some discursive practices that might perhaps serve as models.

So what if we turned our attention away from the ones who set the tone and provide the models for the way we keep talking about the conflict, and looked elsewhere, at people who seem to have started to look at their differences and conflicts openly and are working toward peace as well as they can—even if not always on the level of the state and politics? Seeds is about communication on a person-to-person basis; however, many of the graduates are now in their thirties and seeking organizational ties with each other in which the work can be carried on. What would they say now about the conflicts in which their countries are involved, and how would they say it? How would they explore their disagreements now? How would the discursive practices they learned at Seeds of Peace camp and the discursive practices they learned in their professions and the discursive practices in their cultures diverge and converge and interact?

I believe that we should seek out these transversal and micropolitical spaces. The question is not just about nation states and political solutions and the way we talk about those. At the political level, conflicts are inscribed with language that addresses political constituencies in the desired way at a particular time. At times, that language will be etched with religious and nationalist and racial or ethnic coding that consolidates a political base at the same time that it makes political cooperation impossible. The political advancement of peace and cooperation often depends on prior advances in economic and other kinds of social cooperation. It is a commonplace that people strive to defend the peace when they have something to lose—good jobs, schools, a working justice system, security, stability, prosperity. Trans-conflict discursive practices that succeed in advancing these factors need our attention. This is especially the case because the "Israeli-Palestinian conflict" is not a single conflict but is many conflicts.

So *where else* do people talk about the conflict in ways that do not sink into the patterns we are all so familiar with? If part of the problem with talking about the conflict is that we are talking about many conflicts all at the same time, let's look at the way people talk when they are being practical about one conflict—say about water. The Geneva Initiative and a Quaker group sponsored dialogues between Palestinian and Israeli engineers in August of 2008. The participants reported success. Retired US Ambassador John McDonald mediated the dialogue, and said: "When you get good engineers together to work on problems, they speak the same language no matter what countries they come from."[3] The "same language" means here not only that the content of what was spoken concerned engineering and that the vocabulary was technical, but also that the discursive practices of engineers, the way engineers describe and work toward solving problems, were also the same. They knew how to use a common language, took turns speaking, characterized what each other had said, gave accurate summaries of work completed, and so on. Shaul Arlosoroff, a director of the Israeli national water company who participated in the dialogue, stated, "Not much more is needed to submit [the draft] to the final negotiating team." Geneva Initiative Palestinian executive director Nidal Foqaha added, "The meeting's output is beyond our expectations." I believe it would be helpful to investigate the way these meetings were set up and organized—who spoke to whom and for how long and in what way and about what and under what rules of protocol. Again, I would like to refocus, to magnify these discursive events and to put them at the center so that we could learn from them, and experimentally imitate them.

Here is another example. Global Hosted Operating System is a company whose CEO and Israeli employees live and work in West Jerusalem and Tel Aviv. Its thirty programmers work at the company headquarters in Ramallah, in the West Bank. The CEO has never been able to visit the headquarters. The Palestinian employees travel into Israel for meetings but are often delayed at checkpoints and sometimes forced to miss meetings altogether. The employees all worked together through the fighting in Gaza, although no one found it easy. Employees admit that discussions about the endless conflict can get heated—especially when they get together in person. But they say that these conversations have never degenerated into shouting matches. They have plenty of nonpolitical problems to solve. They *are* economic development in the West Bank. They *are* what peace looks like. How do they manage this discursively? How are their heated discussions conducted? What are the things they do *not* say to and about one another? Why are their discursive triggers not pulled? Why does their discourse *not* degenerate and force them apart? What are the discursive practices that allow them to cooperate in their common business and to explore the conflicts that divide their peoples?.[4]

Every time we invite speakers to campus, we give them power and influence. Every time we design a discursive space and hold an event, we affirm the appropriateness of that form. People follow our leads, especially our students. I suggest that we do this all more deliberately and that we think of the productive examination of discourse as a more practical and experimental project, one focused at least as much on successes as on failures. The discourse of political leaders and of political experts and of leaders of political advocacy organizations may not be the best discourse for us to study. The study of discourse focused on the most contentious, high level political controversies may not yield much more than we all already know. It may be much more illuminating to study the trans-conflict discursive practices of those who are pursuing the more specific politics of starting up and developing businesses, solving engineering problems, and educating the young in transcultural communication.

Even more importantly, we cannot forget the point, which is to change the current state of discourse about the Israeli-Palestinian conflict in the United States. This will be accomplished not simply through the acquisition of more knowledge about current discursive practices, but also through using our institutions and our positions to engage in an examination of discourse that is practical and experimental. We can begin by studying the micropolitical discursive spaces and practices where trans-conflict cooperation is already occurring, but we can move even further by giving the agents of this cooperation the attention, the forums, the microphones, and the cameras that have for too long been devoted to the people whose discursive practices have led nowhere. Finding these speakers, publicizing them, and giving them the floor in an appropriately designed forum may not be as simple or entertaining or prestigious as landing the well-known speaker who commands crowds. There is no guarantee of success, but it may be much more illuminating and more productive of change in the long run. It would not hurt to try and then see what happens. We may learn something.

Notes

1. Emmanuel Levinas discusses indifference and non-indifference in *Otherwise than Being, or, Beyond Essence*; see especially p. 166ff. Stanley Cavell develops his conception of skepticism throughout his work, perhaps most accessibly in his Shakespeare criticism (2003), but see also *In Quest of the Ordinary*, especially pp. 8–9.

2. All information about Seeds for Peace is drawn from the organization's website: http://www.seedsofpeace.org/. Retrieved 1 September 2010.

3. Quotes concerning the Geneva Initiative water dialogue are taken from "Geneva Initiative Tackles Difficult Israeli-Palestinian Water Issue" retrieved from http://www.internationalwaterlaw.org/documents/regionaldocs/gi-pressrelease-final.pdf, 1 September 2010.

4. The possible cautionary twist here is that such opportunities may be fleeting. All of the above was true when I presented an early version of this essay orally, in March of 2009. However, in April, 2010 the company informed its customers that the competition and the current marketplace made it no longer practical for the company to host the service. It announced that it was still seeking to license its product. I have not been able to discover the impact of this event on the company's business practices or on its employees.

11 Conclusion

Matthew Abraham

How exactly does one go about dialoguing with those with whom one disagrees about the Israel-Palestine conflict, without succumbing to the psychic and historical attachments that all too frequently lead such attempts at dialogue to the same unproductive common places? The essays in this collection advance an ambitious goal: a comprehensive and careful treatment of the often divisive rhetorics surrounding the Israel-Palestine conflict that is focused on producing empathic understanding and increasing cross-cultural identification. Below, I attempt to distill the salient points in each of the essays included within the collection for the purpose of concluding our collective efforts.

Anis Bawarshi's essay reminds us of how history and affective attachments haunt our language usage. We cannot escape the past, as the past finds its way back into how we understand certain words and concepts. Bawarshi's treatment of uptakes should play a pivotal role in advancing conversations about the Israel-Palestine conflict beyond the usual common places. If we hear echoes of anti-Semitism in seeming references to "Zionist influence," we need not shut down these concerns, but should instead contextualize them within a specific rhetorical situation. Arguments that a special relationship exists between the United States and Israel should not be shut down as anti-Semitic speech, but should instead open the way to invitations for evidence and contextualization. As Bawarshi notes, John Mearsheimer and Stephen Walt, the authors of *The Israel Lobby: United States Foreign Policy and the Middle East*, go to great lengths to show that the Lobby is not a cabal or a conspiracy, but a political group devoted to practicing good old fashioned politics. Despite Walt and Mearsheimer's nuanced treatment of how the Lobby operates to shape the US's Middle East policy, they were accused of advancing anti-Semitic conspiracy theories reminiscent of the *Protocols of Zion*. The reverberations around a history of Jewish persecution are quite substantial, shaping how we think of any reference to "Jewish power." Despite this tendency to collocate phrases such as "Jewish influence" with "anti-Semitism," rhetoricians should think about creative ways to conduct discussions about the Israel Lobby, the Israel-Palestine conflict, and anti-Semitism within good-faith frameworks free of accusation, hyperbole, and name-calling.

As I indicated in my essay, it is important to avoid lachrymose narratives about Jewish suffering in the Middle East conflict if they interfere with the accurate comprehension of present events. While conflations of Jewish memory leading up to Nazi Holocaust with the supposed present-day security threats Israel faces are natural and difficult to avoid, critical rhetoricians should work to differentiate the relevant contexts to reduce the affective, transferential, and belated effects of the past, which all too frequently are deformed in the present in the service of a partisan politics. Attempts to hold the present hostage to the past prevent meaningful rhetorical interventions around crucial issues.

By describing the metahistorical aspects of anti-Semitism Amos Kiewe indirectly challenges the claims within the two preceding essays by Bawarshi and Abraham. Kiewe, for example, refuses to identify the rise of worldwide anti-Semitism as being related to the creation of Israel and ongoing hostilities between Israelis and Palestinians, Israel's occupation, etc. Instead Kiewe argues that anti-Semitism has always been part of human history, a malignant and hateful rhetoric that possesses the potential to scapegoat Jews and non-Jews alike. Kiewe helps us to understand anti-Semitism as a broad and pervasive psychological force that exercises an unconscious hold on the collective psyche of a society. Through his thorough historical accounting of anti-Semitism's attraction to those seeking to explain away their own weaknesses and failures, Kiewe cautions us to avoid the tendency of developing simplistic theories about the relationship between the rise of the New Anti-Semitism and Israel's predicament in Middle East as the Jewish State. His powerful analysis of anti-Israel cartoons, widely produced throughout the Arab world, reminds critical rhetoricians of the continued persuasive appeal of historical anti-Semitism in the context of the Israel-Palestine conflict.

Drawing upon the work of Dominick LaCapra and a careful reading of Carol Emcke's *Echoes of Violence*, David Frank shows that the middle voice represents an appropriate method through which to avoid the acting out frequently enacted by those who have been through a traumatic event. By working through such traumatic events, the middle voice enables participants to move past unproductive sticking points that simply repeat an emotionally-laden process. The use of transhistorical, myth-laden, traumatic, and hyperbolic positions and their associated rhetorics is all too common in the context of discussions about who has suffered most in the Israel-Palestine conflict. Indeed, Palestinians and Israelis must work past the rhetorics of Deir Yassin and the Holocaust through the middle voice if they are to engage the crucial issues of their current historical moment. Furthermore, Frank's development of the riparian model of negotiation and territorial pragmatism demonstrates that a shift in emphasis from needs to rights may hold the key to bringing a lasting peace to Israelis and Palestinians.

Robert Rowland's analysis of Netanyahu's and Obama's 2012 speeches to the American-Israel Public Affair Committee raises very interesting questions about the Israeli leadership's continued use of the Holocaust as a political weapon in the context of understanding contemporary threats against Israel. At what point, do comparisons between Israel's current political enemies and the Nazis become counterproductive? Rowland's use of Burke's "terministic screens" to explain Netanyahu's seeming terministic blindness to how Holocaust discourse may actually stand in the way of drawing distinctions between a nuclear-armed Iran and Hitler's Third Reich is very important and useful. I think the kind of Zižekian fantasy frame Thomas Rickert discusses in his *Acts of Enjoyment: Rhetoric, Zizek, and the Return of the Subject* enables a productive reading of Netanyahu's worldview, which appears to be moored to the past instead of the present. Netanyahu's fantasy frame shifts based on a change in Israel's perception of its enemies' intentions in the Middle East. Whether we use Burke's worldview terministic screen or Žižek's conception of fantasy to understand Netanyahu's world view, the imperative remains the same: to maintain a rhetorical flexibility that provides the kind of pragmatic vision necessary for responding to current events, rather than to imagined threats refracted through the prism of the past.

Michael Bernard-Donals' conception of the "exilic" position gives us a third space through which to think about Jewish and Palestinian suffering, without privileging one over the other. Bernard-Donals' description of the controversy that arose around the Madison-Rafah Sister City Project reminds us of the dangers attending the exogamic tendency, that is, the tendency to incorporate the Other into our discourse while speaking for this Other *from* our perspective rather than *to* this Other, from her perspective. The exile, the one who refuses this incorporation of the Other, employs a Jewish rhetorical stance. The exile, as Edward Said points out, does not feel at home anywhere and, as a result, comes to appreciate different types of marginalized experiences. Relatedly, Bernard-Donals's careful consideration of the exilic position through the writings of Levinas and Nancy, encourages us to think about the exile as being developed in a position outside of the dominant discourse and, as a consequence, outside of being heard. This exilic stance makes us aware that when we speak for others we are affirming our own affiliations and communal loyalties, while also marking where the outside resides in relation to the inside, which has been created in relation to ourselves. It is the appreciation of this outside exilic position that must take some precedence when we think about failed attempts to create dialogue about Israel-Palestine, such as the one Bernard-Donals describes in the proposed partnership between Madison and Rafah.

Shai Ginsberg's attempt to talk about civic discourse in relation to architecture charts new territory, so to speak, as it demonstrates how discourse can be conceived in novel ways. Ginsberg's insightful reading of Amichai's poetry on Jerusalem provides us with a new conception of how rhetoric works in and structures space through architecture. As Ginsberg notes, "[Jerusalem] is a space that allows for co-habitation, it allows for the humanist poetic of identification as the logic of such co-habitation (at least from a Jewish perspective); but that space does not necessarily yield a dialogue, a discourse, civil or otherwise." I see some strong resonances between Bernard-Donals' and Ginsberg's contributions, as both are seeking to locate more nuanced and subtle ways to engage those with whom we disagree. By using Amichai's poetry as an attempt at mediation, Ginsberg points the way toward a material instantiation of the exilic position articulated by Bernard-Donals. Although Ginsberg speaks in his essay of a "civil discourse," instead of a "critical rhetoric," he is imagining how to productively engage the Other through Amichai's ruminations on the power of architectural design space.

By using Fisher's narrative theory, Michael Kleine gives us a heuristic through which to form empathic attachments to Jewish and Palestinian suffering, without privileging one over the other. By breaking down the warrants informing extremist rhetorics on both sides, Kleine provides an analysis of why extremism often emerges out of cycles of oppression.

James Crosswhite demonstrates that it is not enough to theorize about how to discuss the Israel-Palestine conflict; we have to commit to working within our local environments to ensure that the same voices do not frame and dominate the conversation. Indeed, as Crosswhite writes, "This will be accomplished not simply through the acquisition of more knowledge about current discursive practices, but also through using our institutions and our positions to engage in an examination of discourse that is practical and experimental." Responding to Crosswhite's call for engagement requires more than just innovation, it also requires persistence and courage. Ultimately, these essays ask us to be less certain about the positions we have established—and the answers we have formulated—in relation to the Israel-Palestine conflict. If we can convince our colleagues that a certain epistemological humility is in order when talking about the conflict, without succumbing to dogmatism in the process of advancing this position of expressed humility, we will move a long way toward fulfilling the rhetorical aims of this collection.

Contributors

Matthew Abraham is Associate Professor of English at the University of Arizona. His scholarship has appeared in *JAC, Cultural Critique, South Atlantic Quarterly,* and *Logos: A Journal of Culture and Society.* He is the author of *Out of Bounds: Academic Freedom and the Question of Palestine* (Bloomsbury, 2014) and *Intellectual Resistance and the Struggle for Palestine* (Palgrave, 2014), as well as the co-editor, with Erec Smith, of *The Making of Barack Obama: The Politics of Persuasion* (Parlor Press, 2013). Matthew won the Rachel Corrie Courage in the Teaching of Writing Award in 2005.

Anis Bawarshi is Professor of English and former director of the Expository Writing Program at the University of Washington. He is currently Program Profiles Editor for the journal Composition Forum and is co-series editor of Reference Guides to Rhetoric and Composition. His publications include *Genre: An Introduction to History, Theory, Research, and Pedagogy* (with Mary Jo Reiff); *Genre and the Invention of the Writer: Reconsidering the Place of Invention in Composition; Scenes of Writing: Strategies for Composing with Genres* (with Amy Devitt and Mary Jo Reiff); *A Closer Look: A Writer's Reader* (with Sidney Dobrin); *Ecologies of Writing Programs: Program Profiles in Context*; and recent articles and book chapters on genre, uptake, invention, and knowledge transfer in composition.

Michael Bernard-Donals is the Nancy Hoefs Professor of English and the Vice Provost for Faculty and Staff at the University of Wisconsin-Madison. He is also an affiliate member of the Mosse/Weinstein Center for Jewish

Studies. His most recent work includes *Jewish Rhetorics: History, Theory, Practice*, co-edited with Janice Fernheimer (Brandeis University Press, 2014)

James Crosswhite is Professor of English at the University of Oregon. He is the author of *The Rhetoric of Reason: Writing and the Attractions of Argument* (University of Wisconsin Press, 1996) and *Deep Rhetoric: Philosophy, Reason, Violence, Justice, Wisdom* (University of Chicago Press, 2013).

David Frank is Professor of Phetoric in the Robert D. Clark Honors College at the University of Oregon. His research and teaching interests feature what James Crosswhite has recently termed "deep rhetoric," the study and practice of reason expressed in argumentation seeking justice. Professor Frank's research agenda incorporates rhetorical theory and history, with a focus on Chaïm Perelman's new Rhetoric project, argumentation, the rhetoric of the Israeli-Palestinian conflict, and the rhetoric of Barack Obama.

Shai Ginsburg is an assistant professor of Hebrew and Israeli culture at the department of Asian and Middle Eastern Studies at Duke University. He writes about Hebrew rhetoric in the context of modern Jewish nationalisms and Israeli cultures. He is the author of *Rhetoric and Nation: The Formation of Hebrew National Culture, 1880–1990* (Syracuse UP 2014) and the translator into Hebrew of Paul de Man's book *The Resistance to Theory*.

Amos Kiewe (PhD, Ohio University, 1984) is a professor of Communication and Rhetorical Studies at Syracuse University. He co-authored *A Shining City on a Hill: Ronald Reagan's Economic Rhetoric, 1951–1989* (Praeger, 1991); co-edited *Actor, Ideologue, Politician: The Public Speeches of Ronald Reagan* (Greenwood, 1992); he edited *The Modern Presidency and Crisis Rhetoric* (Praeger, 1994); co-authored *FDR's Body Politics: The Rhetoric of Disability* (Texas A&M University Press, 2003); authored *FDR's First Fireside Chat: Public Confidence and the Banking Crisis* (Texas A&M Press, 2007); authored *The Rhetoric of Hate: Seeking an end to Anti-Semitism* (Trubador, 2010); and the co-edited of *The Effects of Rhetoric and the Rhetoric of Effects: Past, Present and Future* (University of South Carolina Press, 2015). His published work also appeared in journals such as *Communication Studies, Communication and Religion, Legal Studies Forum, Journal of American Culture, Argumentation and Advocacy*, and *Southern Communication Journal*.

Michael Kleine is a professor in the Department of Rhetoric and Writing at the University of Arkansas at Little Rock, where he teaches courses in first-year writing, persuasive writing, composition theory, rhetorical history and theory, and language theory. His published articles have appeared in *Rhetoric*

Review, Rhetoric Society Quarterly, Technical Communication Quarterly, Communication and Religion, Journal of Business and Technical Communication, JAC: A Journal of Composition Theory, Journal of Medical Humanities, Journal of Teaching Writing, The Writing Instructor, ex tempore (a music-theory journal), *Journal of Psychological Type, Centrum,* and *Composition Forum.* He has published book chapters in *The Philosophy of Discourse* and *(Re)Visioning Composition Textbooks.* And he has published poetry on Italian art and literature in *Poem* and *The Formalist.* In 2006, he published, with Parlor Press, *Searching for Latini,* a book-length study of Brunetto Latini, the teacher of Dante.

Robert C. (Robin) Rowland is a Professor in and Director of Graduate Studies of Communication Studies at KU, where he teaches rhetoric and argumentation. He has written more than seventy-five articles, book chapters, and proceedings essays and has had research appear *QJS, Rhetoric and Public Affairs, Communication Theory, Philosophy and Rhetoric, Communication Monographs,* and numerous other journals. He has published three books, including *Shared Land/Conflicting Identity: Symbolic Trajectories of Israeli and Palestinian Symbol Use* (with David Frank, Michigan State University Press, 2002), which won the top national award for rhetorical criticism, the Kohrs-Campbell Prize. His most recent book is *Reagan at Westminster: Foreshadowing the End of the Cold War* (with John Jones, Texas A & M University Press, 2010). Based on this book and roughly a dozen refereed articles on the rhetoric of President Reagan, he was asked to present the keynote in a panel on Reagan's rhetoric jointly hosted by USC and the Reagan Presidential Library as part of the Reagan Centennial celebrations. In 2011, the National Communication Association honored his research in rhetoric with the Douglas W. Ehninger Distinguished Rhetorical Scholar Award

Index

Abraham, Matthew 32, 100, 101, 177, 187
Abbas, Mahmoud, 16, 70, 96, 106, 107, 143
Adler, Felix, 95
Adwan, Sami, 93, 109
Ahmadinejad, Mahmoud, 45
Aliya, 162
Alterman, Nathan, 152
American-Israel Public Affairs Committee, 48, 111, 113–114, 119–120, 127, 129
Amichai, Yehuda, 151, 158, 170–172
Anti-Defamation League 12
Arafat, Yasir, 16
Arlosoroff, Shaul, 184
Auschwitz, 59, 120–121, 123, 125, 128, 146, 149
Avishai, Bernard, 126, 131, 143

Badiou, Alain, 78
Balfour Declaration, 68, 91, 99, 104
Barak, Ehud, 16
Barghouti, Mourid, 9, 11
Bar-On, Dan, 109
Begin, Menachem, 112, 124, 128–131
Ben-Gurion, David, 160
Bialik, Hayyim Nachman, 152

Bloch, Chana, 156, 171–172
Boyle, Francis, 136
Brennan, Teresa, 38
British Mandate 73, 104
Bronner, Ethan, 125, 130
Buber, Martin, 92
Burg, Avraham, 21, 47
Burke, Kenneth, 8, 73, 91, 112, 120, 130
Bush, George W., 127

Carter, Jimmy, 8, 15, 17, 18, 19, 24, 50, 54, 57
Catholic Church 65, 66, 72, 74
Cavell, Stanley, 176, 185
Chomsky, Noam, 79, 100, 101
Clinton, Bill 14, 48, 96, 107, 109, 141
Clinton Parameters, 141
Cohen, Eliot, 12
Cohen, Shaul, 142, 147
Corrie, Rachel, 8, 18, 25, 26, 27, 28, 30, 31, 32, 33, 35, 36, 37, 38, 42, 45, 47, 49, 50, 51, 53, 54, 55, 56, 59, 60, 79, 100
Crowley, Sharon, 39

Dagan, Meir, 125
Damascus Affair 67

Darwish, Mahmoud, 9
Davis, D. Diane, 87
Deir Yassin, 132, 133, 134, 135, 145, 149, 188
DePaul University 8
Dershowitz, Alan, 12, 17, 50
Dreyfuss Affair 67
Duke, David, 8, 14, 18, 19
Durban Conference, 70, 80

Eban, Abba, 41, 97, 107
Ellis, Marc, 33, 47
Engel, Eliot, 12

Finkelstein, Norman, 8, 56, 57, 100
Fisher, Walter, 90
Fleming, David, 9
Freadman, Anne, 13, 15
Freire, Paulo, 92, 98
Frienlander, Saul, 135
Fuss, Diana 23

Gaza, 8, 9, 10, 11, 18, 19, 21, 25, 26, 30, 31, 34, 36, 54, 70, 79, 80, 81, 82, 96, 101, 105, 106, 108, 110, 126, 136, 175, 184
Geneva Initiative, 140, 141, 147, 149, 183, 185
Glenn, Cheryl 52, 53
Gordon, Neve, 44
Goren, Shlomo, 166
Gouri, Haim, 152
Grant Mufti of Jerusalem, 71, 104
Greenberg, Zvi, 152

Habibi, Emile, 9
Halevi, Yehuda, 158, 172
Hamas, 34, 46, 80, 82, 96, 107, 126
Hass, Amira, 9, 10, 11
Hezbollah, 34, 96, 103, 107, 108, 109, 126, 137, 138
Hitler, Adolph, 46, 69, 70, 71, 73, 112, 122, 123, 124, 129, 132, 133, 137, 138, 139, 188
Horowitz, David, 179, 180
Huntington, Samuel 43
Hussein, Rashid, 9

International Solidarity Movement, 18, 29, 30, 34, 36, 54, 55, 60, 87

Iran, 45, 103, 116-129, 188,
Israel Lobby, 19, 20, 48, 49, 57, 58, 59, 60, 187
Israeli Defense Forces 34
Israeli Nationality Law, 162

J Street, 48
Johns Hopkins School of International Advanced Study 12
Johnstone, Henry W., 137, 146, 148

Khalidi, Rashid, 134, 135, 146, 147
Khalidi, Walid, 9, 145
King, Martin Luther, Jr., 92
Klein, Menachem, 141, 147
Kronfeld, Chana, 156, 171

LaCapra, Dominick, 43, 56, 133, 146, 188
Landler, Mark, 125, 130
Lapidoth, Ruth, 147
Law of Return, 160, 161, 162, 163, 172, 173
Leff, Michael, 179
Levinas, Emmanuel, 83, 88, 89, 176, 185
Lewis, Bernard, 69, 75
Loar, Yitzhak, 47
London Review of Books, 12

Makdisi, Saree, 9, 19
Massad, Joseph, 49, 56
Mbeki, Thabo, 141
Meir, Golda, 11
Mishol, Agi, 152, 170
Mofaz, Shaul, 126
Morris, Benny, 11, 105
Mosse, George, 155, 171

Nachträglichkeit (belatedness), 43
Nancy, Jean-Luc, 85
Netanyahu, Benjamin, 111, 120, 129
Newton, Adam Zachary, 82
Nostra Aetate, 66

Obama, Barack, 24, 54, 111, 129
Olbrechts-Tyteca, Lucie, 137, 147, 148
Olmert, Ehud, 107, 126, 131, 143
Omer-Sherman, Renan, 157, 171
Ong, Walter, 93
Oren, Michael, 113
Oz, Amos, 140, 155

Palestine: Peace Not Apartheid, 15, 50
Papper, Illan, 44
Pasha, Ziwar, 68
Pearlman, Wendy, 9
Peled, Yossil, 121
Peres, Shimon, 113
Pinker, Steven, 147
Prophet Muhammad 62, 66, 68, 72, 74
Propp, Vladimer, 92
Protocols of the Elders of Zion, 12, 13, 50, 58, 67
Psalm 137, 76, 86, 89

Qutb, Sayyib 68

Ratcliffe, Krista, 4, 93
Reagan, Ronald, 127, 131
Reich, Wilhelm, 48
Rickert, Thomas, 56, 188
Ricoeur, Paul, 63, 74
Sacco, Joe, 19

Said, Edward, 5, 8, 9, 25, 31, 47, 55, 58, 99, 101, 110, 136, 189
Salaita, Steven, 8, 18, 21
Schultz, Debbie Wasserman, 113
Seeds of Peace, 181, 182, 183
Segev, Tom, 11, 44, 130
Shalom Aschav, 136
Shemer, Naomi, 166, 171
Shlaim, Avi, 44, 146, 149
Simon, Bob 8

Technion, 102
Toulmin, Stephen, 91
Truman, Harry, 114, 119
Tuqan, Fadwa, 9

United Nations (UN), 9, 50, 56, 74, 118
United Nations Partition Plan, 84

Warnick, Barbara, 179
Washington Post, 12
West Bank, 8, 9, 16, 17, 24, 46, 48, 82, 96, 106, 107, 108, 109, 117, 126, 136, 144, 184
Wiesel, Elie, 120
Worsham, Lynn 23

Yad Vashem, 134

www.ingramcontent.com/pod-product-compliance
Lightning Source LLC
Chambersburg PA
CBHW021857230426
43671CB00006B/424